INTRODUCTION TO VISUAL LITERACY

A GUIDE TO THE VISUAL ARTS AND COMMUNICATION

Deborah Curtiss

D1558542

PRENTICE-HALL, INC.   ENGLEWOOD CLIFFS, NEW JERSEY 07632

Library of Congress Cataloging-in-Publication Data

CURTISS, DEBORAH, (date)
    Introduction to visual literacy.

    Bibliography: p. 247
    Includes index.
    1. Art—Terminology.   2. Visual communication—
Terminology.   I. Title.
N34.C87 1986   701′.4   86-12206
ISBN   0-13-498833-7

© 1987 by Prentice-Hall, Inc.
A Division of Simon & Schuster
Englewood Cliffs, New Jersey 07632

All rights reserved. No part of this book may be
reproduced, in any form or by any means,
without permission in writing from the publisher.

Printed in the United States of America

10 9 8 7 6 5 4 3 2 1

ISBN 0-13-498833-7

Prentice-Hall International (UK) Limited, *London*
Prentice-Hall of Australia Pty. Limited, *Sydney*
Prentice-Hall Canada Inc., *Toronto*
Prentice-Hall Hispanoamericana, S. A., *Mexico*
Prentice-Hall of India Private Limited, *New Delhi*
Prentice-Hall of Japan, Inc., *Tokyo*
Prentice-Hall of Southeast Asia Pte. Ltd., *Singapore*
Editora Prentice-Hall do Brasil, Ltda., *Rio de Janeiro*

CONTENTS

Preface

Introduction to Visual Literacy is designed to be accessible to all persons who have an interest in their visual perceptions, who wish to know and see more. Although it was developed as a text for first-year college students, it should also be useful as a reference and guide for all studio, art history and art appreciation students; educators of all levels and fields; professional visual communicators, artists, and designers; visual arts support personnel such as curators, museum and gallery people; visual journalists; and the general educated public.

Most books on the visual arts are written either for the passive appreciator of art, or for persons concerned with the how-to aspects of making art. This book differs from these approaches in that it illuminates the process of visual communication for creator and receiver alike.

Persons who have consciously made visual statements, no matter what medium or how modest, are better equipped to comprehend and appreciate the visual statements of others. Likewise, artists and communicators who are aware of their responses to visual phenomena—who know their own preferences, predilections and limitations, and who have learned to hear and validate the responses of others no matter how different—are strengthened in their ability to make meaningful and effective visual statements.

Over the years as I have come to grips with my own efforts to comprehend and make paintings, I have also, through teaching, helped many students to find and develop their own visual literacy. This book has emerged from my experiences of working with others, artists and non-artists alike, who have desired to improve their visual communication skills. These skills, and thus also *Introduction to Visual Literacy*, include the basic symbolic vocabulary of visual arts and communication and the verbal vocabulary that is used to discuss visual experience. Interwoven throughout this book are concepts of visual literacy—the cognitive and manual processes of visual thinking, problem solving, and creating—that facilitate visual comprehension and expression.

The illustrations were selected to represent a broad spectrum of visual expression from both in and out of the mainstream of visual arts and communication. In order to right the imbalances and slights of the past I deliberately sought examples by women and minorities. I also sought, with mixed results, works that reflect the deeper values—those that this book attempts to articulate—that underlie effective and meaningful visual statements for all time.

WHY VISUAL LITERACY?

From 75 to 80 percent of human sensory perception is visual; ten percent of vision is in the eye and 90 percent in the brain; and at least 60 percent of forebrain activity—cognition, memory, and emotion, as well as perception—is linked with vision. Considering these facts, it is shocking that visual perception, understanding, and expression are so neglected by modern education. The neglect of visual literacy is especially reprehensible in this age of proliferating visual communication. It is my fervent hope that the concepts and skills of visual literacy will be integrated into educational programs at all levels: it is too central to human intelligence to be limited to the minority of students who elect to take art classes.

Even for those who do study art, the vocabularies and concepts are often so deeply embedded in the process of acquiring skills—or as in the case of art history, they are embedded in the historical context—that they have little immediate accessibility to the student. *Introduction to Visual Literacy* endeavors to bring these vocabularies and concepts to the fore for the enrichment of all.

A NOTE TO EDUCATORS

The material presented in *Introduction to Visual Literacy* has been offered as a four-semester-hour credit course at a university, as a three-hour-per-week semester-long non-credit workshop at an art college, and as a three-credit course at a community colllege. In no instance was the material covered in total; assimilation of the many complex aspects of visual literacy is a lifelong process. I would expect however that the essential concepts and processes of visual literacy could be achieved in a full-year course of three credits per semester. Ideally there would be a balance of verbal learning with lectures, discussions, and writings; passive visual learning with primary examples, slides, and films; and active learning with hands-on visual problem-solving and creating experiences including drawing, collage, and photography.

In an art school or college, where prior visual training is assumed, I think the curriculum would fit well into a three-credit one-semester course, especially if it is integrated with a foundational studio curriculum. For the art history major, it could likewise be presented in one semester to establish vocabulary and introduce art-creating processes. I have found twenty students to be the optimum class size.

The Visual-Verbal Connection

One phenomenon observed in my community college classes was a dramatic improvement in writing skills by some students. From their first paper on how their heritage has affected their visual awareness (see chapter 17), to their final essay, a thorough analysis and evaluation of an original work of art or design, there was considerable growth in their handling of language. While this deserves further study, I can conjecture two interrelated explanations. First, as students become more visually aware, their descriptive writing skills improve. (Writing teacher, Pearl Rosenberg, also has found that, when students are required to draw a subject before writing about it, the quantity and quality of their ideas and writing, imagination and description, increase exponentially.) Second, some students may have a natural predilection for visual learning that previously had been neglected and/or discouraged. In a course of study where visual thinking is validated, where students are encouraged to perceive and create interrelated and interlocking whole images and structures, they may better grasp the idea of unlocking other structures such as language. Thus, writing about topics, ideas, and perceptions piece-by-piece in a linear verbal statement is aided by visual-spatial awareness. Visually dominant learners, I suspect, need to learn how to see parts of a whole, and the relationship of one part to the whole, in order to express themselves effectively with words.

Visual Literacy for Pre-college Students

The concepts, vocabularies, and processes presented in *Introduction to Visual Literacy* can and should be made available to young learners from birth onwards. Research has shown that infants thrive on stimulating, interesting, and challenging visual environments and experiences; and toddlers delight in expressing themselves with appropriate visual media—drawing implements, paints, clay, and building-blocks.

The elements of visual expression (part II) should be introduced at the same time as the letters of the alphabet. This learning can be strengthened by exploring in pictures where and how these elements are used. Young students can celebrate their knowledge of the elements by making visual statements comprised of the simpler elements such as dots, lines, shapes, colors, and textures. The compositional principles (part III) should be learned in the classroom along with grammar. Both composition and grammar are syntactical and, as concepts, are mutually reinforcing.

Photography, incorporating visual awareness and acumen, should be taught by age ten. Frequent discussions of visual experience, and of the communications and structures of a variety of visual examples, should be encouraged. Illustrating writings with drawings, collages, and photographs should be common and comfortable practice. Students can make visual statements in a variety of media as organs of communication and expression, both as complements to, and alternatives to, verbal communication.

In teaching these skills in the classroom and the photo lab, no pretense of making art should be made. These skills are neither a distraction from, nor a substitute for, the important activities of the art room; they reinforce all creative expression. Moreover, they are relevant to the cognitive activities of reading, writing, mathematics, and science.

At puberty, young people leave their uninhibited expressiveness and become cognitively and conceptually hungry for drawing skills. Thus this is the time for special art classes to teach perspective (chapter 3) and transformative vision (chapter 10). From teaching adults I learned that if these skills are not acquired before the age of 25, possibly earlier, they are never going to be mastered. Puberty also marks the end of the instinctive compositional sense that all young children possess. Therefore this is a time to introduce the compositional exercises given for the chapters of part III. The exploration of craftsmanship and media (part V), art history and styles (part IV), and visual thinking (part VI) are continuous as appropriate to age levels, abilities, and interest.

At all ages we should actively nurture visual imagination by encouraging closed-eye visualization of stories, history, games, and fantasy.

ACKNOWLEDGMENTS

I first encountered the concept of visual literacy in 1977 when I read *A Primer of Visual Literacy* by Donis A. Dondis. It struck a deep resonance within me, especially Dondis's hope that others would grapple with the issue as well. While teaching drawing and painting at the Philadelphia Museum of Art from 1972 to 1976, I had begun to codify some of my concerns about visual awareness and the verbal articulation of visual experience. This led, with the support of Professors Wayne Johnson and Robert Schwoebel of Temple University, to my teaching a course of my own design, Visual Awareness, from 1977 to 1982. It was during this time, with much encouragement from my Temple students, that parts I through IV and part VI of this present book were developed. Educators Pearl Rosenberg (University of Pennsylvania) and William B. Russell (Philadelphia College of Art) also waded through the early inchoate drafts.

Part V, *Formats, Media, and Techniques for Visual Expression,* could not have been written without the patient and generous expertise of a number of my colleagues, many of them at Philadelphia College of Art where I taught from 1976 to 1984: Jack Andrews, Yvonne Bobrowicz, Renée Weiss Chase, Sharon Church, John Columbus, Frances M. Cox, Oddy Curtiss, William Daley, Gerald Greenfield, Suzanne Reese Horvitz, Roland Jahn, Jerome Kaplan, Gretchen Klotz, Ruth Lozner, Robert McGovern, Bob Miller, Larry Mitnick, Scott Nemtzow, Barry Parker, Sharon Helmer Poggenpohl, Thomas Porrett, Peter Rose, Warren Seelig, and Robert B. Worth.

Professors Bobbye Burke and Madeleine Cohen of Community College of Philadelphia gave me the opportunity to use the near-final manuscript for Art 101 Visual Communication in 1984. My students there provided perceptive and gratifying feedback. One of them, Anne Woods, possessed the skills, intelligence, and fortitude to type the entire manuscript—parts of it several times—at a more than human pace, proof-read, and help prepare the index.

Had I realized the quantity of tedious clerical work, the exhaustive looking, and the expense of traveling entailed in acquiring illustrations, I doubt that this book ever would have been started. As difficult as it was, this task would have been impossible had it not been for the generosity of the artists, galleries, and businesses most of who made photographs available at their expense. Although many are identified in the captions, I wish to express my deep appreciation to those who sent work, and who, through their questions and responses, provided significant encouragement in completing a job that kept me from my studio far too long.

At Prentice-Hall, Norwell F. (Bud) Therien, Jr. acquisitions editor, first signed me up to complete this book, and together with his assistant, Jean Wachter, fielded my many questions, concerns, and frustrations. Doug Gower was a thorough copy editor who seemed to know the difference between which and that. Lisa Domínguez coordinated the production which involved many persons, including Otto Bartz who did the layout, whom I have not had the pleasure to meet. To them and to all the publicity and sales staff who will take *IVL* out into the world, I tender my thanks.

My children, Gretchen and Jeremy, have been stalwart supporters as have all my family and friends. Especially noteworthy is William M. Hollis, Jr.; poet, pianist, and painter, whose clear thinking helped hone some fine points and bring the final manuscript together as an artful whole.

To all, my heartfelt gratitude and appreciation.

This book is lovingly dedicated to my parents,
Oddy and Roy, Jr.,
who certainly knew how to nurture creativity.

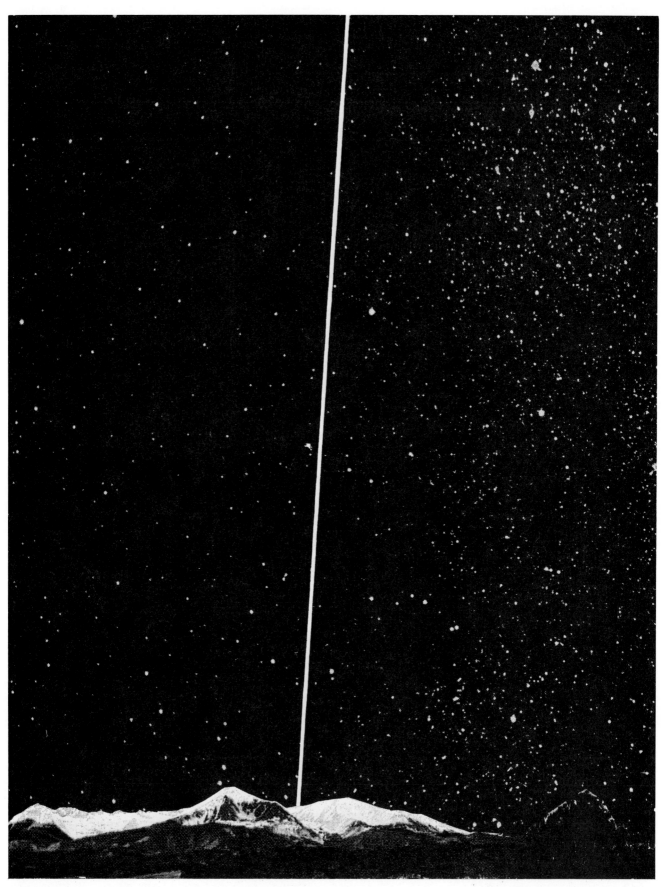

I Al Wunderlich. *Lightflight Project*. Collinated (non-diverging) white beam strobe light shining from orbiting space shuttle to earth; conceptual art, simulated photograph. *Courtesy of the artist.*

WHAT IS VISUAL LITERACY?

The term *visual literacy* has been in use since about 1970, having arisen from the proliferation of visual communications: television, electrographic (instant) printing, and computer technology. Yet, as a concept, visual literacy is applicable to all forms and media of visual expression.

In verbal literacy—the ability to read and write a language—no distinction is made as to the typographic font, format, or method used for the act of verbal communication via the written word. Similarly, the concept of visual literacy—the ability to understand (read) a variety of visual examples, such as painting, sculpture, film, and architecture, *and* the ability to express oneself (write) with at least one visual medium—is relevant to all visual arts and design disciplines as well as to visual communications.

Indeed, visual literacy is pertinent to the entire visible world in which we live.

Basic to becoming visually literate are two vocabularies: the marks, symbols, and visual elements that are used in making visual statements in any medium; and the words that are used to describe our perceptions and efforts. These vocabularies comprise one of the two central themes of this book. The other theme, visual literacy as an integral part of our activity in the world, addresses the cognitive and organizational processes—visual thinking, comprehension, problem solving, and creativity—that facilitate visual communication for both creator and receiver.

SUGGESTIONS FOR USING THIS BOOK

Because the acquisition of vocabularies in visual arts and communication—vocabularies that are both extensive and rich—is one purpose of this book, I have attempted to be concise and clear. Discourse and description have been kept to the minimum necessary to clarify a point; there is little fleshing out of information for the purpose of reinforcement and assimilation. A bibliography has been provided for readers who might desire deeper and broader discussions of the many topics.

The book is designed and written as a guide to visual arts and communication, and its scope and organization is clearly outlined in the table of contents. Each part and chapter contains introductory paragraphs and concluding summaries. Reading these introductions and summaries, from the beginning to the end of the book, provides an accessible overview of the various conponents of visual literacy.

In this part, chapter 1 contains the basic vocabulary and concepts of visual communication, and chapter 2 addresses the need for improving and strengthening one's visual acuity by providing some ''calisthenics'' for the eyes.

To become visually literate, one must continually reinforce one's reading with active experiences in analyzing and making visual statements. The appendix contains exercises, organized by chapter, that my students and I have found to be effective toward improving visual literacy. Some of these exercises can be applied immediately to the illustrations provided.

In reading the book straight through, one should proceed at a comfortable pace for comprehending each concept. The material is such that one can focus on topics of particular relevance and skip those that are, for the time, not as pertinent. The order in which one becomes visually literate is not as important as eventually putting it all together into a whole that is mean-

ingful and useful to one's own visual statement making.

Part VI, ''You as Visually Literate,'' can be particularly helpful when one is stuck on a visual problem. Chapter 16 lists blocks to creativity and paths to creative endeavor, and chapter 17 taps the rich resource of one's own visual heritage. At any point on the road toward visual literacy, either chapter can be helpful in stimulating imagination and developing problem-solving strategies.

This book has been designed to be used also as a reference. All the terms are listed in the index.

We all develop visual literacy in our own unique way. So the procedure you use with this book is not as important as its validity to you in terms of *your* learning. It is hoped that by using it as both a guide and a resource, you will acquire the basic vocabularies, both verbal and visual, that will help you in expressing your experience in receiving, comprehending, and making visual statements.

VISUAL STATEMENTS AS A MODE OF COMMUNICATION

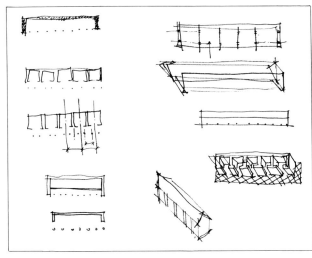

1-1 MARGO LEACH. Informal architectural sketches. *Courtesy of the artist.*

BASIC TERMINOLOGY

Visual awareness is a degree of alertness and interest in visual things. People who are visually aware keep their eyes open to the world and respond to visual experience by sharing their observations with others. Visually aware people know from their experience that visual objects, spaces, and relationships contain a great deal of information, interest, pleasure, learning, and enjoyment that can be gained simply by looking—feasting one's eyes, as it were.

Visual communication is the sharing of information through primarily visual means. One learns the language of visual communication through making, doing, and using, just as we learned to speak, read, and write. It is natural for humans to make things and to communicate. *Visual communication* allows us to utilize and celebrate these two fundamental activities. And, just as we enjoy watching or playing a sport more when we know the rules of the game, when we understand the rules and language of visual arts and communication, we will be able to participate more actively in their comprehension and creation.

Visual Literacy

The term *visual literacy* has often been applied to connote electronic media used to communicate information, such as computers and television. Herein the term is reclaimed to apply to *all* media of visual expression. **Visual literacy** is the ability to understand the communication of a visual statement in any medium *and* the ability to express oneself with at least one visual discipline. It entails the ability to:

> understand the subject matter and meaning within the context of the culture that produced the visual work (Part I)
> analyze the syntax—compositional and stylistic principles—of the work (Parts II, III, and IV)
> evaluate the disciplinary and esthetic merits of the work (Parts V and VI), and
> grasp intuitively the *Gestalt*, the interactive and synergistic quality of the work (Part VI).

Visual literacy involves an awareness that can transcend subject matter, an ability to see significant visual relationships and to recognize that these visual relationships have their own organic reality and communicative substance.

The ability to enter into the realm of visual experience and creation is one of the highest cognitive abilities: it engenders experimentation and curiosity; it is ever enriching of experience and of human intelligence. Both the understanding and making of visual statements are based upon knowledge and experience, and both involve a complex array of thoughts and activities.

	Maker	**Designer/Communicator**	**Artist**
	no formal training personal purpose minimal conscious intent	extensive formal training client-oriented problem-solver highly conscious intent	usually has formal training self-expression both conscious and unconscious intent
Examples of visual statements	one's appearance, clothes one wears	fashion design, design of useful objects	crafts: jewelry, weaving, pottery
	rooms one decorates or organizes	interior, architectural, environmental designs	sculpture, environmental art
	informal maps, doodles, sketches snapshots	graphic designs, illustrations photo-journalism, movies, television, video	drawings, prints, paintings photographs, art films, video

1-2 Find your place on this chart.

Visual Statements

An object or collection of objects created or assembled for the purpose of being seen and experienced is herein called a **visual statement**. The term is used generically to include many sizes, shapes, formats, and methods of fabrication from a vast range of materials and techniques.

Visual statements are made by a *maker* (designer or artist) for a *receiver* (viewer or audience). Every human being is a **visual statement maker**. Every sighted person is a **visual statement receiver**.* The degree to which a visual statement maker is conscious of making visual statements, the formal training one has had, and the nature of the intent of that maker, determine whether one is a *maker*, a *designer*, or an *artist* **(1-2)**.

Sometimes the visual statement *maker* determines the outlines of a visual statement—for example, with the shape of a painting or photograph, the mass of a craft object or sculpture, or the time of a film or performance work. At other times, the visual statement *receiver* sets the parameters of a visual statement—when looking at a scenic view one might include all of one's visual field, or limit it by two clumps of trees that frame the view; in experiencing a room or installation art work, one might set the parameters to include only one or two walls, or the floor plan and arrangement of objects on it; or with a

building, the parameters might be limited to the façade and the front lot setback from the street. As a visual statement receiver, you must be aware of the choices, both the maker's and your own, that determine what is included in a visual statement.

Intent

Intent, that is, having in mind something to be done or brought about, is a complex issue. Both makers and receivers of visual statements must realize that what is intended is not always what is received.

In any given visual communication, both the maker and receiver are contributing *equally* to the communication process, to the exchange of information, feelings, and perceptions through visual means. Each may differ on the interpretation of a specific visual statement, but it isn't because one is right and the other wrong or because the maker failed to communicate adequately. Because visual communication is not a precise medium, it is not limited to the sharing of factual information.

Visual statements are affective, intuitive, and general. They complement verbal communication by providing expressions of experience that would be arduous or impossible to articulate verbally. Thus, when the maker and a receiver learn of their different interpretations of a visual statement, this knowledge can become a source of growth. As different human beings, each with a distinct heritage of experience and learning (see chapter 17), they can recognize the validity of different ways of seeing and experiencing, and can use each others' responses as an expansion of their own experience.

---

*Blind persons receive visual information through expansion of their other senses, primarily through touch (haptic perception). While the scope of this book cannot include unsighted sensory awareness, it is hoped that the descriptions will be useful for unsighted persons in understanding better the nature of the visual communication.

Content

Visual statements are comprised of *content* and *form*. **Content** is the subject, information, story, and meaning of a visual statement. It is all that a visual statement depicts and is about, a composite interaction of subject matter with the substance or meaning of the visual statement. Visual statements made in the past, or about the past, contain historical content. There may be narrative content, where a story is told through visual means. The content of a visual statement may be futuristic, fantastical; emotional, mystical, philosophical, religious; informational, or political.

Symbols and **emblems** are marks and shapes that have come to stand for or connote something, the meaning of which has been agreed upon by a group or culture (**1-3**). Symbols can simultaneously convey content and provide form in visual statements (**1-4**). To interpret the *content* of a visual statement, we must be initiated into an understanding of the signs, methods, and symbols used in its creation. The disciplines of art history and semiotics offer opportunities for deeper study of content and its interpretation than can be provided here. Keep in mind, however, that content includes, or is modified by, the interpretive perceptions of the viewer. Your interpretations, no matter how far removed from the intent of the maker, are a valid part of the visual communication.

For most people subject matter dominates visual experience, often excluding awareness of the *form* (**1-5**). But for visual literates, awareness of form is in balance with awareness of content.

1-3 Symbols in common usage.

1-4 Roger van der Weyden (Flemish, 1399-1464). *Christ on the Cross. John G. Johnson Collection, Philadelphia, PA.*

Form

Form is the structure of a visual statement.* *Form* is comprised of both physical properties and theoretical concepts.

The **physical properties** are the visual statement's *format* (shape and size) and its *medium* and *technique* (materials and methods with which it is made).

---

*The word *form* is used in visual communication in two significant ways. In addition to the definition given here, it is also used to connote the visible shape of an object. See chapter 3.

1-5 FRANCES M. COX. *W. Wilson Goode Campaigning for Mayor.* 1983. Photograph, $5\frac{3}{4} \times 8\frac{3}{4}''$. *Courtesy F. M. Cox.*

1-6 EDNA ANDRADE. *Moonrise.* 1983. Acrylic on canvas, 30 × 30″. While a moonrise may have inspired this painting, its communication is dominated by form to the extent that its formal aspects become the primary content. *Courtesy of the artist and Marian Locks Gallery, Philadelphia, PA.*

The **theoretical components** are the visual *elements*, such as line, shape, and color; its *composition* or design (the principles that determine the underlying organization); and its *style* or character.

Form includes the idea behind the shape, style, and structure of the elements, which work together in such a way as to support and communicate the content of the visual statement.

Coming to understand the formal aspects of a visual statement is crucial to becoming visually literate, and thus form receives more emphasis than content in this book (**1-6**).

SUMMARY

A visual statement contains content and form. Content is subject matter and meaning. Form is comprised of a format, visual elements, principles of composition and design, and the medium and techniques used in its making. A visual statement is made by a maker (designer or artist) for a receiver (viewer or audience).

Visual literacy is the ability to understand visual statements in any medium *and* the ability to consciously make visual statements in at least one of those media.

SEEING AND AWARENESS 2

2-1 Photography class, East Tennessee State University.
Courtesy of the Art Department. Photo: James Sledge.

Visual literacy begins with visual awareness. To become visually aware we need first to turn to the physiological means by which we receive visual messages, namely the eye-brain mechanism. Vision is a profoundly complex process, about which much is known but about which there remain many questions. Neurophysiology, perception psychology, and ophthalmology are but a few of the professions seeking further understanding of how we see.

It is estimated that visual perception comprises 75 to 80 percent of our sensory input. Moreover, of our visual perception, about 10 percent is in the eye and 90 percent is mental. Clearly, if we expand that 10 percent, the 90 percent will expand accordingly!

PHYSIOLOGY OF THE EYE

Let us look at some of the basic physical features of the human eye. The eye is more or less spherical in shape. In the front is an opening, the **pupil**, protected by a clear, transparent **cornea**. Through the cornea and pupil light enters the interior of the eyeball, passes through a flexible biconvex **lens**, and projects the image of what one sees onto the **retina** at the back interior of the eye (**2-2**).

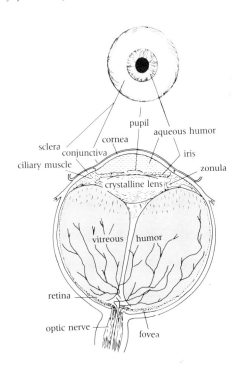

2-2 Diagram of the human eye.

7

The retina is comprised of about 132 million nerve cells, of which 125 million are rod-shaped cells (called **rods**) that distinguish light and dark; and 7 million are cone-shaped cells (called **cones**) that perceive color. The **optic nerve** carries the information from the retina in the form of electrical impulses to the brain, which decodes the messages and processes the information as vision.

In a small area of the retina at the back of the eye near the optic nerve, the cones are packed together very densely. This is known as the **fovea**, and it is responsible for our ability to focus, to see detail. The remaining area of the retina is used for **peripheral** vision, vision which is necessary for our perception of a broad visual field.

The eye also has muscles. The **iris** is a muscle that regulates the diameter of the pupil, making it small in bright light and large in dim or dark circumstances (to allow as much light as possible to enter the eye). The pupil ranges in diameter from 1 to 8 millimeters. Muscles attached to the eye and connecting with the eye socket enable us to move our eyes up and down, left and right, and around. This mobility permits us to **scan** a broad visual field without moving our heads.

In perceiving the visible world, we use our two eyes. When we look at an object through one eye and then the other, we see slightly different things. This **binocular** vision enables us to perceive depth and distance. But when we make a representational drawing, we must resolve these two slightly different images into one point of view. The camera, with a single lens, is **monocular**.

Psychologists of perception maintain, quite convincingly, that much of visual perception is *learned* and, moreover, that it is subject to modification through learning. Thus one can improve and expand visual perception. We can strengthen and sharpen it through exposure and exercise.

When one is learning a new skill or activity, it is often part of the training to strengthen relevant muscles and improve coordination. No one would expect to be able to swim a mile or ski a slalom without preparation. Similarly, depending upon the extent to which we are accustomed to using our eyes, we may need to strengthen and sharpen our visual apparatus. The following are exercises for the improvement of foveal, peripheral, and scanning vision. It is recommended that one or more of them be practiced daily for 3 to 6 weeks, or until strength in focused, peripheral, and scanning vision has been achieved.

Please be advised that these exercises will not improve impaired vision. They assume that any visual impairment you might have has been corrected to the extent possible by corrective lenses.

EXERCISE FOR FOVEAL VISION

This exercise, adapted from *The Zen of Seeing* by Frederick Franck, is known as "blind contour drawing."* Since it requires total visual attention and is in the form of a guided meditation, it will help to have someone else read the exercise slowly and quietly. In addition to improving foveal vision, it can also aid eye-mind-hand coordination and, for some people, lead to the peaceful effects of an alpha state of meditative consciousness.

First, find an object of visual interest to you. It may be a flower, a crumpled tissue, a sleeping pet, a picture, or whatever. It should be complex—a simple form will not hold your interest for very long. Additionally, you will want a comfortable place to sit, a pen or pencil, and a piece of plain paper attached to a pad or taped to a table, desk, or lapboard.

To begin the exercise, close your eyes and become aware of yourself sitting in space. Allow yourself to relax while taking several slow, easy and deep breaths. Feel your tensions gravitate downward and out of your body.

Think of a time in which you were dazzled or amazed by a visual experience. It may have been a sunset, your first flight in an airplane, a striking skyline, or whatever. Really sense the intensity of your total awareness at that time, the drinking in of everything you were seeing, free of any editing. In that original experience, you were really *seeing* with total and undivided attention. Permit that quality of seeing to dominate this exercise.

When you feel you are participating in that original quality of seeing, free of expectations and distracting thoughts, open your eyes and look at the object you have chosen. For the remainder of the exercise, keep your eyes on that object and look at nothing else.

Continue to look at the object, permitting your eyes to wander around it as if they are explorers in an uncharted land. Keep looking at the object until you feel that there is nothing in the world but you and the object.

With your eyes *continuously* on the object, take your pen in hand and allow it to follow on the paper whatever your eyes see. Feel as if, with the point of your pen, you are caressing the outlines of the object.

Do *not* look at your paper. For now, what you draw does not matter at all. Keep exploring with your eyes, in ever greater detail, all the subtle ins and outs of your object. Allow your pen to follow wherever your eyes go, and whatever they see.

*Franck, Frederick, *The Zen of Seeing* (New York: Knopf/Vintage, 1973).

Do not take your pen off the paper, but keep it constantly exploring just as your eyes are doing. Feel free to draw on top of parts you have already drawn. Do not expect the drawing to be at all recognizable. It is merely a record of a visual journey.

Don't let your eyes wander from the object, and don't try too hard. There is no need to think about what you are drawing, but merely permit your hand to follow what your eyes see.

Let the pen explore the interior edges and shapes of your object. Let it stroke and caress and discover.

This is an exercise and an experiment—an experience in seeing with undivided attention. The goal of the exercise is to extend your duration and quality of seeing with your foveal vision. The experience is successful if you feel as if you have become the object, regardless of what has appeared on the paper (**2-3**).

Work to extend the time and quality of this exer-

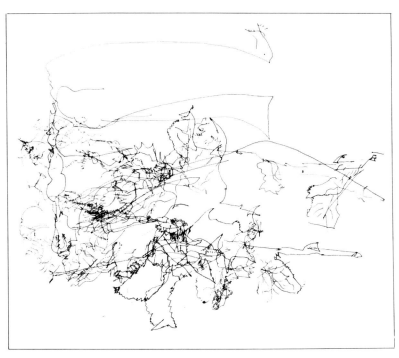

2-3 Student "blind" contour drawings of a rose and of non-drawing hand; students concentrated on looking at the object, not the drawing.

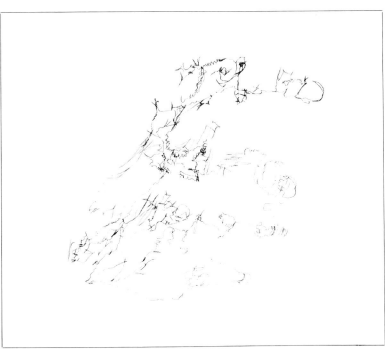

cise, but don't get lost with it. Forty-five minutes is a good cut-off time.

As a special reward, allow yourself to do a regular drawing of the object you exercised with. This time look at the paper as well as the object—and discover representational drawing.

Hint: See the forms as *abstract shapes*, not as known things.

EXERCISE FOR PERIPHERAL VISION

This exercise is the opposite and complement to the exercise for foveal vision. It is similar in that it is a meditative exercise, and you don't look at your paper. But in this exercise you do not move your eyes at all; you keep them on one point. The point should be a very clear one, and not particularly interesting: the center of a doorknob, the corner of a table, or the dot of an *i* on a magazine cover.

Again, assume a comfortable position with pen or pencil and have a secured piece of paper oriented horizontally. Close your eyes for a minute or two, and breathe slowly to relax and divest yourself of extraneous thoughts. When you have reached a state of clear-minded relaxation, open your eyes and look at your chosen point.

While looking at it, feel around the edges of your paper with the fingers of your drawing hand. Run your fingers around the perimeter again, this time (while keeping your eyes still focused on the point) be conscious of the outer edges of your visual field and relate them to the edges of your paper: left side to left edge, top of your visual field to the top edge of the paper, and so forth. (Your visual field is not exactly rectangular, but it is close enough for this exercise.)

Keeping your eyes fixed on your point, put your pen to the paper and draw all that you are conscious of in your visual field. Approximate all the relationships of shapes and forms that you see. They won't be clear, so your drawing won't be either. But that doesn't matter. We are not making art, nor are we even trying to make a representational drawing. This is an exercise in strengthening peripheral seeing.

You are in good company if you feel a little helpless and foolish while doing this exercise. You may also feel an irresistible urge to sneak a peek in order to catch a detail. Instead, enjoy this opportunity to be informal, playful, and imperfect.

This exercise is successful when you discover that you can see much more and in greater detail than you ever realized, even when not looking at whatever you are drawing. The experiment is successful if you feel that you have embraced the entirety of your visual field and have expanded your awareness (**2-4**).

2-4 Student "blind" peripheral drawing; eyes are kept focused on a point, and only what one sees around the periphery of the visual field, without looking at either the field or the drawing, is drawn.

EXERCISES FOR SCANNING VISION

In essence, when we scan things with our eyes we are selecting discrete bits of information from a broad visual field. There are several ways to improve the speed and accuracy of scanning vision. Many games are excellent for this purpose: any fast game with a ball, such as squash or basketball, provides a wealth of visual information that is continuously processed and acted upon.

Card games, especially forms of solitaire that require laying out the whole deck face-up, also demand a great deal of scanning vision. An especially challenging one is to lay out the cards face-up in nine overlapping columns, having respectively 9, 8, 7, . . . 2, 1 cards in each. Seven cards are left over, and may be played at any time, but once put in play they must remain in play. The object is to get the four suits in sequence from Ace to King played above the card spread. The spread is reordered by moving *only one card at a time* into descending numerical sequence, alternating black and red suits. A card may be placed in this order or in an open column and may be moved any number of times to effect the objective. It is a difficult game, but it can be won. And regardless, you are getting in a lot of scanning exercise while strategizing.

Here is another scanning exercise you can do anywhere, one guaranteed to shorten a wait in line or any boring situation. Pick a color or type of object in your immediate environment and, while keeping your head in a fixed position, roll your eyes to the fullest extent in all directions, counting as quickly as possible the objects of that color or shape or type which you see. This is a very quick exercise, so do it several times, changing the category, or even combining categories, to have more objects to enumerate.

Doing puzzles (500 or more pieces), mazes, seek-and-find word games, and so forth are all good scanning exercises. They not only engage foveal and scanning vision, but entice us to coordinate seeing with problem solving. They deal with complex and sometimes chaotic situations that require visual ordering and organization to make sense.

Can we ever again feel guilty for "wasting time" while engaging in these games?

SUMMARY

Visual literacy begins with visual awareness. An expanded and strengthened use of our eyes to perceive the visual world with interest, breadth, and depth, can lead to expanded mental capacity as well.

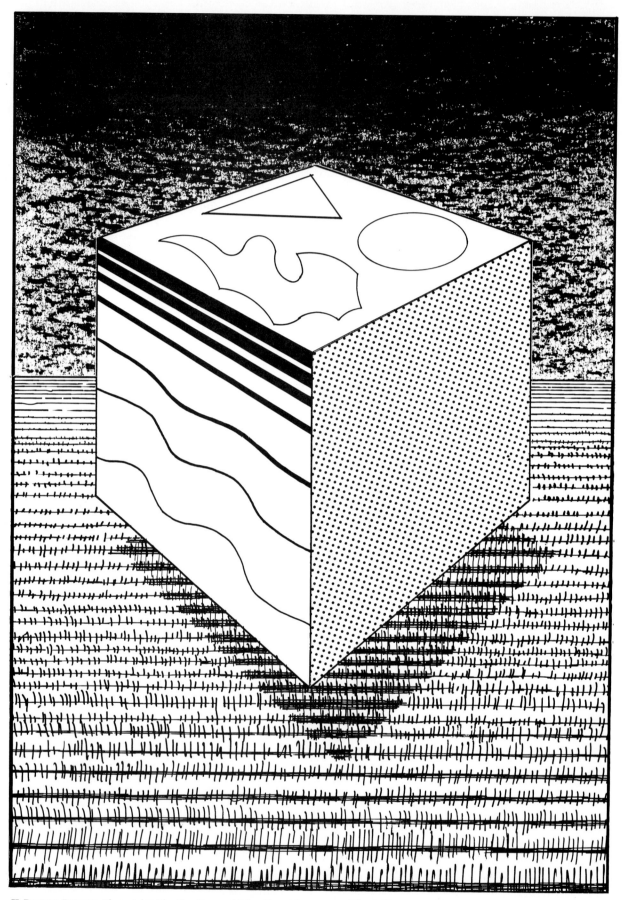

II Beverly Benson. *Elemental Celebration*. Pen and ink, oil pastel on paper, 7¾ × 6″. *Courtesy of the artist.*

THE BASIC ELEMENTS OF VISUAL STATEMENTS

Whenever a visual statement is made—whether photographed, sketched, painted, or constructed—it is comprised of what are known as the basic visual **elements**: certain constituents that are given and irreducible. Irrespective of the format and medium—such as film, paint, clay—the elements are basic, usable, and applicable to all visual statements.

The **basic visual elements** are: point, line, shape, mass, texture, space, time, movement, color, and value.

A visual statement may not include all of the *elements*; their use is determined by such factors as medium, object depicted, and the choice of the visual statement maker.

THE DIMENSION ELEMENTS

3-1 SUSAN ROSENBERG. *Mask, Milk & Men.* 1983. Photograph, shot from underneath a piece of thick plexiglas. *Courtesy of the artist.*

Dimension is the size, magnitude, or measurement of a thing, usually in terms of its height, width, thickness or depth, and duration. A visual statement referred to as "dimensional" usually means it has the third dimension, depth, which includes volume.

ZERO DIMENSION

The simplest, minimal unit of visual communication is that of the point. Theoretically a **point** has no dimension and is defined in terms of the intersection of lines. Its concrete manifestation is the **dot**; but for us to see a dot, ● it must be on something, such as this page (a two-dimensional format), or located in space, such as

a speck of dust floating in the three-dimensional area of our immediate environment.

Two dots imply a line, that is, we can connect them and have a one-dimensional object (**3-2**). Three dots, when not in a line, imply a triangle, a two-dimensional shape (**3-3**).

Dots also group and attract (**3-4**).

Used collectively, depending upon their density, dots are the means of half-tone photographic reproduction used in newspapers, the tones created in stip-

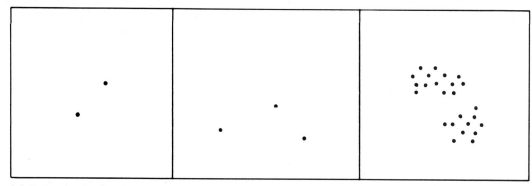

3-2 Two points imply a line.   3-3 Three points imply a triangle.   3-4 Random dots group and attract.

ple drawings, and comprise the patterns—through varying densities of electronic impulses—created by video or television. Dots used repetitiously can thus create illusions of light and shadow (half-tone reproduction), texture, and pattern (**3-5**).

3-5 Dots of varying density and size create the illusion of light and shadow as in half-tone reproduction.

ONE DIMENSION: Length

A **line** can be thought of as a string of points so densely placed that we no longer can see them as distinct. A line can also be thought of as the history of a point's movement. Because it is made with movement, a line tends to be experienced as moving, restless. "Flow of line is the most musical element in the visual arts, continually urging us on in time," says Kenneth Clark in *The Nude*.* Movement can be suggested through a gestural use of line, repetition of line, and the activity of lines (**3-6**).

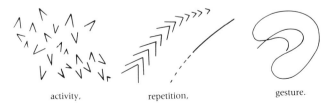

activity,   repetition,   gesture.

3-6

*Clark, Kenneth, *The Nude* (New York: Pantheon, 1956), p. 102.

Line tends to be definitive and has a broad range of qualities. *Straight* lines may be drawn mechanically with a straight-edge to guide the pencil on paper. A line may be *horizontal, vertical, diagonal,* or *slanted* (**3-7**).

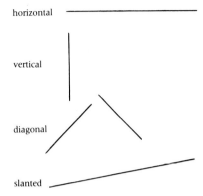

horizontal

vertical

diagonal

slanted

3-7

Placing an arrowhead on these lines makes them *directional* (**3-8**).

3-8

Directional lines may also be *curved* and *changing* (**3-9**).

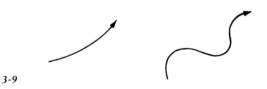

3-9

Two straight lines may be *perpendicular* or *parallel* (**3-10**).

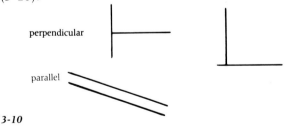

perpendicular

parallel

3-10

Lines may *converge, diverge,* and *intersect* (**3-11**).

converge

diverge

intersect

3-11

Lines also may curve, giving us qualities that include *wavy* and *serpentine* (snaking) (**3-12**).

3-12

Curving lines can also be *calligraphic*, influenced by lettering and handwriting (**3-13**).

3-13

A drawing devoid of shading, made only with line, is called a **line, outline,** or **contour** drawing. A drawing of circular and organic forms, such as plants or the human figure, would be a **curvilinear** drawing (**3-14**), whereas a drawing of boxes or architecture

3-14 Jill Moser. *Untitled.* 1984. Graphite, oil crayon on mylar, 31 × 36". *Courtesy of the artist. Photo: Pelka/Noble.*

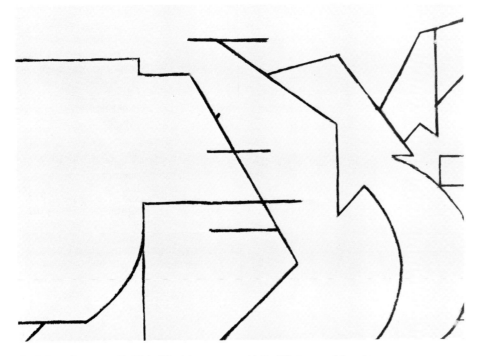

3-15 ELKE SOLOMON. *Untitled.* Oil stick on paper, 44 × 60″. *Courtesy of the artist.*

would be **rectilinear** in quality (**3-15**). Curving lines can also be parallel (**3-16**).

3-16

When a straight line changes into a curved line, it is called a **compound** line (**3-17**).

3-17 A compound line has both straight and curved segments.

Lines may also be clear or sketchy, thick or thin, smooth or jagged, hard or soft; they may swell and taper or be uniform; they may vary in length, density, and direction (**3-18**).

3-18

Lines drawn repetitiously to create the illusion of light and shadow are known as **hatched** lines. Hatching may be parallel, following contours, or made with crossing lines (**3-19**). The repetition of lines can also

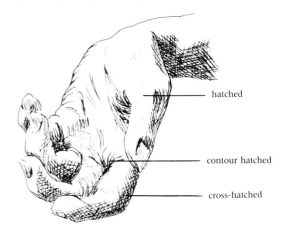

3-19 Hatching, cross-hatching, and contour hatching.

create the illusion of texture or create patterns on two- and three-dimensional surfaces. A common linear pattern is that of the **grid** as utilized in graph paper (**3-20**).

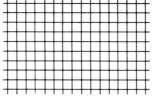 

3-20 A grid and a grid pattern.

3-21 PENNY KAPLAN and CAROLEE THEA. *Ceremonial Conjecture.* 1981. Earth work at Morris Museum of Arts and Science, Morristown, NJ, one acre. *Courtesy of the artists. Photo: Donald Madson.*

The expressive potential of line is vast. The quality of a line or line drawing can convey a broad range of emotion, energy, touch, direction. Lines can define, search, point, and measure. As the first manifestations of visual record keeping, line is imbued with a rich history that includes the formation of symbols, letters, and numbers, the basic components of written communication. The use of line in diverse media such as earthworks (**3-21**) and skywriting and tape (**3-22**) lead us to recognize its ever-evolving potential.

3-22 ABE ROTHBLATT. *Les Amis* (detail). Line drawing with produce tape on wall and partition, 14 × 30′. *Courtesy of the artist. Photo: Joe Mikuliak.*

TWO DIMENSIONS: Length or Width + Height

A point moves to make a line, and when a line moves to come back to itself, it makes a **shape (3-23)**. A

3-23 A moving point creates a line, and a moving line that comes back to itself creates a shape.

shape states its own limits that identify it from any other shape or space. This may be accomplished with line, or by a contrast of value, color, or texture **(3-24)**. Shapes can be categorized as *geometric, natural/organic, abstract, nonobjective,* or *compound.*

Geometric shapes are formed with straight lines or evenly curved lines. They can be categorized according to fundamental structures such as the *triangle, rectangle, circle,* and other *polygons* **(3-25)**.

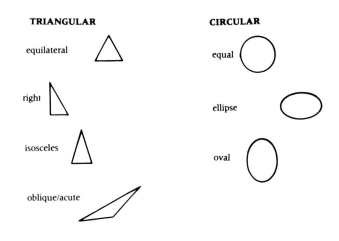

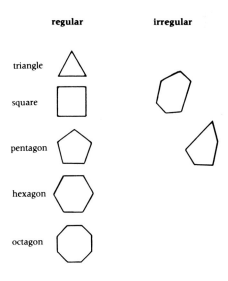

3-25 Geometric Shapes.

3-24 PALOMA CERNUDA. *In My Father's Room.* 1985. Charcoal on paper, 84 × 60". *Courtesy of the artist.*

There are several two-dimensional shapes that are important to recognize for their function in creating the illusion of depth. They are the **trapezoid** (**3-26**) and the **diamond** (**3-27**), which are formed

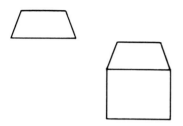

3-26 A rectangle becomes a trapezoid when seen in a foreshortened position.

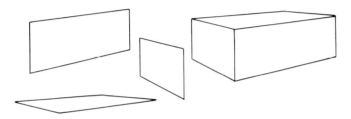

3-27 A foreshortened rectangle seen from one of its points looks like a diamond.

when a rectangle is depicted perspectively; and the **ellipse** (**3-28**), which is the shape a circle assumes when depicted perspectively. Ellipses are constantly

3-28 A foreshortened circle forms an ellipse.

curving—there are no flat or pointed areas—and they are symmetrical around both the vertical and horizontal axes (**3-29**).

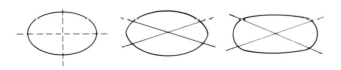

3-29 A correct ellipse and two common errors in drawing ellipses.

A relatively new regular shape is that of the **rectoid**; a rectangle with rounded corners most commonly seen in the shapes of television screens and airplane windows (**3-30**).

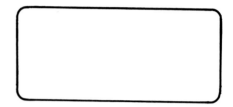

3-30 A rectoid.

Natural, organic, or **biomorphic** shapes possess complex interrelationships found in nature, living things, organisms, and include flower and plant shapes, egg and amoeba shapes (**3-31**).

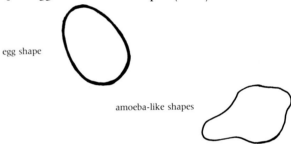

egg shape

amoeba-like shapes

3-31 Organic shapes.

Abstract shapes are derived from nature, but are simplified or distorted to reduce an object to its essence (**3-32**).

3-32 Abstract shapes.

Compound shapes incorporate both geometric and organic aspects, and often are **nonobjective**, that is, have no reference to any known object or form (**3-33**).

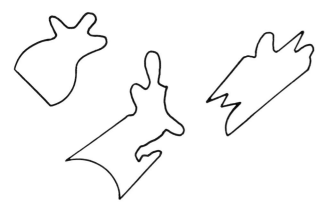

3-33 Nonobjective compound shapes.

When a curved area of a shape protrudes outward it is **convex**, and when it curves inward it is **concave** (**3-34**).

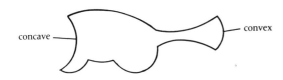

3-34 A concave and convex segmented shape.

Flat, two-dimensional shapes exist on a **plane** and are known as planar. **Planar** or two-dimensional formats, such as paper or canvas, are surfaces on which designs and images may be drawn, painted, projected, or printed.

Before exploring the illusionary techniques that can be used in drawing and painting, let us first establish the vocabulary for the third dimension.

THREE DIMENSIONS: Height + Width + Depth

Depth exists on both actual and implied levels. In three-dimensional visual statements such as sculpture, architecture, and furniture it is **actual**. The distinctive characteristics of an actual 3-D form are its **mass**, the substance and bulk of a solid body of material, and its

volume, the space that it occupies. Actual three-dimensional forms thus exist **in-the-round**, in the dimensions of ordinary reality.

As with 2-D shapes, 3-D forms may be *geometric, natural/organic,* and *freeform.* The Platonic **polyhedra** are constructed by combining the regular geometric shapes (**3-35**).

Tetrahedron—comprised of 4 equilateral triangles.

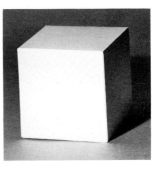

Cube—comprised of 6 squares.

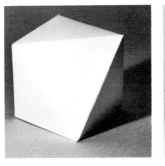

Octahedron—comprised of 8 equilateral triangles.

Dodecahedron—comprised of 12 pentagons.

Icosahedron—comprised of 20 equilateral triangles.

3-35 RICHARD MOSES. *The Platonic Polyhedra. Courtesy of the artist.*

Common but irregular polyhedra are the **box**, comprised of six rectangles, and the **pyramid**, comprised of four triangles on a square base (**3-36**). Two common regular 3-D forms are the **cylinder**, created

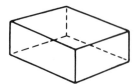

3-36 A box and a pyramid.

by rotating a rectangle on its bisecting axis, and the **cone**, created likewise by rotating a triangle (**3-37**).

3-37 A cylinder and a cone.

A complex regular 3-D form is the **geodesic dome**, composed of a grid of triangular faces that approach the shape of a sphere or segment of a sphere (**3-38**). The ball or **sphere** is also a regular

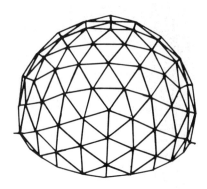

3-38 A geodesic dome developed and designed by R. Buckminster Fuller.

three-dimensional form. An **elliptoid** is a 3-D mass formed from ellipses (**3-39**).

3-39 A sphere and an elliptoid.

Compound three-dimensional forms are a combination of planar geometric shapes together with curved forms such as concave and convex segments of a sphere or elliptoid (**3-40**). **Freeform** 3-D masses are

3-40 Joyce de Guatemala. *Varanel Tzel* (The Guardians). 1982. Highly polished stainless steel with texture of stainless steel weld beading, 6′ to 10′ high. *Courtesy of the artist and Marian Locks Gallery, Philadelphia, PA.*

3-41 ALICIA PENALBA. *The Sparkler*. 1957. Bronze on carved stone base, 47 × 27¾ × 25". *Courtesy of the Hirshhorn Museum and Sculpture Garden, Smithsonian Institution, Washington, DC.*

3-42 ARLENE LOVE. *Eight Figures on a Piazza* (detail). 1984. Epoxy bonded graphite on slate base, 18" maquette for life-sized work. *Courtesy of the artist.*

primarily nongeometric and are characterized by their irregularity and unpredictable shapes. They may derive inspiration from botanical or animal forms (**3-41**). **Figurative** forms are based upon human or animal figures, and may be manifest in either a realistic or abstract mode (**3-42**).

Some three-dimensional forms are simplified by a reduction of depth. Coins and medals have a narrow edge and two sides, the **obverse** (or *recto*) and **reverse** (or *verso*). **Relief** sculpture minimizes actual depth and is presented as part of a wall or other flat surface. Also known as *bas relief*, relief sculpture attaches figures to a background and can incorporate techniques of shading to create the illusion of greater depth (**3-43**).

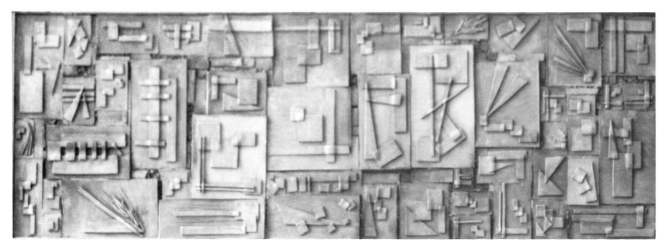

3-43 RIMA SCHULKIND. *Untitled Wall.* Stoneware with iron wash, 2'9" × 8'. *Courtesy of the artist.*

Texture

Texture, the tactile quality of a surface best perceived through the sense of touch, exists on both
actual and illusional levels. The **actual texture** of
three-dimensional forms is inherent in the material
from which an object is made: wood, metal, clay,
fibers, and so forth. A visual statement maker can
choose materials for their inherent textures and can
also create textures that are rough or smooth, hard or
soft, regular or irregular. Actual texture can also exist
in two-dimensional formats such as intaglio printing
and painting. A highly textured surface is one in which
the texture is evident to both eye and touch.

As mentioned above under the section on
one-dimension, textural qualities can be achieved
through illusion. When paintings, prints, and especially photographs represent texture, it is known as
visual texture (3-44).

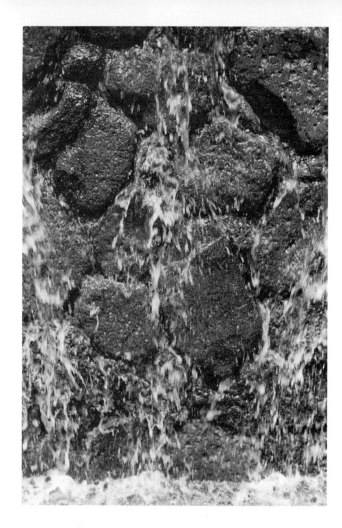

3-44 Photographs of texture: **A.** Susan Rosenberg. *Water, Hawaii.*
1982. Photograph. *Courtesy of the artist.*

B. SUSAN ROSENBERG. *#33 Leaves, Hawaii.* 1982. Photograph. *Courtesy of the artist.*

24

C. SUSAN ROSENBERG. *90 dozen eggs.* 1981. Photograph. *Courtesy of the artist.*

D. Pennsylvania Academy of the Fine Arts, Philadelphia PA. *Courtesy of the PAFA. Photo: Jules Schick.*

Three-dimensional Space

Extending upward or outward from earth, **space**, so far as we know, is limitless, empty, and void. As well as expanse, distance, and void, space is both the interval between and the emptiness contained by objects (**3-45**). In our ordinary world we encounter many barriers and limits so that space does not seem so vast, unending, and overpowering. Some of these limitations are natural, such as a cliff, or the edge of a forest. Many are human-made, such as buildings. Buildings create a space into which we may also enter; the space enclosed is an **interior space** (**3-46**). The space around the building or between buildings is an **exterior space** (**3-47**). Visually literate persons do not perceive these spaces as *voids*, but acknowledge them as meaningful and integral parts of the ongoing dialogue between form and space. This dialogue (look around the room in which you are now sitting) can be calm or rambunctious, ordered or chaotic, cheerful or gloomy, or a host of other qualities, because the space between objects is part of the visual organization. The interaction of 3-D objects and space is omnipresent in our world.

3-46 JULIE JENSEN. *London Tube.* 1980. Photograph, $9\frac{1}{4} \times 5\frac{3}{4}''$. *Courtesy of the artist.*

3-45 PHYLLIS BAKER HAMMOND. *Clay Gateway.* 1983. High-fired stoneware, $8' \times 39'' \times 18''$. Background: *Excavations.* 7' high high-fired stoneware. *Courtesy of the artist and Pindar Gallery, New York. Photo: Ned Manter.*

3-47 STEPHEN CAPRA. New York City. 1985. *Courtesy of the photographer.*

Illusion

Illusion is a deception that is achieved through a variety of devices such as implication, suggestion, and sleight-of-hand. We have mentioned already how lines can suggest movement (a fourth-dimensional, time reality), and how line and light-and-shadow can give the illusion of texture (a 3-D reality). An important use of illusion in visual statements is that which creates the volume and depth of 3-D reality on a two-dimensional, planar format.

In two-dimensional pictures, whether drawings, paintings, or photographs, the illusion of depth is created through two basic means: light-and-shadow, and perspective. **Chiaroscuro** (Italian for clear-dark), an effective tool for modeling shape with light-and-shadow to create the illusion of volume, is discussed in chapter 4. **Perspective**, meaning a single pictorial point of view, is a system of rules that provides for the natural and realistic recession of space, and for the proportions of objects in that space to appear the way we actually perceive them.

Aerial or **atmospheric perspective** is the rendering of distance and depth by modifying the tone and/or color of objects perceived as receding from the picture plane. Saturated or bright colors tend to come forward due to their more intense presence, while muted colors and values appear to recede. Likewise, a clear atmosphere advances while fogging suggests recession. These phenomena are based upon our own real-world experience where the combination of our optical limitations and the earth's atmosphere softens colors as they become more distant from us.

Placement refers to the location of an object in a picture plane. An object placed lower in a picture plane is perceived in the **foreground** and as closer than objects placed higher, in the **background**. This is due to our own orientation on the earth: objects close to us are near our feet, but when they are distant from us they appear up toward our eye level (**3-48**).

Objects **overlapping** another object also appear closer or in front, even when the two objects are on the same line (**3-49**).

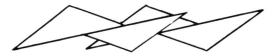

3-49

Stacking one above the other can also suggest the illusion of depth (**3-50**).

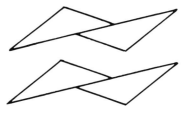

3-50

Areas in sharp **focus** tend to stand out while those depicted more softly or fuzzily tend to recede. This is a device used most often by photographers, but it can be used in drawing and painting as well (**3-51**).

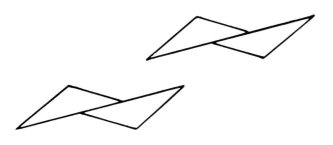

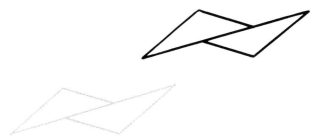

3-48

3-51

3-52 ALBRECHT DÜRER. *Draughtsman Making a Perspective Drawing of a Woman.* C. 1525. Woodcut. *Courtesy of the Metropolitan Museum of Art, New York, Gift of Felix M. Warburg, 1918.*

Linear perspective—so called because it involves the use of lines, real or implied, to provide the illusion of space—also known as **structural illusion**, was devised during the Renaissance. Artists would look through a grid from a fixed point of view to render exactly what appeared through each square of the grid on the picture plane. Here is a print by Albrecht Dürer (1471–1528) showing one of the devices he used to train his eye to see perspectively (**3-52**).

To be sure to sight monocularly (with one eye) from the same point of view for the entire drawing, Dürer affixed an obelisk (the four-sided shaft topped with a pyramid) to his desk. Using a frame with wire or thread strung across at regular vertical and horizontal intervals, and a paper of the same size with the same intervals drawn upon it, the artist would have proceeded, square by square, to depict exactly what he saw. This process is also known as the "window view" of art. Dürer has depicted the model in a side view for us, but as seen by the artist in the print, the figure would be seen in a *foreshortened* position with her knees much closer to the artist than her head.

Foreshortening is created by the combination of two physical-visual phenomena: diminution/enlargement, and convergence/divergence. **Diminution** refers to objects appearing smaller as their distance from the observer increases, and **enlargement**, as that distance decreases (**3-53**). **Convergence** refers to lines or edges of objects, which in three-dimensional reality are parallel, coming together as they recede from the observer. The obvious example is a straight

3-53 JULIE JENSEN. *Paris July 1980.* Photograph, 13 × 8½″. *Courtesy of the photographer.*

3-54 Allan D'Arcangelo. *Number One of Road Series 2.* 1965. Synthetic polymer on canvas, 81¼ × 121⅛". *Courtesy of Hirshhorn Museum and Sculpture Garden, Smithsonian Institution, Washington, DC.*

stretch of road: as it recedes, the sides **converge**; as it comes toward us, the sides **diverge (3-54)**.

The point at which the sides of the road converge is called a **vanishing point**, which is located on the **horizon line**. This last term has enticed young artists to assume that the horizon line is determined by some place in the distance where the earth and sky meet. In fact, the horizon line is determined by the viewer's *own eye level*, so **eye-level** is a better term for the location of vanishing points of convergence.

Here is a box drawn as it would be seen below us (**bird's-eye-view**), at our eye-level, and above us (**worm's-eye-view**). Notice what happens to the horizontal edges of the box when they fall *at* our eye-level (**3-55**).

One of the challenges that many art students face is that of looking at one's drawing surface at an oblique or foreshortened angle (see **3-52**). When attempting to draw objects accurately, it is wise to have the drawing paper as close to alignment with the

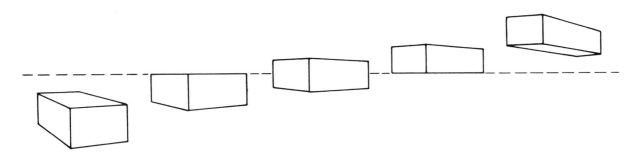

3-55 Boxes depicted below, on, and above eyelevel.

objects as possible. Naturally, if it were directly in line with the objects, it would block them from view. But finding a position as close to perpendicular as possible to the **central ray of vision**—and as directly in front of the artist as possible relative to the object—can reduce the likelihood of distortion caused by having the paper horizontal or askew (**3-56**).

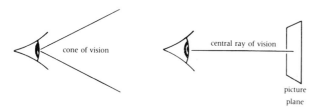

3-56 Awareness of one's own eye location and direction is very important when drawing realistically.

When perspective was developed during the Renaissance, many painters delighted in creating paintings with one point of convergence, known as **one-point perspective**. This worked well for a space into which the viewer could seem to enter, but, when objects appeared to come forward toward the viewer, distortions would occur unless the face of that object was parallel to the picture plane (**3-57**).

Thus **two-point perspective** was born, in which the vanishing points are to the left and right of the picture plane. The boxes in **3-55** are drawn in two-point perspective. The back vertical edges are shorter than the front vertical edge due to both diminution and convergence. All the top and bottom edges of the right face of the boxes converge to one point on the eye-level line to the right of the page, although this point is beyond the edge of this page. Likewise, the horizontal edges of the left face of the boxes converge to an eye-level point at the left edge of the depicted eye-level line.

When there is no convergence to a vanishing point but the actual parallel dimensions are kept parallel or undiminished, the diagram so drawn is called **isometric,** or **parallel perspective** (**3-58**). We are so accustomed to seeing convergent perspective that objects in isometric perspective seem distorted or askew. Parallel perspective is commonly used in drawing-plans for industrial design and architecture. What we *know* about an object—that the front and back edges, for example, are in fact equal in length—can inhibit the accurate seeing of the back edge as shorter due to its greater distance from us. This is a common error of beginning drawing students.

Linear perspective provides the underlying struc-

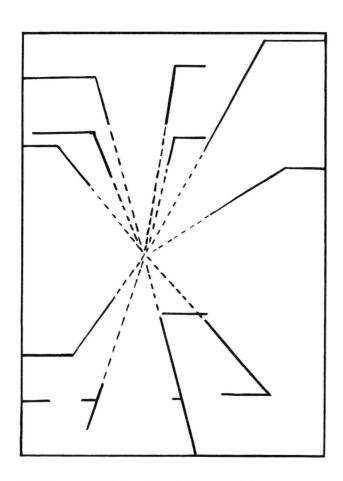

3-57 Master of the Barberini Panels. *The Annunciation. Samuel H. Kress Collection, National Gallery of Art, Washington, DC.*

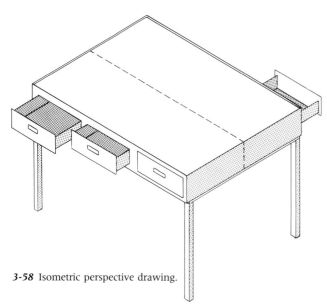

3-58 Isometric perspective drawing.

ture by which objects can be projected backward in depth, forward, to the side, above, or below one's eye level. **Three-point perspective** can be used in a variety of situations, such as drawing buildings from below looking up (**3-59**), or when looking down a street of buildings (**3-60**). Then there is convergence to a central point as well as to the right and left.

Multipoint perspective can be used in a variety of situations: in the painting of ceilings—*sotto in su,* (from below upwards)—and in Cubism, where artists deliberately depict a subject from several perspectives or points of view simultaneously (**3-61**). These multiperspectives are an attempt to communicate a passage both around an object and in time.

FOURTH-DIMENSION: Time and Movement

The fourth dimension in visual communication is somewhat different from the theoretical fourth dimension of mathematics. It is that of **time**, and implies a sequence of events. It is most pertinent in film, video, performance art, and happenings. These media all engage aspects of duration, repetition, rhythm, periodicity, and episodicity, all of which are dependent

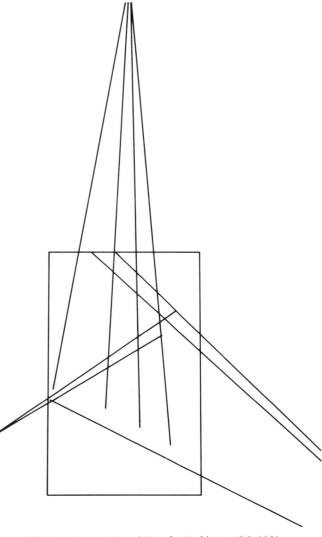

3-59 JULIE JENSEN. *Masonic Temple, Washington, DC.* 1981. Photograph, 13 × 8½". *Courtesy of the artist.* Diagram indicating points of perspective outside of picture plane.

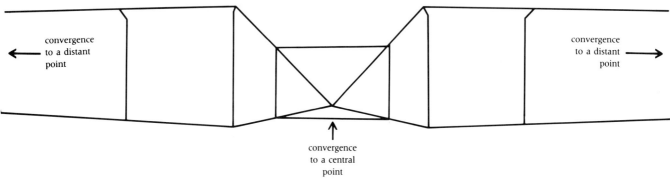

convergence to a distant point ←

convergence to a distant point →

↑ convergence to a central point

3-60 Pitti Palace, Florence, Italy. Diagram of 3-point perspective. *Photo: Gregory Benson.*

3-61 JUAN GRIS. *Breakfast.* 1914. Pasted paper, crayon, and oil on canvas, $31\frac{7}{8} \times 23\frac{1}{2}''$. *Collection, The Museum of Modern Art, New York. Acquired through the Lillie P. Bliss Bequest.*

upon time passing, of a period between events, for their perception.

Time should be considered as part of all visual communication. Instantaneous recognition of a picture, when compared to describing the image verbally, may be a fact. But the experience of a painting or sculpture engages a viewer for a longer period so that more meaningful perceptions and appreciations transpire. Assimilation of form and content requires lengths of time and repetition to achieve knowledge and appreciation. Likewise, architecture requires time for a tour to experience its manifold parts. A photograph, in its depiction of an instant in time, has made time stand still. Yet that splinter of time persists henceforth for continued perception.

In visual statements time exists in real, illusionary, and metaphoric modes. Historical paintings, for example, offer the past in the present, and some depict different eras within one painting (**3-62**). Fantasy and futuristic works project the present into the future (**3-63**). Timelessness or endurability, and timeliness and propriety, are metaphoric qualities that can be part of the content of static (nonmoving) visual statements.

3-62 MASTER OF KAPPENBERG. *Christ before Caiaphas.* C. 1500-25. The attire and furnishings depicted in this painting are of sixteenth century Europe, not those of Christ's lifetime in first century Palestine. *John G. Johnson Collection, Philadelphia, PA.*

3-63 YVES TANGUY. *Naked Water* (L'eau nue). 1942. Oil on canvas, $36\frac{1}{4} \times 28''$. *Courtesy of Hirshhorn Museum and Sculpture Garden, Smithsonian Institution, Washington, DC.*

3-64 CLAES OLDENBERG. *Icebag Scale A.* Programmed kinetic sculpture: red polyvinyl material, lacquered wood, hydraulic and mechanical movements; height: 3 to 16 feet, 18' diameter. Created for Art and Technology Pavilion, World's Fair, Osaka, Japan, 1970. *Courtesy of the artist and Gemini G.E.L., Los Angeles, CA.*

In the time-oriented media of film, video, and performance art, motion and movement are an integral element. With motion, objects or persons change position over a period of time. **Cinema**, movie film, comes from the root *kine*, Greek for movement. **Kinetic** sculpture is sculpture with moving parts (**3-64**).

Beyond the fourth dimension, we enter into dimensional realms of meaning and value, myth and metaphor, in which numerical classifications approach, for now, the unnecessary or absurd. Visual statements have a long history of achieving profundity in the expression of inner realities and cosmic dimensions. But our language tends to be inadequate to articulate these qualities with much consensus. So rather than risk losing ourselves in those exquisite ephemera, we will proceed to a couple of very important elements of visual communication, those of color and value.

SUMMARY

The dimension elements of visual experience are point, line, shape, mass, texture, space, time, and movement. Each has a dual existence in visual statements, for they exist both in actual reality and through implication and illusion. They have concrete reality in the format and materials of visual objects while they simultaneously participate in the communication of a vast range of illusory and metaphoric content.

Color and Value

4-1 HELEN FRANKENTHALER. *Buddha*. Acrylic on canvas, 74 × 81″. *Courtesy of the artist and André Emmerich Gallery, New York. Photo: Stephen Sloman.*

COLOR

Color is the sensation aroused in one's mind, as received by the eye-brain visual mechanism, in response to the radiant energy of certain visible wavelengths of reflected light. The computer can generate sixteen million different colors of which the human eye is capable of discerning about one million. Yet we have names for fewer than one hundred, the majority of which are borrowed from objects possessing that color, such as orange, violet, and avocado.

LIGHT

Light is the parent of color: the sunlight of our environment contains the wavelengths of all visible color. A beam of light passing through a transparent polygonal body, called a **prism**, is **diffracted** into the **spectrum** of rainbow colors: red, orange, yellow, green, blue, indigo, violet. These *spectral, prismatic,* or *diffracted* colors are the purest colors, and obtainable through the diffraction of light only. In making visual statements, spectral colors are available in light projections, holographic engravings, and computer terminals. With the use of pigments or color film, however, the brilliance and purity of spectral colors can only be approximated.

When light falls on an object it divides, or **refracts**, into rays that are either **absorbed** by the object or **reflected** by it. For example, grass absorbs all the spectral colors except those light waves we have named green, which it reflects. Thus we perceive grass as green. Objects that are white reflect almost all light and absorb minimally, while black absorbs most light and reflects minimally.

Any given color is considered to have three principal properties: *hue, saturation,* and *value.* The **hue** is the color itself, its location in the spectrum and color wheel and, often, its namesake. **Chroma** is the degree of intensity of a color, and **local color** refers to the actual color of an object.

Saturation is the purity, vividness, and intensity of a color, the degree to which it is unadulterated by white, black, its complement, or a thinning agent. **Highly saturated** colors are often brilliant in their effect while colors **low in saturation** are soft, subtle.

The **value** or **tone** of a color refers to its degree of lightness or darkness relative to white or black. Black-and-white photography reduces colors to values or tones. A **high value** is light in color, whereas a **low value** is a dark color. **Local tone** refers to the inherent lightness or darkness of an object.

COLOR MIXTURES

There are two kinds of color mixture: **subtractive**, which refers to pigment, and **additive**, which refers to light. Each has its own processes and effects.

Subtractive Color Mixture: Pigment

The mixture of pigments is called *subtractive* because, with most mixtures, a darker color results and light reflectance is lost. Theoretically there are three **primary hues** from which all other hues may be mixed or derived: *red, yellow,* and *blue*. They cannot be derived from any other colors, and form the **primary color triad**.

Mixture of any two of these primary colors gives us the **secondary colors**: red and yellow make *orange,* yellow and blue make *green,* and blue and red make *violet*. These form the **secondary color triad**. By juxtaposing these two triads, we form the **color wheel**, and by adding the **tertiary** or **intermediate colors**, which are derived from the mixture of a primary with one of its neighboring, or **adjacent** secondary colors, we get the **color circle** comprised of twelve hues (colorplate **1A**). In between the twelve basic hues is a continuum of hues, gradating from one segment of the circle to another. **Analogous** colors are those colors immediately next to a given hue on the color circle and usually centered about a primary or secondary color.

Colors directly opposite one another on the color wheel are known as **complementary colors**. For example, green is the complement of red; blue and orange, and yellow and violet are complementary pairs. Mixture of complementary colors, or of the three primary colors, yields neutral colors that are not hues. These rich and varying mixture-colors have not had a specific or definitive term in common usage. In my classes I use the term **co-mix** to connote a complex mixture of colors: those mixed with their opposites, or with gray.

Additive Color Mixture: Light

The mixture of light is called **additive** because each mixture contributes more light and, when combined, colored lights create white light. In additive color, the **primary** colors are *red, green,* and *blue*. Mixture of any two of these colors gives the **secondary** colors: red and green make *amber,* green and blue make *cyan,* and blue and red make *magenta*. When all three primaries are mixed together, they create white light (containing all colors, as in the sunlight's spectrum), as do pairs of complementary colors (colorplate **1B**). This is why, in the theater, every stage light can have a different colored gel over it, but when they are all turned on together, the stage is flooded with white light.

Aside from these different phenomena in the color mixture of light, the terms such as hue, chroma, saturation, complementarity, and so forth are used in the same way as with the mixture of pigment colors. Color mixture with lights is important for color photography, video, film, electrographics, as well as for stage lighting. It is also used in color printing, which relies upon the optical mixture of small dots of color, discussed below.

VALUE—TONE

Light and Shadow

Black-and-white photography, *chiaroscuro* drawings, and **grisaille** (French for gray tones) paintings depict contrasts of light and shadow or value and tone without color. These media are therefore **achromatic**, without chroma.

Light is directional, and the side of an object away from the light source is in **shadow**. This phenomenon of **light and shadow** greatly enhances our

4-2 Julie Jensen. *The Nose* 1977. Photograph, 13 × 9". Where are the shadows cast, attached, and contained? *Courtesy of the artist.*

ability to see and navigate in the world. Likewise, its depiction in visual statements gives a sense of substance, of three-dimensionality to two-dimensional pictures (**4-2**).

A shadow may be **cast, attached,** or **contained**, and it gives important information as to the location of an object relative to others in a visual statement (**4-3**).

Color and Value

A **tint** is a hue mixed with white, and a **shade** is a hue mixed with black or its complement. When dealing with color mixture in painting, the modeling of forms to create the illusion of volume is made through a modulated **toning** down with dark colors, a **heightening** with bright colors, and a **lightening** with light colors. A **highlight** is a small area of light color surrounded by dark (*see* **4-3**).

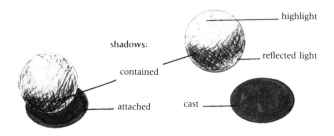

4-3 Kinds of light and shadow.

A **color scheme** is comprised of the dominant colors in a given area such as a painting or a room. An array of colors or color combination can be called a **palette**—a term borrowed from the surface on which a painter lays out and mixes colors. When one hue is mixed with varying quantities of black or white only, and comprises the color scheme of a work, it is called **monochromatic** (one color). **Bichromatic** and **trichromatic** refer to two and three color combinations. A color scheme using many colors is called **polychromatic**, while one using tones of gray from white to black is called **achromatic**.

Areas of a picture can modulate gradually from light to dark values, creating a **confluent** or **blended** quality; or they can change through a constant or step-by-step **gradation**; or they can change abruptly with **contrast**.

COLOR NOTATION, MEASUREMENT, AND EXPERIMENTATION

Several schematic systems, most notably those of Munsell and Ostwald, have been devised to attempt to organize colors into a coherent whole. These systems succeed in combining the color wheel with the gray scale, but color mixture requires another dimension to demonstrate combinations of nonneighboring hue families (colorplate **2A**).

There are electronic devices, **spectrophotometers**, that measure light reflectance and color wavelengths. These can be useful in technical photography, filmmaking, holography, and industrial color matching. The isolated reflectance of a single color as measured will be of little purpose for visual creators in general, for color must always be considered *in context*. Environmental variables, such as lighting, texture, adjacent colors, and spatial relationships all affect color perception and experience.

Color phenomena are of interest to professionals other than visual artists and communicators. Physicists are interested in optical properties of color and the electromagnetic spectrum. In recent years the **laser** (light amplification by stimulated emission of radiation), comprised of intense beams of one amplified wavelength, has been found to have many applications in physics and medicine, as well as in holography. Painters have many colors to use because chemists are engaged in an ongoing search for new synthetic pigments. Designers draw upon the knowledge of color and its effect on human behavior as studied by psychologists.

COLOR AS SUBJECT

Color as subject has certain properties or effects. As Josef Albers in *Interaction of Color* says,

> In visual perception a color is almost never seen as it really is—as it physically is.
> This fact makes color the most relative medium in art.
> In order to use color effectively it is necessary to recognize that color deceives continually.*

Thus we have the color **agent**, the autonomous physical properties of a given color as it has been discussed in sections above, and the color **effect**, its **exponential aspect** and its perception.

The discrepancy between a color as *agent* and as *effect* can be independent from personal preference. For example, an orange color on a red background will look yellower than it actually is, yet that same orange on a yellow ground will look redder. This phenomenon, called **simultaneous contrast** and **color induction**, is the deceptive or relative aspect of color. In simultaneous contrast, objects of the same color and size appear brighter or duller, or larger or smaller, due to the effect of the grounds on which they are placed (colorplate **2B**).

*Albers, Josef, *Interaction of Color* (New Haven, CT: Yale University, 1975), p. 1.

Another effect of color is that of psychological or emotional **temperature**. It is agreed by subjective consensus, as well as by the physical wavelengths of reflected colors, that the longer wavelengths—red, orange, yellow—are considered to be **warm, hot,** and the shorter wavelengths—blue, violet—are considered to be **cool, cold**. Those in the middle, such as green, can be of **neutral** temperature. There are physical exceptions to these associations, such as the blue flame of a gas stove or the much hotter white heat of molten steel. These exceptions, however, do not seem to carry the psychological clout of red-hot and ice-blue.

Colors can appear to advance or retreat. Generally speaking, warm and bright colors **advance**, while cool or drab colors **recede**. (See aerial perspective under *Illusion* in chapter 3.)

The qualities of color that create temperature, space, mood, movement, and so forth, are known as the *exponential* aspects of color. They are different from the *autonomous*, physical aspects of color: hue, value, and saturation.

COLOR CONTRAST

Color perception can be enhanced through contrast, juxtaposition, and comparisons of differing colors. There are a number of possible **contrasts** from which to choose: hue, temperature, value, light-dark; color-wheel location, complementarity; and saturation, quantity, and visual impact. Some contrasts are **harmonious**, pleasing to the eye. They seem to go together, or create **consonance**. **Disharmonious** and **dissonant** colors seem to fight and are visually disturbing.

With color contrasts, some colors will appear to **dominate** while others, by comparison, will be **subordinate** or subservient.

Color **confrontations** occur when two or more contrasting colors are placed so that they create tensions, pulsations, dissonances, color changes or vibrations. Two bright colors of nonadjacent hues, when juxtaposed with one another, can yield a very active edge, known as **vibration** or vibrating colors (colorplate **2C**). This can be optically attracting but visually disturbing when experienced over a period of time, for unrelieved color intensity is self-defeating.

Colors that are toned down with their complement or grays are sometimes described as **dead** color. **Matte** or **flat** colors are lacking in shine or sheen, or variation of tone or hue. Color areas having a high degree of variation can appear **luminous**. Luminosity can be enhanced through the use of **transparent** color—that which allows a lot of light to pass through.

Colors that allow some light to pass are known as **translucent**, whereas those that allow no transmission of light or color are **opaque**.

Iridescent, interference, or **opalescent** colors are those which reflect two or more different colors, depending upon the angle of light falling on them relative to the eye of the observer. This reflectance is known as **luster**, and can be seen as well on metals and luster glazes in ceramics. **Fluorescent** colors contain special pigments that are activated by ultraviolet light waves. These light waves are invisible to the human eye but are present in sunlight and in fluorescent and ultraviolet light bulbs. These light sources cause the fluorescent pigments to appear to glow intensely. **Phosphorescent** or **luminescent** pigments have a chemical that activates when exposed to light. The phosphorous pigment retains the light-activated chemical reaction when light is removed and glows in the dark. This glow fades with time and must be reactivated through recurrent exposure to light (**4-4**).

When assessing the impact of color, and color combinations, it is important to remember that what is perceived can often be different from what actually, physically is. The perceptual, exponential aspects are the ones that are of greater importance in visual communication.

PERCEPTUAL AND PSYCHOLOGICAL ASPECTS OF COLOR

A saturated color can stimulate the perception of its complementary color, known as **successive contrast** or **after-image**. This phenomenon is caused by fatigue in the cones of the retina of the eye. When you look at a bright red, for example, only the red receptors of your eye are stimulated. They become fatigued, and the blue and green receptors take over for relief. Thus when you look away from the red onto a light neutral color (white), you will see the after-image of the red shape in blue-green or cyan. This is an **optical** effect. The rods of the retina have a similar reversed light-dark response to looking at a light or out a window.

Optical mixture is created when broken color comprised of small dots is employed. Also known as **pointillism**, the eye blends the dots, red and blue, for example, into larger areas of a mixed color, magenta-purple. Just as collections of dots are used in black-and-white halftone reproduction, pointillism is used in some color reproduction processes. Best known is the four-color separation process where dots or screens of magenta, yellow, cyan, and black are

4-4A DEBORAH CURTISS. *Court.* 1978. Acrylic, mica powder, and phosphors on unprimed linen canvas, 50 × 52". *Collection of Teresa Benzwie. Courtesy of the artist.*

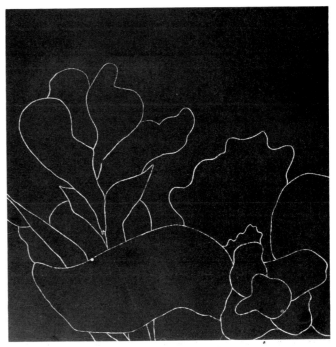

4-4B *Court* photographed with time-exposure in the dark, revealing the phosphorescent drawing.

combined in varying densities to reproduce color (colorplate **3**). Since the eye is actually doing the blending of these color dots, the process is the additive mixture of light rather than the subtractive mixture of actual pigments.

The foregoing has dealt primarily with that of perception, the psychophysiological and physical processes that enable us to see colors, differentiate one from another, or engage in optical color mixture. Another level of color involvement is emotional. "I am feeling blue," "He's green with envy," "She's in a purple rage," are examples of general color associations. Personal color preferences tied to our emotions and personality also exist. For example, some people may find a bright yellow room sunny and uplifting while others may experience it as cloying and intrusive.

Color asserts a great influence in our lives. It is a most emotive element, capable of creating moods, and of communicating a rich variety of qualities. It has power to unify, vary, or provide accent in the composition and design of visual statements. Whether consciously or not, we all engage in an ongoing process of

response to the color around us. As we become involved in making visual statements, an increased sensitivity to color and value is inevitable. Life is never dull to one who is attuned to the power and playfulness of color.

SUMMARY

Color and value are visual elements that contribute greatly to the variety of visual perception and experience. Colors are more than physical properties, for they have effect, lend qualities of temperature, placement, harmony, and changing appearance to visual statements. The contrast of light-and-dark values is crucial to our perception both of the world around us and of visual statements.

Point, line, shape, mass, texture, space, time, movement, color, and value comprise the basic elements from which all visual statements, irrespective of medium or format, are made.

III Joseph Lev. *Late Light*. Photograph, 12 × 10″. *Courtesy of the artist.*

III
COMPOSITION AND DESIGN:
THE SYNTAX OF VISUAL STATEMENTS

Composition is the order, organization, and orchestration of a visual statement. It is the underlying structure that, when successful, supports and combines the elements into a coherent, unified whole.

The compositional syntax affects the life of a visual statement, the length of time it holds the interest of its audience. A well-designed composition can support a vast variety of appearances and solutions to visual problems, whereas a poorly composed visual statement cannot be salvaged by sumptuous color, splendid technique, or any other gimmicks or feats.

Learning to see and evaluate composition and design is one of the most important steps in becoming visually literate. This process entails looking beyond the content of a visual statement, and even beyond many of its elements, in order to see how it is held together. This involves learning to extract the *underlying forces* and events that comprise the *skeleton*, the *articulate form* of its structure. Seeing this way feels like having "x-ray" vision.

In good composition the underlying structure is strong enough to support the dynamics of contrasts, alignments, proportions, balance, and associations of the elements. These dynamics, unlike the elements, are nonmeasurable, nonquantifiable *qualities* that contribute in manifold ways to the character of the statement.

There are infinite ways to organize the elements in any given visual composition, for both the elements and the organizational principles of composition are endlessly variable. Moreover, the elements themselves have intrinsic compositional power:

Line for coherence, thrust, and movement
Texture for rhythm
Value for illusion of volume and depth
Color for variety, unity, and accent
    and so forth.

With so many possibilities from which to choose, a visual creator employs a highly complex process of decision making. This process synthesizes theoretical concepts (chapter 5) with visual sensitivity and personal, subjective preference (chapters 16 and 17).

In our daily lives we are continually affected by the considerations and products of designers. The clothing we wear, the furniture we live with, the utensils we use, the buildings we live and work in, the newspapers and magazines we read, and the cars we drive have all been *designed*. These designs may be good or bad, but chances are, if they are well designed they have been subjected to the organizational principles described in this section. In chapter 5, the principles of composition are identified and defined. Some methods for discovering the underlying structure of visual statements are provided in chapter 6. In chapter 7, methods are recommended for utilizing compositional principles when making your own visual statements.

Unity

Scale, orientation, proportion, balance

Dominance/subordination, focal points

Repetition, rhythm

Contrast, variety, energy

Tension, conflict, resolution (unity).

Basic Principles of Visual Composition

5-1 BENEDICT TISA. *Rickshaw* (Bangladesh). Photograph, $4\frac{3}{4} \times 7''$.
Courtesy of the photographer.

The basic processes and **principles** by which visual statements are organized are:

Unity
Scale, orientation, proportion, and balance
Dominance/subordination and focal points
Repetition and rhythm
Contrast, variety, and energy
Tension, conflict, and resolution (unity).

UNITY

Unity is the sense of cohesion, of oneness, the umbrella under which a great deal of visual activity can take place. Whether experiencing a two-dimensional, three-dimensional, or time-oriented visual statement, a viewer needs to have a sense of coherence and unity if the effect is to be maximized.

The opposite of unity is chaos, and chaos breeds confusion, not communication. When unity is evaluated, the *entire* format of a visual statement must be taken into consideration.

Unity can be achieved in a multitude of ways:

Shapes and forms may be contained and well placed within the format.
Lines of force, energies, and focal points may cohere and achieve balance within the format.

A harmonious color scheme can provide powerful unity despite other divergent activity.
Value and texture have unifying potential.

Whatever the means employed, the most significant unity is one which has **Gestalt**, the working together of all the elements and organizational principles to create a whole that is greater than the simple sum of its parts, a totality that has a sense of magic and power.

All of the following principles of visual organization must be considered in terms of their contribution to, participation in, or contrast with the overall *unity* of a visual statement.

SCALE

Scale is a size comparison with a constant, most often the human form. Thus, in visual statements, we have the **miniature**, which is tiny in size. There are **small-scale** sculptures that can be set upon a table or shelf. **Life-size** works depict the human figure within the normal size range of human beings. **Large-scale** works need floor space or a whole wall to be dis-

5-2 Beverly Pepper. *Excaliber.* 1975-76. Black painted steel, 32 × 40 × 60'. Federal Building, San Diego, CA. *Courtesy of the artist and André Emerich Gallery, New York.*

played. And **monumental** works are much larger than lifesize, usually requiring display out of doors (**5-2**).

ORIENTATION

We are essentially vertical beings on a horizontally perceived earth. This is our **orientation**. Whether or not we are conscious of this, we are constantly comparing what we see with the primary underlying qualities of vertical and horizontal. Objects in our environment that are skewed from these perpendicular axes tend to attract attention, to disturb. Walking into a funhouse, where no verticals or horizontals exist, is "fun" precisely because it is a disorienting and unexpected experience. Imagine living in such an environment; the disruption and disorientation would fatigue you and can result in vertigo and illness, both mental and physical. When askewness is *purposely* part of the meaning of a visual statement, it can be justified (**5-3**). Otherwise it distracts from and conflicts with the statement's message. Except for occasional thrills and attention-getting devices, human beings seem to want stable orientation both in our environment and in the visual statements we make and see.

PROPORTION

Proportion refers to the relationship in size of individual parts to one another and to the whole. Varying sizes affect visual weight, location, and emphasis in a visual statement. A well-proportioned visual creation

has stability, elegance, grace, harmony, and sense of purpose.

Proportions found in nature and in theory (mathematics) have greatly influenced human-designed objects. One of these is known as the **golden section** or **golden mean**, discovered by Euclid during the third century B.C. In it, the ratio of the smaller segment of a line to the larger segment is the same as that of the larger segment to the whole line (**5-4**). This proportion, while recurring in nature and art, does not insure good design, however, and often can lead to a static, lifeless appearance.

In A.D. 1202, the Italian mathematician, Fibonacci, found a manifestation of growth in nature that extends the golden mean. Numerically it is expressed by any number in the sequence as the sum of the previous two numbers. Thus, 1,1,2,3,5,8,13,21,34,55,89 . . . .

Good proportion is usually judged according to ideals that have been culturally established. Proportional qualities both affect and are affected by stability, scale, and balance.

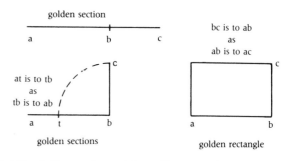

5-4 The Golden section and the Golden rectangle.

5-3 MARGARETTA GILBOY. *Persephone & Hades*. 1983. Oil on canvas, 22 × 28". *Courtesy of the artist and Marian Locks Gallery, Philadelphia, PA.*

BALANCE

Balance—the quality of weight distribution on either side of an imaginary central vertical axis—is a refinement of orientation. Balance is affected by proportion and contributes to equilibrium and unity in visual statements. The sense of balance can differ according to personal perception and depends, to a degree, upon one's sensibility, feelings, and preferences. Thus there may be variance in the experience of balance in visual statements. However, ranges of balance and imbalance are largely agreed upon and can be extracted from a visual statement for assessment and discussion. Balance in visual statements may be formal, informal, or radical.

Formal Balance

The most obvious example of **formal** balance is **symmetry**. There are three basic kinds of symmetry: bilateral, translational, and rotational. **Bilateral** (axial or mirror) **symmetry** is the most common. It is based upon organization on either side of an implied or actual axis of reflection (**5-5**).

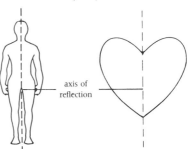

5-5 Bilaterally symmetrical shapes.

Translational symmetry is also known as **frieze** symmetry from its frequent use in decorative bands at the tops of buildings. It entails the repetition of a design element in a single direction (**5-6**).

5-6 Translational symmetry.

Rotational symmetry (known also as central or radial symmetry) is achieved by rotating around an axis that is perpendicular to the page and is perceived as a point (**5-7**). **All-over** symmetry is pattern itself (see below).

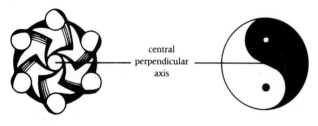

central
perpendicular
axis

5-7 Rotational symmetry.

Symmetry does not always insure balance. The heart for example can be considered top-heavy, lacking the repose we associate with balance. The examples of bilateral symmetry (**5-4**) have vertical axes that give a sense of poise. What if we tilt the axis or make it horizontal? Then the human form does not appear quite so balanced (**5-8**).

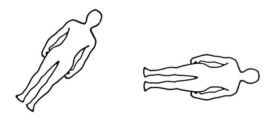

5-8 Bilateral symmetry does not guarantee balance or stability.

While symmetry is fascinating both visually and theoretically, placement and use within a visual statement determine whether the various symmetries are balanced. **Asymmetry** is the absence of symmetry either in form or composition. **Informal** symmetry is achieved when a composition has the underlying simplicity of bilateral symmetry, but the forms within that composition are not exactly the same (**5-9**).

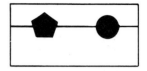

5-9 An example of informal symmetry.

Informal Balance

If all visual statements were formally or symmetrically balanced, what a dull visual world this would be! Balance and repose can be achieved more subtly than through rigid equality, and while this **informal** balance may not be as dynamic, vital, and alive as radical balance, it plays a significant role in many visual statements. The perception and creation of *informal balance* requires sensitivity to the relative weights of shapes, forms, colors, textures, and energies within a given visual statement. Included in this awareness is an acknowledgement that negative spaces have weight and presence as do depicted objects or positive forms. For example, a shape placed on one side of a composition can appear more balanced than that shape placed slightly off-center (**5-10**).

5-10 Negative or open space also has weight. The diagram on the left is more balanced than that on the right.

An informally balanced visual composition has equilibrium. It tends to be stable, relatively simple, harmonious, and ordered. Informally balanced compositions tend to be calm, understated, consistent, and rhythmic.

Radical Balance

Radical or **occult** balance employs contrast and energy to create an interest and tension within a statement. More extreme than informal balance, it is obviously asymmetrical and may be dramatic, irregular, active, and spontaneous. It is dynamic and alive. *Radical balance* is eye-catching and is used in visual statements where the purpose is to attract attention (**5-11**). In the hands of one sensitive to opposing weights of size, placement, color, and space, radical balance can be employed to great and powerful visual effect. Additional qualities used for contrast and radical balance in composition are: instability, sharpness, intensity, turbulence; fragmentation, multiplicity, complexity, irreg-

5-11 HELEN FRANKENTHALER. *Phoebe.* 1979. Acrylic on canvas, 81½ × 100¾". *Courtesy of André Emmerich Gallery, New York. Photo: Geoffrey Clements.*

ularity; extravagance, accent, boldness, intricacy, dissonance; variation, distortion, stress; and randomness, diffusion, episodicity.

Clarity is desirable in the use of asymmetry and radical balance—an awareness of purpose. While the most exciting visual statements often employ radical balance, care is required to avoid ambiguity and arbitrariness. In evaluating balance, remember that color and value have visual weight too.

When assessing balance in a visual statement, there are two approaches. One is to imagine a vertical axis down the center of the visual statement as you are looking at it. Then weigh each side in terms of the visual weights of shapes, colors, and forms, and compare one side with the other. The second approach is to do the weighing first, of left and right, and then place the imaginary axis so the weights of each side are similar.

If the axis falls in the center of the format, the visual statement is formally or informally balanced. If it falls to the left or right of the center, it is asymmetrical and may be informally balanced (close to center), radically balanced (distant from center but possessing an equilibrium, a "rightness" of position), or **unbalanced**: lacking in repose, equality, or equilibrium; disturbing and lopsided.

DOMINANCE/SUBORDINATION

The relationship of **dominant** and **subordinate** aspects of a visual statement is another dynamic in its organization. The most obvious example of this dynamic is the **figure-ground** relationship, also known as the positive form–negative space contrast.

The *figure-ground* relationship is a major structural differentiation in visual statements. **Figure** refers to the *dominant* shapes and objects whereas **ground** connotes both the background and the ground-plane (earth or floor), which are *subordinate*. These contrasts are also called **positive** (form) and **negative** (space) (**5-12**).

FOCAL POINTS

Using instruments to measure and record eye movement, perception psychologists have studied the scanning process employed when looking at pictures. The eye tends to stop at several places: a point of entry, usually one or two areas that are returned to again and again, and a point of exit. These points or areas to which the eye repeatedly returns are the **focal points**, centers of attention or interest.

Focal points are set apart through accent, emphasis, contrast, and association. If there is only one focal point, it may be the lone tree in a landscape or a particularly bright color. But most often there is more than one interest center (**5-13**). The placement of focal points in relation to the edge of the format is an important component of a visual statement. If a focal point is too near an edge, the eye might wander out of the picture and stay out. If the center of interest lacks focus,

5-12 Julie Jensen. *New York, March 1977.* Photograph, 12⅝ × 9″. *Courtesy of the artist.*

5-13 DEBBERA STELLING. *K.V.S., Mental Vigor . . . Conjoined Mutuality,* state two. 1984. Inked collagraph on paper, $19\frac{1}{2} \times 29''$. *Courtesy of the artist.*

5-14 NICHOLAS AFRICANO. *The Shadow #3.* 1979. Oil acrylic, and wax on masonite, $49\frac{1}{2} \times 73\frac{1}{2}''$. *Courtesy of Holly Solomon Gallery, New York.*

strength, or climax, a viewer will not be sufficiently rewarded to give more than a glance.

There is a kind of visual dance that a viewer does between two or more focal points (**5-14**). The maker of visual statements can place focal points so as to entice and involve the viewer in this active participation of seeing.

RHYTHM

Rhythm is a recurrence or repetition of accents and intervals that are similar enough to establish both order and continuity. It is thus intrinsically proportional and unifying (**5-15**). Its most obvious manifestations are regular *texture* and *pattern*.

Pattern is a system of organization and/or repetition of a shape, form, or **motif**—a designed representational or nonrepresentational 2-D or 3-D form. Patterns have many manifestations in our environment: Fences, porch railings, brick and stone work are examples of three-dimensional pattern; and printed fabric, wrapping papers, and wall and floor coverings often use pattern designs (**5-16**). Patterned

motif   pattern

5-16 From a design motif a pattern can be created through regular repetition.

materials offer interest, for they contrast with solid color and shapes while their predictable, often symmetrical repetitions simultaneously offer a sense of

5-15 VINCENT VAN GOGH. *Starry Night.* 1889. Pen and sepia ink on paper, 47 × 62.3 cm. *Courtesy of Kunsthalle, Bremen.*

order and organization. Patterns, as an interaction of the basic visual elements, can have much variety and expressive quality. They may be calm and soothing, or jumpy and enlivening; radical or conservative, sweet or pungent . . . .*

CONTRAST

Contrast is associated with opposites or polarities, some of which are: light-dark, bright-dull, linear-painterly, clear-unclear, hot-cold, fast-slow, and so on. It is because of contrast in color, shape, form, and especially value that we are able to clarify visual experience and communicate more readily with visual means (**5-17**). When using contrast expressively to achieve dynamic or dramatic effect, one takes into account the basic human need for opposing and complementary actions. The absence of contrast would result in an intolerably dull visual world, but the unbridled use of opposites without structure and restraint would result in instability and chaos.

*Pattern recognition, the process by which we cognitively classify visual experience, not only the specific use of *pattern* as defined here, has recently been acknowledged as critical to human function and intelligence. It is a subject of ongoing research by perception psychologists, neurophysiologists, and visual communicators.

VARIETY

Variety is diversity. Variation may be applied to the elements, subject matter, format, medium, techniques, and design principles. Many design theorists refer to a unity/variety connection in which one must have the other, and each must be in evidence in a visual statement: unity for its cohering power, variety for its interest.

ENERGY

Energy exists in visual statements in a variety of ways and levels. On an *actual*, concrete level, **energy** is expressed through motion and light in film and video, or in the reflected light of two-dimensional and three-dimensional visual statements. On an *implied* level, energy is expressed through the use of dynamic elements such as diagonal lines, jagged shapes, scattered objects (**5-18**), or intense, vibrating colors.

Objects, whether actual or depicted, have **lines of force**, which imply direction or thrust. Coming to see these directional, energetic forces is an exciting aspect of becoming visually literate, of learning to assess compositional structure (chapter 6).

5-17 FRANCES M. COX. *Communication.* 1980. Photograph, $6\frac{1}{4} \times 9\frac{1}{2}''$. *Courtesy of the artist.*

5-18 JOHN DOWELL. *To Plan and Move on a Round.* 1980. China ink and watercolor on paper, 30 × 22″. Inspired by the rhythm, presence, and energy of music. *Courtesy of the artist.*

CONFLICT/RESOLUTION

When looking at the underlying structure of a visual statement, relationships of:

figure to ground format,
energies to the format, and
focal points within the format,

can be evaluated for their contribution to or distraction from proportion, balance, and unity. Inevitably, areas of **tension** and **conflict** will be revealed. Once exposed, their appropriateness to the purpose of the visual statement can be assessed. And whether they are to be left in conflict or resolved to contribute to a dynamic and interesting *Gestalt* can be decided.

The tension that arises from conflicts, clashes, or oppositions can heighten interest in a visual statement; and for some quick attention-getting statements, such as posters, there may be little purpose in providing resolution. But in lasting visual images, another element or principle may be employed in such a way as to create a unified field, a **resolution**, for the conflict. For example, a harmonious color scheme could hold together active and divergent energies, or thrusts of lines and shapes. Similarly, a calm, subdued pattern could resolve a wildly polychromatic color expression.

Several methods of compositional analysis are provided in chapter 6. They may assist you in the evaluation of a visual statement's underlying structure and formal substance.

SUMMARY

The operative components of visual composition are the following: unity, scale, orientation, proportion, balance; dominance/subordination, focal points; repetition, rhythm; contrast, variety, energy; tension, conflict, and resolution (unity). Composition is about structure, and above all, about relationships: the relationship of one shape or form to another, and each to the whole; of one color to others, and the color scheme throughout; the relationships among forces and directions, of positive and negative, of large and small, and so forth. Getting these complex interrelationships to work together, so that the completed visual statement is somehow more than the sum of its parts, is an integral purpose of visual statement makers.

ANALYSES OF COMPOSITION IN VISUAL STATEMENTS

6

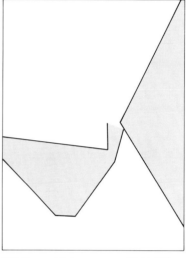

6-1 NORA JAFFE. *Grasp.* 1974 Pen and ink on paper, 24 × 18".
Courtesy of the artist.

The best way to learn the importance of composition and to recognize and evaluate it is to analyze a variety of visual statements. In this chapter are several analytical methods that will facilitate your ability to recognize compositional merit. Not every analysis is suited to every visual statement, so they may be applied as appropriate.

The most effective learning is that which is experientially reinforced. So our methods here call for using tracing paper over reproductions from magazines. Art magazines are good, but photographs and advertisements from any magazine can be just as valuable. In doing these analyses, we learn to extract the *substructure*, the given *relationships* of forms and energies. With hands-on practice, recognition of strong or weak composition becomes increasingly easy and rapid. Seeing a visual statement's structure can eventually become nonanalytical and intuitive, and almost instantly recognizable.

These analytical procedures form a learning process that nurtures awareness of compositional structure. The goal is to learn to evaluate composition as a viewer, to share our visual perceptions and knowledge with others, and as visual creators to integrate sound composition into our visual statements.

One readily available source of visual statements (in a 2-D format) is the illustrations in this book. Alas,

due to time and budget limitations, I could not acquire only exemplary, visually literate examples. Rather than bemoan this, I came to realize that you the reader would benefit by analyzing and evaluating (chapter 16) visual statements over a broad range of organizational and esthetic merit. Therefore I encourage you to apply all of the following analyses to the pictures contained herein, and to the book as a whole. Decide for *yourself* whether they are well composed or not, and why.

DIAGRAMMATIC ANALYSIS

Visual statements may be reduced to schematic or diagrammatic sketches in order to extract and clarify the compositional and proportional structure. By reducing the subject matter to simple geometric shapes, for example, proportional relationships of weight, sizes, and masses can be revealed (*see* **6-1**).

Basic Shapes

Many visual statements can be divided into **basic shapes**, such as triangles, rectangles, and circles, or parts thereof. Thus simplified, how the shapes relate to

3

one another and to the overall composition can be analyzed.

The basic shapes can reveal relative weights of the objects depicted. These weights affect balance and symmetry. The basic shapes can also reveal stability/instability. An interesting and dynamic composition, as revealed by a basic shape diagram, is quite different from a static and dull one.

As in all of these analyses, the tracing must be accurate and include the outline of the whole format. Taping the tracing paper to the picture will prevent inadvertent slips (*see* **6-2, 6-3, 6-4**).

Element Location and Function

In a complex composition that uses most of the elements, it is desirable to look at each *class* of element and understand its relationship and interrelationships within the format of the visual statement. Each class—whether dot, line, shape, mass, texture, color, or value—sets up a kind of internal conversation, cohesion, or substructure that both calls for and establishes its own compositional integrity.

This concept of the interrelationship of elements is similar to the lines of a fugue in music. In the fugue each line has its own melodic and rhythmic integrity as it stands alone, but when all the lines are played together they contribute to a powerful harmonic whole.

To understand the relative power of one class—in this case, *color*—we will analyze the location, shape, and size of each major color in a composition by tracing them on separate sheets of paper. In this method, we use colored pencils or marking pens to match the colors extracted, permitting the affective presence of each color to be considered (colorplate **4**).

This analysis of element location and function can be applied to *value* as with black-and-white photographs. Levels of gray from white to black are extracted for their interrelationships. White, black, and three to five gradations of gray are usually sufficient steps for this study. It may involve grouping and simplification of the tones, and thus provide an exercise in tonal discernment and interrelatedness as well.

Analyses of this nature are effective with regard to classes of *line* qualities in drawings or prints; and with *shapes*, *forms*, and *textures* in any medium. Whatever method of classification is used, *the purpose is to become sensitive to the internal relatedness that each class of each element has within the whole of a visual statement.*

6-2 Keiko Hara. *Verse 4.5.2.1.* 1985. Monoprint, litho/drawing, 40 × 30". *Courtesy of the artist and The Print Club, Philadelphia, PA.*

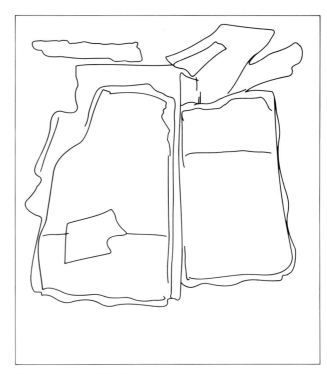

6-3 DEBORAH REMINGTON. *Zanthus*. Oil on canvas. 1983. 74 × 67″. *Courtesy of the artist. Photo: Pelka/Noble.*

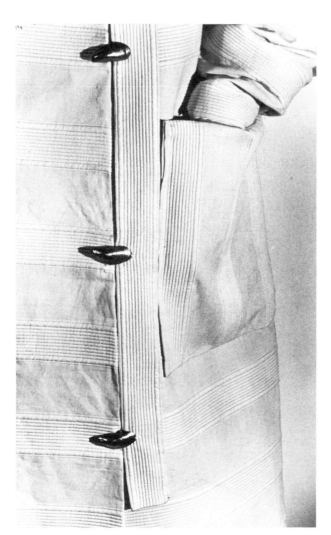
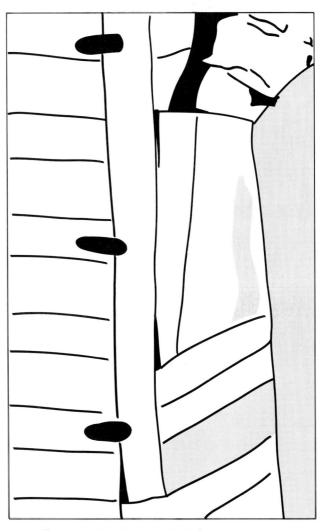

6-4 ILSE BING. *Photographe de Mode* (for Harper's Bazaar 1934). Silver print, 11 × 7″. *Courtesy of Zabriskie Gallery, New York.*

Lines of Energy

Doing a tracing to determine the lines of energy, force, direction, and thrust can reveal how energy flows throughout a visual statement. A **construction-line** diagram of these forces will reveal whether they conflict to create tension or confusion, whether the composition is lifeless and dull, or whether they serve as a unifying force (**6-5**).

Lines of force, direction, and thrust are located at the *center* of a wholly depicted object and its parts. This central line is the average, or median, as estimated by eye when looking at the outer edges of any given shape or form. Thus, in the human figure, a line down the center of the torso, the center of each arm and each leg, and the center of the neck and head give a slightly disjointed stick figure, but one in which the directional lines are clear (**6-6 A-B**). In partially depicted objects, or where high contrast creates a strong line at the edge of a form, that edge may express more thrust than does the center of the form (**6-6 C**). In analyzing lines of force, the viewer must decide where the greatest directional energy lies. Subjective interpretations and preferences may influence these perceptions.

The actual direction, thrust, of these implied lines affects the balance and stability in a visual statement.

Verticals are poised and horizontals are stable, reposed. Slanted and diagonal lines are active, always pushing to straighten up to vertical or fall down to horizontal. Their denial of gravitational pull is what makes them active, forceful. Are diagonals contained within the composition, or do they thrust out of the format and take the viewer's gaze with them? Similarly, curved lines of force can keep the eye of the viewer returning to the central part of the format, or they can fling it out and away forever.

When lines of force have been extracted, and the outline of the format provided, these lines can be analyzed for their contribution to unity or chaos, balance or imbalance, energy or dullness, rhythm or irregularity, and conflict or resolution. Lines of force that are choppy and helter-skelter do not make a good composition (**6-6 D**).

Focal Points

A diagram locating focal points relative to the whole format can reveal substructure, whether it holds the viewer's attention or invites a viewer to move on. These focal points often are interrelated with the directional lines of force and can be located on any of the above analytical tracings (**6-7, 6-8**).

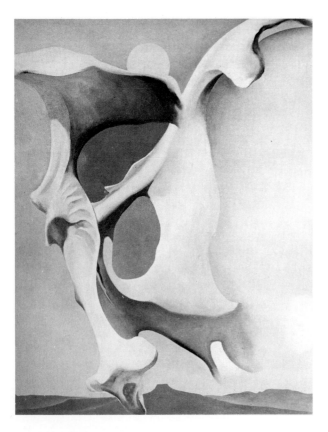

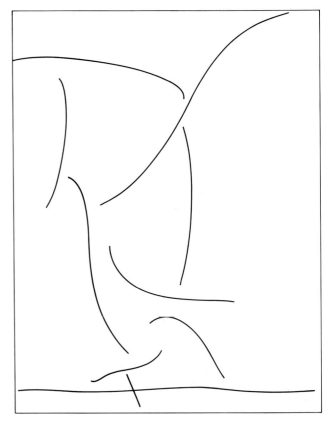

6-5 Georgia O'Keeffe. *Pelvis with Moon.* 1943. Oil on canvas, 30 × 24″. *Collection The Norton Gallery of Art, West Palm Beach, FL.*

6-6A WILLIAM S. MOUNT. *The Painter's Triumph.* 1879. Oil on canvas, $19\frac{1}{2} \times 23\frac{1}{2}''$. *Courtesy of Pennsylvania Academy of the Fine Arts, Philadelphia, PA: bequest of Henry C. Carey.*

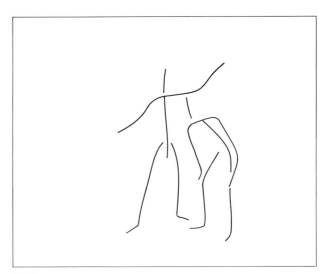

6-6B

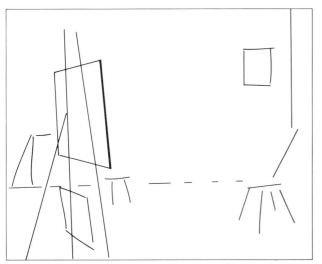

6-6C Selected lines-of-force diagram of **6-6A.**

6-6D Lines-of-force diagram for **6-6A.** What a mixed-up, unresolved composition!

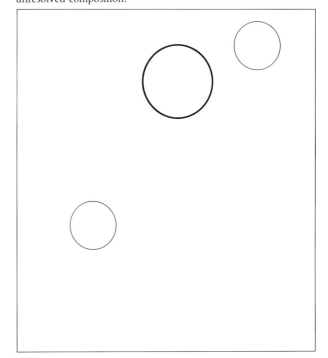

6-7 DEBORAH REMINGTON. *Zanthus* and diagram of primary and secondary focal areas.

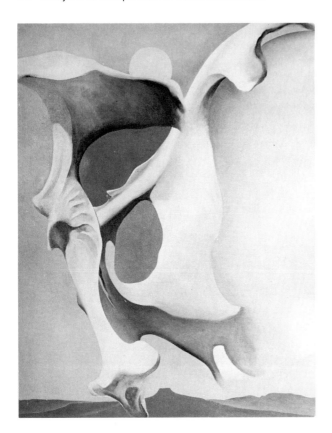
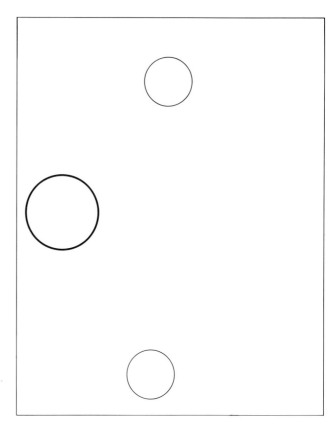

6-8 GEORGIA O'KEEFFE. *Pelvis with Moon* and diagram of primary and secondary focal points. Both the lines of force diagram (**6-5**) and this focal points diagram reveal a restless, unstable underlying structure. The horizon line near the lower edge of the canvas and a muted color scheme—soft grays and blues—provide contrasting stability and calmness. *Collection The Norton Gallery of Art, West Palm Beach FL.*

ANALYSIS OF COMPOSITION AND DESIGN IN THREE-DIMENSIONAL AND TIME-ORIENTED VISUAL STATEMENTS

The format of this book does not permit an effective compositional analysis of either three-dimensional forms; visual statements requiring time for their experience, such as film; or the spatial aspects of architecture and environmental design. Yet compositional analyses of dimensional visual statements are no less important. Therefore, it must be up to the reader to apply these basic principles and procedures to such works. Here are some tips.

The dimensions of depth and time add much complexity to sensing underlying structure. With sculpture, for example, it is desirable that it be visually effective when viewed from any point around its 360° periphery. To quote one author on this subject:

> A photographer attempting to represent fully three-dimensional sculpture has a unique problem. If there can be one best picture of a sculpture, the sculptor has failed.*

*Hall, Donald, *As the Eye Moves . . .* (New York: Abrams, 1977), p. 13.

Thus the analysis of a visual statement in the round, or over time, is far more complex than that of a two-dimensional painting, print, or photograph having a single point of view.

One must scan 3-D and 4-D visual statements (thus *both* are sequential) and construct an intuitive sense of the whole. The view around a building, an object of design, or a sculpture, or the length of a film or video are looked at with the "x-ray vision" we've acquired from analyzing the underlying structure of 2-D visual statements. One analyzes very rapidly, too rapidly for detailed explication, a sequence of 2-D perceptions of 3-D and 4-D works. The viewer then synthesizes these diagrammatic impressions into an intuitive sense of whether the work is visually well composed or not. The only way to do this effectively is *first* to have become proficient in all the analyses of 2-D visual statements given above.

As viewers, we have the opportunity to develop awareness of composition in sequential visual statements every time we go to the movies or watch TV. How well composed, two-dimensionally, is every frame, every instant? How does the whole move from beginning to end? Is it well paced, or do sections lag or rush by with no time for assimilation?

6-9 CH'I PAI-SHIH. *Loquats and Grasshopper.* C. 1940. Ink and watercolors on paper, album painting. *Courtesy of the Philadelphia Museum of Art, Philadelphia, PA.*

THE IMPORTANCE
OF COMPOSITIONAL ANALYSIS

Unlike the rules of grammar in language, the syntax of visual statements is not definitive. That is, there is no one way to organize the components of composition because they all contain an infinite number of variables. Only through learning about these components, and being conscious of them, can we evaluate the construction of a visual statement. Sensitivity to composition enables us to assess whether it supports the intent and content of a visual statement, and whether the visual statement is structured well enough to survive the test of time.

No method of compositional analysis is appropriate for every visual statement. Depending upon the visual elements and compositional principles employed, one form of analysis may be more effective than the others in revealing the compositional substructure.

To resist a hard-sell, or to choose to purchase a work of art, or to reject the past in forging new directions in the development of one's own art, knowing compositional principles is a source of strength and is crucial to becoming visually literate. When we learn to understand composition in visual statements, irrespective of medium and format, confidence in assessing the visual world is a rich reward.

ANALYZING ART
OF OTHER CULTURES

The foregoing analyses may or may not be applicable to visual statements created by cultures other than our own Euro-American culture. In the mid-1970s, the author of this text embarked upon an intensive investigation of Chinese and Japanese art, culminating in a three-month study of Chinese ink painting in Hong Kong and Taipei. It was learned, painfully, that Western concepts of spatial organization were an impediment to learning experientially the basis upon which one stroke implies the next in this centuries-old tradition of painting. One must experience art of other cultures according to the values and standards by which it is made, not by what we know from our own tradition (**6-9**).

SUMMARY

Diagrammatic analyses made with tracing paper over reproductions of photographs, graphic designs, drawings, paintings, and prints are helpful in learning to see the composition of visual statements. Subjects of analysis include diagrams of basic shapes, colors, values, energies, and focal points. Once one is proficient in analyzing two-dimensional visual statements, one can intuitively evaluate three-dimensional and time-oriented visual statements by using this acquired "x-ray vision" sequentially.

These analyses, together with your knowledge of the elements and your understanding of the functions of compositional syntax in visual statements, provide you as viewer with the ability to comprehend the form of a visual statement in any medium.

USING COMPOSITIONAL PRINCIPLES IN THE MAKING OF VISUAL STATEMENTS

7

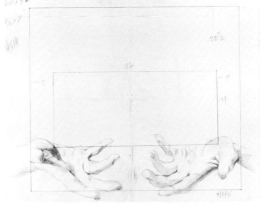

7-1 DEBORAH CURTISS. *Ynap Hands-d.* 1985. Graphite on paper, $8\frac{1}{2}$ × 11″. Drawing of hands cropped and diagrammed to show location in painting. *Courtesy of the artist.*

The principles of composition were presented in chapter 5 in the order they are most often encountered in the process of *making* a visual statement. It must be remembered, however, that the strategies for making visual statements vary tremendously with the maker, with the medium, and with the prevailing influences of the time. Thus, what follows is not a strategy; it is a guideline for you as visual creator to become more conscious of the compositional principles during your creative process.

To begin, you may wish to make **compositional** or **preliminary sketches** to work out the basic organization of your proposed visual statement. These may establish balance, relationships of positive and negative, directions of linear movement, placement of focal points, the value structure, and points of view (**7-2**). In making these sketches—small ones are known as **thumbnail sketches**—you will become aware of **counterpoint** or **contrapuntal forces**, the playing off of one subject or element against another, often its opposite. The sketches will also allow you to **edit** your composition by **cropping**, or cutting off, any undesirable elements (*see* **7-1**).

UNITY

Intrinsic to the satisfactory completion of a visual image is a sense of *unity*. Unity is a concen from start to

7-2 SHERMAN HOEFLICH. *Gordon Craig.* 1964. Pen-and-ink sketches, $8\frac{1}{4}$ × $5\frac{5}{16}$″ each. *Courtesy of Alber Gallery, Philadelphia, PA.*

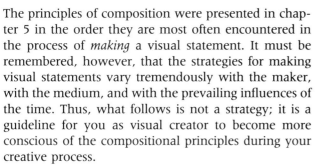

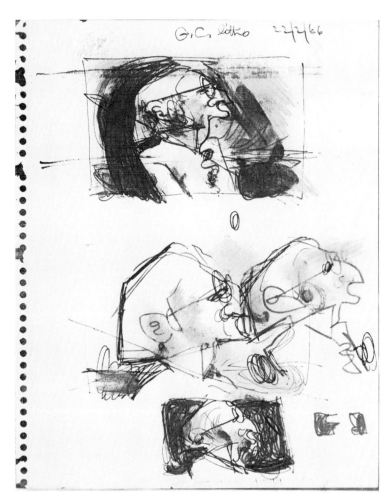

7-3 SHERMAN HOEFLICH. *Studies for Gordon Craig lithograph.* 1966. Red and black ink, wash on paper, 10 × 8″, *Courtesy of Alber Gallery, Philadelphia, PA.*

finish. Some aspects of unity are determined by the format we choose while others are achieved in the combination of the elements and medium within the format **(7-3)**. The challenge is to step back periodically from involvement with elements, medium, and technique to assess how these various components are working, in visual terms, toward the whole.

SCALE

Scale is decided at the outset when the format is chosen, **(7-4)**. The function of the visual statement and its anticipated placement in the world affect the decision of size. In some media the scale of a work may change during its making: it may get larger, smaller, longer, or shorter. Any such modifications require a reassessment of the scale of the work relative to its purpose.

ORIENTATION, PROPORTION, BALANCE

Orientation, proportion, and balance are ongoing concerns from beginning to end of the visual expression. Visualize a poised vertical axis resting on a stable hori-

zontal base; whether actual or implied, it provides an orientation within which activity and variation can take place in a visual statement. Proportion and balance evolve throughout the process of making a visual statement. So when we pause to assess unity, these principles can be effectively evaluated as well:

How is each shape or form proportioned within itself?
How does it fit in with other shapes or forms?
And how do they all relate to the whole of the format?
How do the shapes, forms, colors, and values affect the visual weight?
And how do they balance with other weights on opposite sides of the central vertical axis?

Asking these questions throughout the process of making a visual statement reduces the possibility of getting lost in space and time **(7-5)**.

DOMINANCE/SUBORDINATION, RHYTHM, AND FOCAL POINTS

Dominance/subordination and positive/negative are ongoing, evolving considerations, part of the building and creating of a visual statement. Shapes, forms, colors, and textures are arranged rhythmically or arrhyth-

62

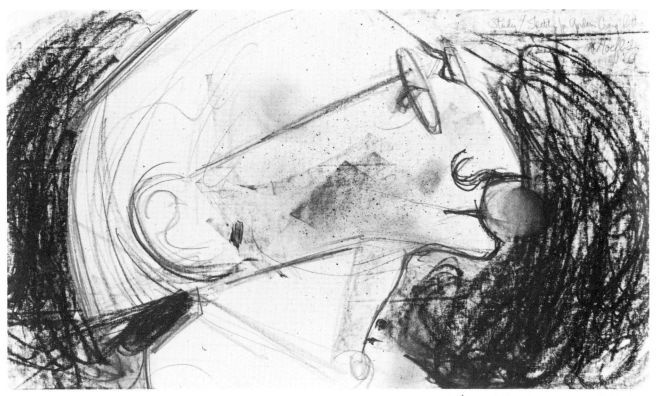

7-4 SHERMAN HOEFLICH. *Gordon Craig Study Sketch.* 1966. Pencil and litho crayon on paper, 8 × 13¾". *Courtesy of Alber Gallery, Philadelphia, PA.*

A/P

#1

Gordon Craig #4

Hoeflich '66

7-5 SHERMAN HOEFLICH. *Gordon Craig.* 1966. Lithograph, artist's proof #1, 9 × 16½". *Courtesy of Alber Gallery, Philadelphia, PA.*

7-6 SHERMAN HOEFLICH. *Gordon Craig #4.* 1966. Lithograph 7/15, 9 × 16½″. *Courtesy of Alber Gallery, Philadelphia, PA.*

7-7 SHERMAN HOEFLICH. *Gordon Craig #4.* 1966. Lithograph, Cancellation proof (as indicated by the x at the bottom), 9 × 16½″. *Courtesy of Alber Gallery, Philadelphia, PA.*

64

mically. Focal points or climaxes are located relative to each other and to the whole format of the visual statement. They can be part of a conscious design or they can emerge spontaneously from the hidden agenda of an evolving artist (**7-6**).

TENSION, CONFLICT, AND RESOLUTION

Intertwined with positive/negative, focal points, and rhythm are contrasts, variety, energy, tension, and conflict. How these components are used, contained, and brought into resolution and a unified whole is a significant part of the *final* stages of making a visual statement. This period is often less active and more reflective. Assessments are made, and the final image, design, form, or sequence is fine-tuned. Thus visual statements can be created so that the total effect is greater than the sum of its individual parts (**7-7**).

Depending upon the medium chosen, some principles of visual organization will be more or less important. In time-oriented works, rhythm and pacing take on keen significance (**7-8**). Three-dimensional works require compositional assessment from all directions. In them, energies and focal points may never be simultaneously visible. But their relationships as we view the work in the round are very important (**7-9**). In

A

B

7-8 James Fuhrman. *Drawings from Graham Class.* Brush and ink on paper. **A** $24\frac{1}{4} \times 28\frac{1}{2}''$; **B** $15\frac{1}{4} \times 27\frac{1}{8}''$. *Courtesy of the artist.*

A

B

7-9 JAMES FUHRMAN. **A.** *Distilled Drawing from Graham Class.* Brush and ink on paper, 14 × 15½ ". **B.** *Calligraphic Form.* Painted welded steel, 48 × 60 × 8″. *Courtesy of the artist.*

7-10 Executive Terrace, King of Prussia, PA. *Photo: Gregory Benson.*

architecture, spatial organization is important both inside and out. The location of a building must take into account its impact upon its surroundings, both visually and functionally (**7-10**). Thus principles of composition are as desirable to the macrocosm of a metropolis as to the microcosm of an intimate drawing.

EVALUATION OF COMPOSITIONAL MERIT

It is appropriate at this time to introduce a simple outline for the evaluation of a visual statement:

1. State what is good about the work: its use of elements, composition, format, materials, media, style, and so forth.
2. State what is not good or inappropriate about the above aspects.
3. Make specific suggestions for improving or correcting these problems.

This three step procedure is effective in evaluating the esthetic merit of a work (*see* chapter 16), and is used in a number of the exercises (chapter 7 and following) in the appendix.

SUMMARY

The principles of visual composition, used as a flexible guide when making visual statements, empower the visual statement maker to create more efficiently and consciously.

Our ability to use these principles rests upon first knowing what they are (chapter 5) and then learning to recognize their presence in visual statements of any medium (chapter 6). Just as a gemstone is cut in certain ways so as to reveal and maximize the brilliance of the gem, visual statements must be thoughtfully and astutely structured (chapter 7) so as to support, enhance, and reveal the substance and content that the visual statement creator makes.

The recognition and utilization of compositional principles are invaluable in becoming visually articulate.

IV FRED DANZIGER. *Landscape with Many Eyes.* Oil on canvas, 48 × 54″. The center panel is painted in a traditional realist style; the panels to the left in increasingly emotional styles: Impressionism, Fauvism, Expressionism; to the right the styles become more analytical: Post Impressionism (Cezanne), Constructivism, and High-Tech (computer-derived). *Courtesy of the artist and Rodger La Pelle Gallery, Philadelphia, PA.*

IV

STYLE

Style is the characteristic way of designing or shaping a visual statement that renders it identifiable as the work of a particular individual, group, region, or period. Stylistic changes occur in visual communication as a reflection of the basic human need for variety. Additionally, the ongoing expansion of media options, the input of individual expression, and the lack of definitive meaning of visual symbols and expressions set the stage for constant evolution.

Development of personal style is an elusive and unspecifiable process. Components include an individual's intrinsic motor abilities, habits, and skills. Knowledge of styles of the past—those we respond to favorably and those we reject—also influence our personal style. As students we may try out various styles to see whether they suit our vision and purpose. By sifting through stylistic possibilities, combining and reshaping them, one can develop a unique **signature**, the identifiable synthesis of elements, methods, and materials employed and/or omitted by an artist, designer, or visual communicator.

On the whole, art historians classify periods of art by highlighting distinctive characteristics of a period and place. This method works well for looking back at times of slower-evolving expression. Today, new developments in both techniques and visual expression are occurring with such rapidity that we are compelled to limit this book's overview to classifications that are basic to the experience of viewing, evaluating, and making visual statements.

In chapter 8, therefore, we will explore the means and concepts that classify visual statements along the representational/nonrepresentational continuum. Chapter 9 is comprised of a selected vocabulary of visual styles, those identifying terms frequently used for classification in describing or critiquing visual statements.

STYLE IN VISUAL COMPOSITION

8-1 LILY FUREDI. *Subway* c. 1934. Oil on canvas, 39 × 48¼″, Public Works of Art Project, New York City. Transfer from National Park Service, U.S. Department of the Interior. *Courtesy of National Museum of American Art, Smithsonian Institution, Washington, DC.*

PICTORIAL MEDIA

Drawing, painting, printmaking, sculpture, photography, film, and video are the **pictorial media**, those capable of (but not limited to) representing images of the world in which we live. In these media, style can be manifested on levels that are embedded in the content and purpose of the visual statement. Certain symbols or modes of depiction can come to stand for a point of view, for example, the ordinary life of working people that was depicted by artists of the Works Project Administration (WPA) during the 1930s (**8-1**).

On an individualistic level, the way an artist handles materials, tools, and techniques can be unique and unprecedented. Such originality establishes that person's contribution to the collective visual vocabulary of style and expression.

On a more general level, visual statements in the pictorial media may be classified as *representational, abstract,* or *nonrepresentational.*

Representation

A visual statement that is **representational** depicts objects and scenes that are recognizable from our experience in the real world. **Realism** suggests representation as closely as possible to the way we see

the real world. **Naturalism** means depicting subject matter as naturally as possible, with no attempt to improve upon nature or flatter the subject. **Trompe l'oeil** (French for "fool the eye") is a work so realistic as to fool the viewer into thinking objects are real rather than painted, made from glazed ceramic, or devised from other artificial materials (**8-2**).

Although there was a move away from realism in the arts in the late nineteenth century, both necessity and choice have kept designers and artists concerned with realistic representation. In recent years there has been a burst of interest in **superrealism**, in which there is a compulsive attention to detail, often on an enlarged scale (**8-3**). Popular too has been **photorealism**, in which photography is used either as inspiration or for the actual imagery of a painting, print, or sculpture (**8-4**).

The subject represented may be a view of the exterior world, such as a **landscape**, a **cityscape**, or a **seascape** (**8-5**). A representational visual statement may depict **interior** spaces such as the inside of a cathedral or a studio. Specific objects of an interior space, or objects placed on a table inside or outside, comprise a composition called a **still-life** (**8-6**).

Depiction of the human figure and the animal

8-2 KATHERINE SCHMIDT. *Gift Wrapping*. 1960. Oil on canvas, 18 × 30". *Courtesy of Zabriskie Gallery, New York. Photo: John A. Ferrari.*

8-3 JANET FISH. *Pink Plates*. 1979. Oil on canvas, 48 × 46". *Courtesy of Robert Miller Gallery, New York.*

8-4 BARBARA MINCH. *Highway Series #2*. Acrylic on canvas, 45 × 55". *Courtesy of the artist.*

8-5 TEMMA BELL. *Esjan*. 1981. Oil on canvas, 24 × 69". *Courtesy of the Bowery Gallery, New York.*

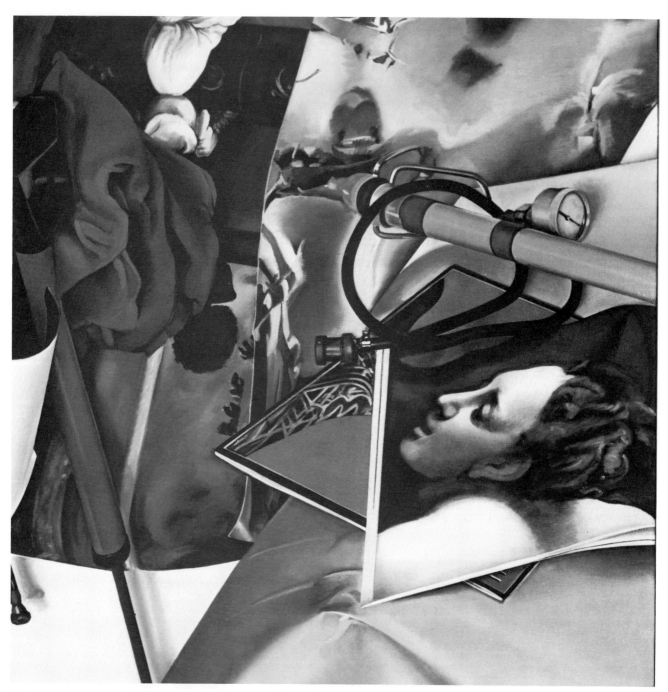

8-6 MARGARETTA GILBOY. *"Egli! lo!"* 1983. Oil on canvas, 24 × 24". *Courtesy of Marian Locks Gallery, Philadelphia, PA.*

and plant kingdoms—whether central to or incidental to a visual statement—is known as **figurative**. The tradition of figurative subject matter, particularly in Western art, includes **portraits**, human figures in a variety of locations (**8-7**), and the **nude**.

Recognizable images are a part of the *content* of a visual statement, but the *way* in which they are depicted pertains to the *style*. In experiencing or making representational visual statements, we must bear in mind that mere recognition of the subject does not

necessarily mean grasping the content. Content has many forms of expression in the purely abstract, formal components of visual statements as well.

Abstraction

In the past century—largely due to the invention of photography, which freed artists from their role of documentors—there was a movement away from realism toward a variety of means of abstraction. On a very

8-7 JOAN SEMMEL. *Siblings.* 1982. Oil on canvas, 56 × 120″. *Courtesy of the artist.*

basic level, all art and visual statements are abstract. The visual communicator selects and *abstracts* from nature that which is to be made, whether it is the materials with which to build a building or the subject depicted two-dimensionally in a photograph or paint-ing. But **abstraction** usually refers to the degree to which the content of a visual statement digresses from the real world as we know it. Thus we may have abstraction that is either *objective* or *nonobjective* in its content.

Objective abstraction is the nonrealistic depic-tion of natural forms. Here, there is a concentration on the essence of the object, but the object itself has been altered or distorted in order to emphasize or reveal qualities that are not otherwise apparent. Such abstract visual statements may have as their source of inspira-tion landscape, still-life, or the human figure (**8-8**).

The range of possibilities in working abstractly is vast. An artist brings personal choice and his or her unique necessity of expression to the process of abstraction. Various schools and techniques of abstrac-tion have evolved at different times in history. One technique is **simultaneous representation**, which connotes the *combining* of more than one point of view (**8-9**). Simultaneous representation sometimes occurs unintentionally in basic drawing classes, when stu-dents lose awareness of their location in space relative to the subject being depicted. In this case, what one knows about the subject gets in the way of seeing it objectively and accurately. It is important to master accurate representation in order to use simultaneous representation with effective intent.

8-8 PAUL KLEE. *Runner at the Goal.* 1921. Watercolor and gouache on yellow Ingres paper mounted on board. $12\frac{7}{8}$ × $9\frac{3}{8}$″. *Solomon R. Guggenheim Museum, New York. Photo: Robert E. Mates.*

A. SUSAN ROSENBERG. *Double Exposure.* 1982. Photograph created with two negatives superimposed. *Courtesy of the artist.*

8-9 Two intentional uses of simultaneous representation:

B. MICHAEL MCGUIRE. *Lady Body Builder.* Photograph created by flipping the negative and exposing the top and bottom halves of the photo separately. *Courtesy of McGuire and McGuire, Jenkintown, PA.*

Nonrepresentation

Nonobjective or **pure abstraction** has no reference to any recognizable representational content. **Nonrepresentational** visual statements are often inspired by formalistic concerns such as geometric shapes, color, gesture, and materials. Nonrepresentation is a realm in which the physical properties of the work, its surface, the elements, and compositional principles are allowed to sing forth expressively, free from most content and contextual associations (**8-10**). The focus is on the work itself, wholly identified with its process of creation (**8-11**).

DESIGN AND CRAFT MEDIA

Architecture, graphics, industrial design, handcrafts, and decorative arts are media in which visual appearance and function are inextricably intertwined.

Form follows function. This was the edict of the Bauhaus, which revolutionized style in design in the 1920s. The idealization of function led to **modernism**, the reduction of form to its essentials, the smoothing out of design elements to create sleek, elegant, purposeful forms.

Yet the functional requirements of designed objects do not limit their style to functionalism alone. Designed objects may make reference to purified classical forms and shapes (**8-12**). Or they may be ornamented, distorted, and reshaped in ways that originate with the designer or craftsperson as a manifestation of creative invention (**8-13**). Unique stylistic embellishments and inventions can serve both as a signature for the designer or craftsperson and as a contribution to the ever-broadening vocabulary of visual expression.

Many influences are reflected in the stylistic manifestations of individuals, groups, eras, and locales. When one considers the unique and identifying characteristics of the signature of one's name, is it any sur-

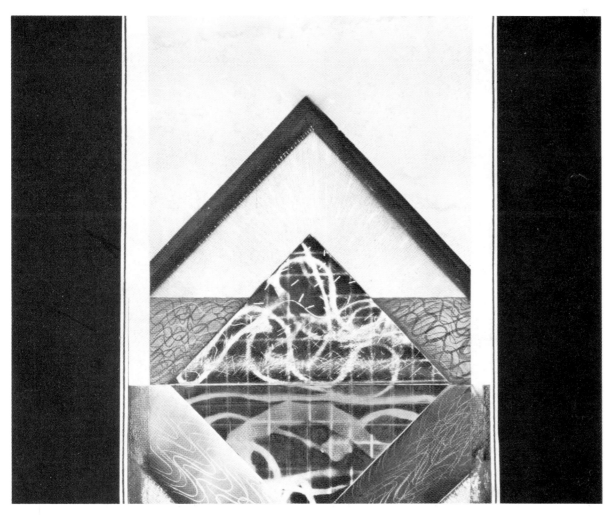

8-10 JAMES DUPREE. *Contained B.R. Light Magenta.* 1983. Acrylic on canvas, 29 × 23". *Courtesy of Sande Webster Gallery, Philadelphia, PA.*

8-11 ANDREW HARPER. *Second Tier*. 1985. Welded steel, 4 × 3 × 3'. *Courtesy of the artist.*

8-12 MICHELLE and DAVID HOLZAPFEL. *Cherry Wood Vase*. 1984. 24 × 13″ diameter. *Courtesy of the artists and Snyderman Gallery, Philadelphia, PA.*

8-13 ROBERT LEVIN. *Color Cup #46*. 1981. Handblown glass, $8\frac{5}{8}$″ × 3″ diameter. *Courtesy of the artist and Snyderman Gallery, Philadelphia, PA. Photo: Dan Bailey.*

8-14 DIANE ARBUS. *Parlor, Levittown.* (Christmas 1963). Gelatin-silver print, 10 × 9½". *Collection, The Museum of Modern Art, New York. Purchase. Copyright © Estate of Diane Arbus 1963.*

8-15 FLORENCE KNOLL. *End Table.* Glass, steel, polished chrome finish, 24 × 24 × 17". *Courtesy of Knoll International, New York. Photo: Mikio Sekita.*

prise that this fundamental ''handwriting'' suffuses what we make as visual statements? It is less direct, perhaps, in such media as photography and design, but artists and designers are continually striving to make their mark of individuality through a ''signature'' theme or concept (**8-14, 8-15**).

SUMMARY

Style, the characteristic way of designing or shaping a visual statement, is embedded in the content, intent, and materials of the work. In pictorial media, style includes choices regarding representation, abstraction, and nonrepresentation. In design and the craft media, style is manifest in the shaping and embellishment of the functional form of the object.

STYLISTIC TERMINOLOGY

9

9-1 SUZANNE HORVITZ. *Fetish and Fantasy.* 1983. Acrylic, photography, and xerography on masonite, 40 × 90″, detail: 40 × 30″. *Courtesy of the artist and Benjamin Mangel Gallery, Philadelphia, PA.*

We are living at a highly individualistic time, and artists, too, develop distinctive styles as an integral part of their communication. This was not always so, for historically a style may have prevailed for many years. Within this century, artistic styles and schools have tended to form by country: *De Stijl* in the Netherlands, *Die Brücke* in Germany, Futurism in Italy, Fauvism in France, and Abstract Expressionism in the United States. At times a style was so intensely celebrated that some paintings, for example those done by Picasso and Braque during Cubism, are indistinguishable from each other except to experts.

More recently we have seen Op Art, Pop Art, Minimalism, New Expressionism, Hi-Tech, and New Wave as stylistic movements. Because of the rapidity of mass communication today, these periods are less confined in time to group or place than they have been in the past.

To delve more deeply into aspects and periods of style would be to enter the realm of the art historian, and this is not a purpose of this book. This chapter includes definitions of the stylistic terms that enter into discussions when making and viewing visual statements. As such, they are an important part of both the visual and verbal vocabularies of visual arts and communication. They have been arranged topically according to similarities of spirit.

CLASSICISM

Classical art refers generally to that of the Golden Age of Greece, 500 to 300 B.C. Classical art subordinates content to form. Design and composition are especially important and are characterized by adherence to standards of ideal proportion. Classical art is realistic, simple, restrained, pure, balanced, symmetrical, regular, and controlled (**9-2**). The Classical spirit has been felt in the following twentieth-century periods.

Cubism, one of the first polemically abstract movements, is theoretical and conceptual in the organization of forms in space. Objects are reduced to planar geometric shapes, hence the name. As a celebration of structure Cubist works represent objects simultaneously from several points of view, resulting in near obfuscation of the object (see **3-61**).

Constructivism is a three-dimensional indulgence in structure and logic (**9-3**). Normally it is geometrically nonobjective and assembled from a variety of materials and processes borrowed from industrial production. The **Bauhaus** was a school of architecture, design, and crafts in Germany, 1919–1933. Upon

9-2 Angelica Kauffman (1741-1807). *Cornelia Pointing to Her Children as Her Treasures.* Oil on canvas, 40 × 50". *Courtesy of The Virginia Museum of Fine Arts, Richmond. VA, The Williams Fund.*

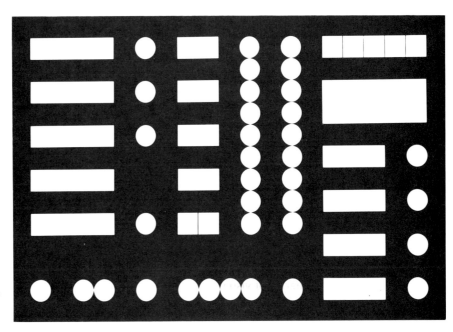

9-3 Sophie Taeuber-Arp. *Schematic Composition.* 1933. Oil and wood on composition board, $35\frac{3}{8} \times 49\frac{1}{4}$". *Collection, The Museum of Modern Art, New York. Gift by Silvia Pizitz.*

the Bauhaus's closing, its proponents migrated throughout the world and guided design theory and production, leading to a dominance of simplicity, clarity and **Functionalism** (form follows function).

Optical Art is a form of perceptual abstraction that generates optical effects in the visual system of the viewer by use of cleanly designed patterns (**9-4**). **Minimalism** is an expression of pure form reduced to its simplest expression.

In **Conceptual Art** the decision-making process of organizing a visual statement becomes the work itself. Here, the art object itself receives low priority while thought processes, theories, and words are presented instead (**9-5**).

Academic art was an outgrowth of the eighteenth-century neo-classical Age of Reason. With an emphasis on explanation and rules, and on a single proper spirit and manner of depicting the world (**9-6**), Academic art came to connote rigidity and dullness. Academicism has been manifest in the twentieth century by **Social Realism**, a depiction of the contemporary scene with idealized and socially conscious content. **Socialist Realism** is blatantly propagandistic, usually reflecting Communist ideology. (Art **academies** today employ a style of teaching in which artists and students work together instead of, or as a supplement to, holding classes of formal instruction. The styles of art taught in this manner, however, are not limited to the Academic tradition.)

ROMANTICISM

The **Romantic style**—often considered the opposite of Classicism—subordinates form to content. There can be an indulgence in the unbridled expression of emotion, passion, and drama; in the exotic, the fabulous, and in the imagination. It is a highly personal art, given to introspection, idealism, and freedom of spirit. **Ornamented** visual statements are sometimes called **Baroque** or **Rococo** from the eras so named (1700–1825) that celebrated spectacular feats of sculptural activity, ornamentation, and colorful painterly lushness (**9-7**).

Gothic refers to intricate, lacy stonework and elongated, sometimes contorted religious aspirations toward a transcendent expression (**9-8**). **Mannerism**, a reaction against the Classicism of the Renaissance, expressed emotion through elongation and exaggeration of light and shadow (**9-9**).

9-4 BRIDGET RILEY. *Current.* 1964. Synthetic polymer paint on composition board, $58\frac{3}{8} \times 58\frac{7}{8}''$. *Collection, The Museum of Modern Art, New York. Philip Johnson Fund.*

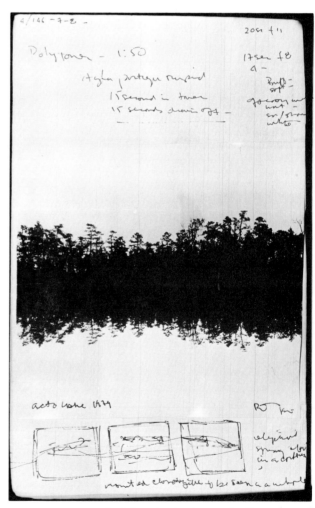

9-5 BENEDICT TISA. *Sketch for Triptych.* Photo and collage, $7\frac{1}{2} \times 4\frac{3}{4}''$. *Courtesy of the artist.*

9-6 CECELIA BEAUX. *Mother and Daughter.*
1898. Oil on canvas, 83 × 44". *Courtesy of
Pennsylvania Academy of the Fine Arts,
Philadelphia, PA. Gift of Frances C. Griscom.*

9-7 FRANÇOIS BOUCHER. *Lovers in a Park.* Oil on canvas. *Courtesy of Timken Art Gallery. Photo: John F. Waggamon.*

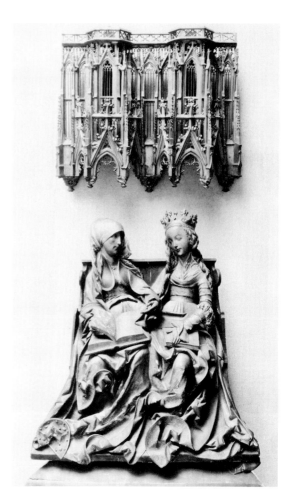

9-8 BENEDICT MASTER, HILDESHEIM SCHOOL. *Education of the Virgin.* C.1510. Wood. *Courtesy of Philadelphia Museum of Art, Philadelphia, PA. Given by Elisabeth Malcom Bowman in Memory of Wendell Phillips Bowman.*

IMPRESSIONISM

Impressionist painting concentrates on the play of light and color on the surface of objects and nature, and in the activity of light and color that exists between an object and the painter's eye. Because the artist breaks color into tiny marks of varying hues, the surface of impressionistic works has a flickering quality (**9-10**). The underlying structure of the objects and forms depicted is often incidental. **Pointillism**, also known as **Neo-Impressionism**, involves the use of these tiny daubs or points of color in a more precise way. Certain colors are juxtaposed with one another so that the eye of the viewer optically mixes and blends them into another color.

The prefix *post-* usually connotes a reaction against the period that preceded it. Thus **Post-impressionism** marked a return to more formal

9-9 ARTEMISIA GENTILESCHI. *Judith and Maidservant with the Head of Holofernes.* C.1625. Oil on canvas, $72\frac{1}{2} \times 55\frac{3}{4}$". *Courtesy of the Founders Society, Detroit Institute of Arts, Detroit, MI.*

9-10 BERTHE MORISOT. *Two Girls.* C.1894. Oil on Canvas, 26 × 21½ ". *Courtesy of the Phillips Collection, Washington, DC.*

consciousness, an increased awareness of the subject/object of a painting. **Genre** drawing or painting refers to the depiction of ordinary, everyday domestic life.

EXPRESSIONISM

Exaggeration, and distortion, and an abandonment of realistic depiction characterize **Expressionism**. It is often polemical, passionate, problematic, and commit-ted to radical ideas and reactions against prevailing taste. Strong color and outline are dominant; finesse and clarity are sacrificed to emotional impact (**9-11**). **Fauvist** works are representational but are characterized by a simplification of shape and an outlandish freedom of color. In **Symbolist** art it is believed that, behind the shapes and colors of a picture's surface, there is something else, another realm, another order of significance and meaning. *Symbols* are used to invoke this other realm (**9-12**). **Surrealism** has had a

9-11 PAULA MODERSOHN-BECKER. *Girl with Yellow Wreath and Daisy.* C.1902. Oil on cardboard, 20 × 18¼ ". *Private collection. Courtesy of Galerie St. Etienne, New York.*

9-12 REMEDIOS VARO. *Harmonie*. 1956. Oil on masonite, 29″ × 36⅝ ″. *Private collection. Courtesy of Jeffrey Hoffeld & Co., New York.*

long history in the depiction of the fantastic and weird. It is often distinguished by unexpected juxtapositions of pictorial ideas and a dreamlike freedom from reason. Works of **fantasy**, imagination (**9-13**), and **psychedelic** imagery (representations of visual experience while under the influence of psychotropic drugs) are outgrowths of surrealism. **Dada** is anti-art that tends to shock and outrage.

Abstract Expressionism engages a high degree of subconscious expression through ''automatic'' or gestural painting that abandons conscious control for a more primal response to color and space. Rigorously nonobjective, it flourished in the United States in the 1950s (**9-14**).

Pop Art of the 1960s shocked when it presented imagery and objects from popular and ordinary culture as high art (**9-15**). This led to **Kitsch**, art made of assemblages of rubbish and commonplace objects. It

and bad-taste **Funk** lean to the eccentric, vulgar, anti-formal, and anti-intellectual. **New Wave** synthesizes Funk with **High-Tech** art, that which utilizes technology both for the creation of its expressions and as a reflection of the changes that technology is making in our lives (**9-16**).

Neoexpressionism is a 1980s movement in both Europe and the United States that is more a reaction to the conditions (catastrophes) of modern life than a development of new visual expression. War, threat of nuclear holocaust, violence, degradation, offensive taste, and funky humor are depicted forcefully and harshly. The works are often narrative (**9-17**), grossly explicit, and rife with oversized, simplified yet violent imagery. Colors are deliberately clashing, and compositional organization is either nonexistent or so emphatically chaotic that narrative content offers the only unifying factor.

9-13 KAY SAGE. *Festa.* 1947. Oil on canvas, 18" × 14". *Private collection. Courtesy of Jeffrey Hoffeld & Co., New York.*

9-14 JOAN MITCHELL. *Girolata.* 1964. Oil on canvas, $101\frac{1}{2}$" × $189\frac{1}{2}$". *Courtesy of the Hirshhorn Museum and Sculpture Garden, Smithsonian Institution, Washington, DC.*

9-15 CAROLYNN HAYWARD-JACKSON. *Ice Cream Mountain*. 1983. Plaster of paris, acrylic and polymer resins, and dyes, 15″ × 14″ diameter. *Courtesy of the artist and Sande Webster Gallery, Philadelphia, PA.*

9-16 REYNOLD WEIDENAAR. *Brooklyn Bridge.* Computerized video image. *Courtesy of the artist and AIVF via Robin White, Media Alliance. New York.*

9-17 SUSAN ROTHENBERG. *Grandmother.* 1983-84. Oil on canvas, 89 × 112½ ". *Courtesy of Willard Gallery, New York. Photo: Geoffrey Clements.*

9-18 Unknown American Artist. *Mahantango Valley Farm* Oil on windowshade, 28 × 35⅜ ". *Courtesy the National Gallery of Art, Washington, DC. Gift of Edgar William and Bernice Chrysler Garbisch.*

Naive art (sometimes inaccurately called primitive) usually is art created by persons who have had no formal art training. It is characterized by a childlike innocence unaffected by the history or tradition of art. In naive art a contradiction arises between a striving for realism and the inability to achieve it. Shapes are usually flat, decorative, static, and spaces are cluttered **(9-18)**. **Pseudo-naiveté** is a characteristic of some New-Expressionists, where formally trained artists are deliberately using the bungled realism and ingenuous-looking compositions of less sophisticated visual creators.

9-19 Philadelphia Art and Fashion Institute, Philadelphia, PA. *Courtesy of Art Institute of Philadelphia. Photo: J.W. Blanco.*

MODERNISM

In design and illustration **Art Nouveau**, or "new art," involved the stylization of elongated, writhing, sinuous botanical forms as motifs in architecture and decorative arts. This—together with influences of the Industrial Revolution—led to the streamlined, simplified qualities of **Modernism**, the stripping of design and form to its essentials. Symmetrical, rectilinear **Art Deco** represented Modern style at its most extreme (**9-19**).

Post-modernism is a collective term for all the art that is created in reaction to the simplified, elegantly proportioned visual statements in the Modern idiom. Thus it is more emotional, expressive, and experimental. We are too much a part of Post-modernism today to have a clear sense of what it is exactly. Characteristics seem to include a dematerialization of the art object, obsession with self-expression and process irrespective of the visual outcome, and a renewed concern with subject matter and meaning.

In the twentieth century artists have striven to be a part of the **avant garde**, the advanced group that gains attention for its unorthodox, experimental treatment of visual expression. With recent developments in mass visual communication, a person or group stays in the avant garde only until the latest trend is broadcast as the next wave of interest.

SUMMARY

Specific technical terms are associated with the character, mode, and idiom of visual statements. This descriptive vocabulary is used to locate and identify the style of a work. Terms in most common usage are Classical, Romantic, Impressionistic, Expressionistic, and Modern.

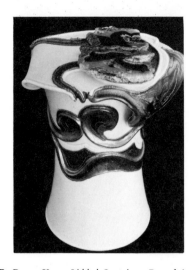

V **A.** PONDER GOEMBEL. *Untitled.* Sepia ink and acrylic wash on watercolor paper, $14\frac{1}{2} \times 10\frac{1}{2}$". *Courtesy of the artist.*

B. DAWN KING. *Lidded Container.* Porcelain with electroformed ornament. *Courtesy of the artist and Works Gallery, Philadelphia, PA.*

C. JULIE JENSEN: *Pari's, June 1980.* Photograph, $3 \times 8\frac{1}{2}$". *Courtesy of the artist.*

D. PIERRE COLLIN. *Maurepas XIV.* 1983. Etching and aquatint, $62\frac{1}{2} \times 28\frac{1}{2}$". *Courtesy of Brody's Gallery, Washington, D.C. Photo: Edward Owen.*

E. NORA SPEYER. *Untitled.* 1983. Charcoal on paper, 30×24". *Courtesy of Gross McCleaf Gallery, Philadephia, PA, and Longpoint Gallery, Provincetown, MA. Photo: Chris Burke.*

F. CLAIRE ZEISLER. *Free Standing Yellow.* 1968. Black jute, yellow and black wool, $48\frac{1}{2} \times 48$", detail. *Courtesy of Helen Drutt Gallery, Philadelphia, PA.*

G. WOOFY BUBBLES A.K.A. CHRISTOPHER HODGE. *Woo World.* Multimedia costume and performance piece. *Courtesy of the artist. Photo: Thomas Moore, © 1983.*

H. JANE STEINSNYDER and MARIE VITALE FOR CASSOWARY. *African Dress.* Cotton oxford cloth with Afghanistani patchwork appliqué yoke. *Courtesy of Cassowary, Philadelphia, PA.*

I. LOUISE BOURGEOIS. *Blind Man's Buff.* 1984. Marble, $26 \times 35 \times 25$". *Courtesy Robert Miller Gallery, New York. Photo: Allan Finkelman.*

V
FORMATS, MEDIA, AND TECHNIQUES FOR VISUAL EXPRESSION

Knowledge about content, basic elements, compositional principles, and style may enable us to comprehend visual statements in any medium. However, to express ourselves with visual means, to become visually communicative and articulate, we need to become familiar with the physical properties and processes of making visual statements.

Within the limited scope of this introduction to visual literacy, a comprehensive approach to media disciplines is impossible. There are too many visual disciplines, and each has its own extensive, rich, and varied possibilities. Therefore, in part V we will broadly identify the disciplines and give a brief overview of the primary techniques. Some of the media are within the skills of beginners—even toddlers use paints—while others require a (sometimes rigorous and lengthy) course of study.

To some extent, all visual statement makers are motivated by the thrill of seeing shape and form come into being: they have taken some materials and tools in hand and created something that did not exist before. *But why choose one medium rather than another?* To attempt to answer that question—and perhaps help you to identify a medium appropriate for you to

explore more thoroughly—we will look at the hidden aspects inherent in each discipline of visual expression. We will also attempt to identify some of the qualities possessed by persons who choose to express themselves within each medium. First, definitions of some terms:

The **format** is the size, shape, and physical composition of a visual statement, such as paper, canvas, a building, or movie. The format has its own character, which is a basic component in a visual statement's organization and structure. As the major substance and support of a visual statement, it is critical that the format be appropriate to the purpose of the visual statement: its expression, anticipated use, placement, function in the world, and intended lifespan.

The **medium** is the physical properties that are used in making a statement visible: graphite, paint, wood, clay, or electronic impulses, to name a few.*

*Many of the media of visual arts involve health hazards. Most books published since 1975 address the hazards of various media and how to work safely. The Center for Occupational Hazards (5 Beekman Street, New York, NY, 10038, 212 227-6220) serves as a clearinghouse for research and information on health hazards in the arts. They also publish a newsletter, books, and pamphlets on the topic.

Each medium has its own dynamic qualities and limitations that convey a unique character to a visual statement. These qualities are elemental to the statement's composition and presence.

Tools are the implements, utensils, instruments, machines, and devices that have been created to facilitate visual statement making. They include pencils, brushes, chisels, drill presses, potter's wheels, cameras, and are far too many to enumerate completely, although many will be identified in the chapters that follow. In using the tools of a visual discipline, knowledge and respect for a tool's possibilities and limitations are necessary, and learning about their use is an integral part of learning a medium and its techniques of manipulation.

Technique is the means employed to achieve an end, a combination of craft and science that a visual statement maker *learns* and draws upon in the use and manipulation of materials and tools of a medium.* Techniques for visual statement making are ever expanding and never fixed. The development of a technique can be an absorbing process, a celebration in and of itself. Care must be taken, however, not to allow technical proficiency, its development and expression, to divert one's attention away from the visual and communicative power of the visual statement as a whole. Technique should neither dominate, impede, nor be subservient to visual expression. It should augment and serve your creative instincts and inner purposes of visual statement making.

Becoming **fluent**, capable of making conceptions materialize in a visual medium, is a lifelong process. Fluency in visual media requires the life-giving breath of an experimenter—an explorer and discoverer who is always searching for better means of expression. In visual expression there are no definitive be-alls and end-alls; there are as many valid responses to a visual problem as there are persons who tackle it. By pursuing the study of a medium, its tools and techniques, one continues to improve in visual expression and evolve toward greater awareness and sophistication.

---

*It is a myth that some of us are born with the talent and ability to express ourselves visually and the rest of us are hopeless cases destined for visual muteness. As one who learned to draw—first took up a pencil with the purpose of representing something I was looking at—when I was 21 years old, I was horrified by my inability (and so were my teachers). But I subsequently did learn to draw with confidence, proficiency, and expressiveness. Perhaps I was fortunate to have learned so late; for it contributed to my knowledge about the process of *learning* to draw and how to help others to learn to see and draw.

CLASSIFICATION OF VISUAL DISCIPLINES

In the chapters that follow, various visual disciplines are grouped under the headings Drawing, Fine Arts, Crafts, Design, Mechanical and Electronic Media, and Multimedia and Intermedia. These classifications have been selected on the basis of the *intent* of the visual statement maker and on the *nature* of the media that are identified in each area. It must be emphasized that *there are no rigid boundaries between these classifications*. All of them overlap, intermingle, cross over, and interrelate in numerous ways. For example, the recent availability of electronic media has affected fine arts in profound and irreversible ways. Electronic copying, electronmicroscopy, and satellite surveillance from and of outer space have provided us with visual information that has enriched our visual imaginations, vocabularies, and options for expression. Likewise, the craft renaissance since 1965 has raised handcrafts to the consciousness of fine art, full of originality and self-expression. So the classifications offered in the following six chapters primarily serve an organizational purpose. They are not to suggest separations between, or a hierarchy among, the visual disciplines. Multimedia art is very much a part of late-twentieth-century visual experience. Drawing, so fundamental to all media of visual expression (even photography, film, and computerized imagery), has been given its own chapter.

All of the descriptions focus upon the dominant and distinctive characteristics of a medium and leave study of the subtler qualities for your investigation. For further reading, refer to the pertinent chapter sections in the bibliography at the end of this book. Subscribing to a magazine that focuses on the use and development of media that interest you is an excellent way to become informed and to stay abreast of current practices in each medium.

CHOOSING A MEDIUM FOR EXPRESSION AND/OR CAREER

Whether as an avocation or a profession, the first considerations when choosing a medium to work in are the same. These considerations have to do with affinities, proclivities, preferences, abhorrences, natural talents, and tendencies—*yours*, no one else's!

Each discipline and medium has inherent imperatives due to its materials, its handling, its tools, its history, and its existential presence. One must not only like the *visual* result of a given medium, but also its feel, its smell, its sound, and the *processes*—often lengthy and arduous—that are part of its manipulation. To accept these imperatives and interact with them in a flexible, creative manner is a rewarding and deeply meaningful experience. One enters a dialogue with a chosen medium, an intimate interaction of one's intuition and intentions with the characteristics of that medium.

Making a career choice based upon anticipated income is putting the cart before the horse in visual arts and communication. One who likes to mush around with clay—gains spiritual fulfillment from the ancient earthiness of its feel; is fascinated with how it dries and shrinks, how it fires to a hard, permanent form—would not necessarily make a good industrial designer; for designers prefer to conceptualize, draw plans, make models, and solve problems for a client or employer. When we are in touch with our affinities and have an opportunity to express ourselves in the medium of our choice, we are more likely to create quality work. We either make our art sufficiently remunerative, or we find alternative ways to support it. Such is the power of a focused creative spirit.

If you were to make a list of visual disciplines and media, how many could you name? Five, ten, forty? In fact they are hard to number for two reasons: one is that there are so many, and the other is that the boundaries between them are so indistinct. But when you consider that all of them have many applications that are professional and remunerative, you begin to understand how many career options exist.*

There is no substitute for hands-on experience in visual arts and communication. Whether for professional or avocational purposes, classes of instruction are available at schools, art centers, and colleges. If you are not already enrolled, it is hoped that the chapters in part V will give you sufficient information and confidence to pursue a visual-arts learning experience.

A PLACE TO MAKE VISUAL STATEMENTS

Depending upon the medium we choose, we will need a place that is conducive to that activity. This could be a drafting table with a good light and a few drawers for

*See the bibliography.

the drawing and design media, a small workbench for jewelry making, a darkroom in a bathroom, a workshop in the basement, or a welding studio in a shed out back.

Most important is that it is a space where materials can be left out. It is time-consuming to pack up and put everything away, and then to get it all out and set it up when you wish to work again. To be able to go back to where you left off, when time permits or the spirit moves, is of great importance. Your work space needn't be fancy. In fact, the more modest it is, the freer you may feel to experiment, to take risks. A workspace that is conducive to your visual expression, and is inviolable for any other activity, is one of the greatest supports you can have.

THE EXPENSE OF VISUAL STATEMENT MAKING

The formats, media, and tools required for visual statements can vary tremendously in their cost to the maker. Works on paper are least expensive, whereas those requiring sophisticated technological equipment can become quite a costly proposition. If we are studying in an art program, we may have access to equipment, have an opportunity to work with it, to explore our affinity with it, before making a commitment to a medium. Graduates from art school programs often enter organizations where equipment is available, or join studios that buy and maintain equipment on a cooperative basis. Some studios, workshops, and fabrication shops rent time on equipment as well. Thus one shouldn't shy away from a particular medium because it requires an array of machines. More often than not there is a creative solution to such problems.

SUMMARY

Each of the disciplines of visual arts and communication uses various formats, media, tools, and techniques in the process of making visual statements. Becoming fluent as a visual statement maker is a lifelong process of discovery and accomplishment.

D RAWING

10

10-1 DEBORAH REMINGTON. *Euros X.* © 1985. Graphite, acrylic crayon, mixed media on paper, 30 × 22″. *Courtesy of the artist. Photo: D. James Dee.*

It is difficult to imagine a human being who has not pushed, pulled, or dragged an implement across a surface to make a mark. It may have been with a toe in the sand, a twig in the dirt, a stone on another stone, a knife blade on wood, or the more refined media of pencil, pen and ink, or charcoal on a piece of paper. Thus **drawing**, the impression of marks on a ground or surface, is fundamental to human nature as well as to all the visual arts.

The kinds of visual statements classified as drawings are many. The basic components of drawing, line and paper, have both been cited as the definitive characteristic of a drawing. *Drawings* have been defined as any medium in which line is the dominant visual element, and likewise as any work on paper. Thus an exhibit of drawings that accepted both these definitions might include pen and ink on paper, watercolor paintings, etchings, collages, handmade paper with no imagery or marks; documents of skywriting, linear designs plowed in the earth; wire sculpture, linear paintings on canvas; architectural plans and renderings; sketchbooks, and so forth.

The most common definition is that **drawings** are comprised of graphic marks on the surface of paper where the paper remains visible as a significant component of the drawing.

Drawings are eclectic in the functions they serve:

Informal: notetaking—quick sketch of something imagined or seen; record keeping—analytical sketch of a detail of something seen; information—map for a friend to find a meeting place (**10-2**)

Descriptive: illustration of specific information or feelings (**10-3**)

Study: a tryout for a work in another medium such as painting, sculpture, handcrafts, or design (**10-4**)

Plan: specific information for fabrication in a design medium such as architecture or industrial design (**10-5**)

Fine art: an end in itself, a manifestation of original self-expression (**10-6**).

THE IMPORTANCE OF LEARNING TO DRAW

Learning to draw implies developing the ability to represent observed three-dimensional objects and spaces on a flat two-dimensional surface so that the illusion of volume, depth, and structure is created that is recognizable as representing the real world (**10-7**). It thus entails a transformation from three dimensions to

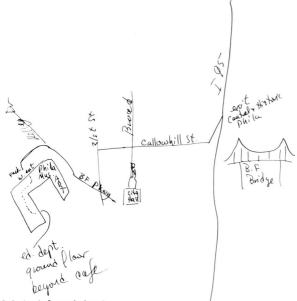

10-2 An informal sketch/map.

10-3 ALICE LEES. *Curving Leap.* 1984. Proposal for kinetic neon figures: fluorescent acrylic paint, pencil on rag paper, $13\frac{1}{2} \times 10''$. *Courtesy of Wallace Wentworth Gallery, Ltd., Washington, DC. Photo: Breger & Assoc.*

10-4 HENRY O. TANNER. *Study drawing for The Resurrection of Lazarus.* Charcoal on paper, $24\frac{1}{2}'' \times 17\frac{1}{2}''$. *Collection of Mrs. Sadie T.M. Alexander on loan to the Philadelphia Museum of Art.*

two dimensions. This **transformative vision** is one of the most complex and profound activities of visual statement making. It entails the ability to look at objects and spaces in the world as if they are a *complex jigsaw puzzle of abstract shapes and tonal variations.* It is these *transformed* shapes and tonalities that one puts down on paper to create the illusion of the objects and spaces one is seeing. Artists who have acquired this ability are informed about the structure of objects in space in ways that can be obtained no other way. This quality of "seeing-knowledge," its substance and meaning, is difficult to describe in words, yet its presence or absence is manifest not only in realistic drawings, but in design plans, photography, sculpture, and all media of visual expression.

Drawing ability is interactive with the organiza-

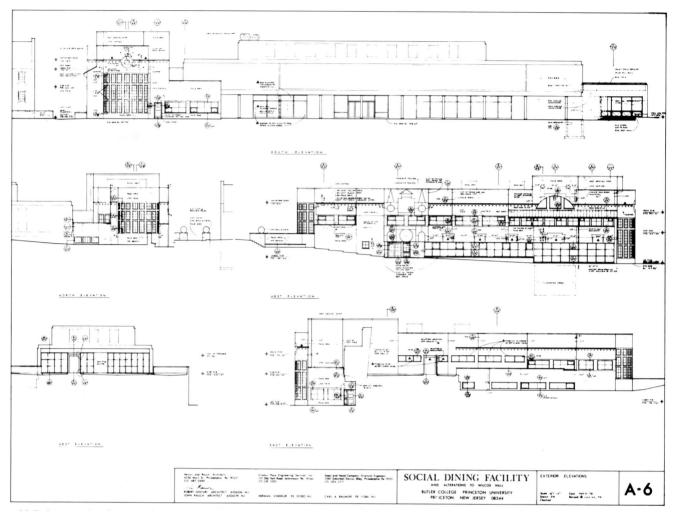

10-5 Construction drawings for Wilcox Hall, Princeton University. *Courtesy of Venturi, Rauch and Scott Brown, Philadelphia, PA.*

10-6 JODY PINTO. *Henry Over an Occupied Sea.* 1983. Watercolor, gouache, crayon on paper, 5' × 7'. *Courtesy of the artist, private collection, Chicago. Photo: Eeva-Inkeri.*

10-7 SHIRLEY FAKTOR. *Bras and Corsets.* 1981. Graphite on Fabriano paper, 100 cm × 70 cm. *Courtesy of Brody's Gallery, Washington, DC. Photo: Edward Owen.*

tional principles of composition so that creating visual statements in any medium is reinforced and strengthened when the visual statement maker is a proficient freehand draftsperson. Even photographers and filmmakers, who use mechanical and electronic devices for their image making, are more perceptive and can make stronger, more sophisticated photographic statements when they have developed a facility in drawing.

Learning to draw is a process of learning to see with undivided attention and uncompromised accu-

racy, of learning to process cognitively what is seen, and of developing manual skills of markmaking. This seeing-thinking-marking is coordinated in a continuous interaction of object, eye, mind, hand, and drawing (**10-8**).

For beginners, learning to draw is best achieved in a basic drawing class. For many persons, drawing is a medium that requires discipline. It is helpful to have a specific time to concentrate on the process, to receive instruction and reinforcement, and to learn from

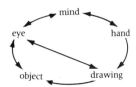

10-8 When you are drawing an object, become conscious of your eye and hand movements, and of your thinking. This awareness is a path to better seeing and mastery.

peers—their mistakes, struggles, and triumphs (**10-9**). If a drawing class is unavailable to you and you are motivated to learn on your own, see the bibliography for books that can guide you on this fascinating journey of learning to see and draw.

If you are phobic about drawing, be assured that you can still engage in the making of visual statements in many other media. In fact, we do it all the time. So don't let your lack of drawing confidence stand in the way of expressing yourself thoughtfully in the media for which you have interest.

TYPES OF DRAWINGS

A **freehand drawing** is made by the human hand with a marking medium or tool, but without assistance from any mechanical device (**10-10**). A **sketch** is a complete visual idea in an abbreviated form; it can be either from observed objects or as a projection of an idea. **Thumbnail sketches** are particularly small, and they are often used to establish basic composition of a proposed visual statement in any medium (**10-11**). A **cartoon**—in addition to those cute drawings created for our entertainment—is a full-scale drawing made for transfer to another surface or for translation into another medium. The **cartoon transfer** is made from a lightweight paper or fabric into which holes are punched (a tailor's perforating wheel works well) along the drawing lines. A silk sack filled with charcoal dust is pounced over the holes to leave a dotted-line diagram of the image (**10-12**).

A **mechanical drawing** uses the tools (compass, straight-edge, and other mechanical devices) and techniques of projective geometry to create illustrative drawings and plans that are precise enough to allow the fabrication of an object from the visual, verbal, and numerical information contained in the drawing or plan (**10-13**).* An **anamorphic drawing** entails the use of a grid to extend, elongate, warp, fan out, or otherwise distort an image (**10-14**). Some anamorphic drawings regain their realistic proportions when viewed at an angle, or in a curved mirror.

A **stipple drawing** is made from dots of varying

*The specific aspects of mechanical and technical drawings have more to do with engineering than with visual literacy, so they will not be explored in any depth in this volume.

10-9 Drawing class. *Courtesy of the art department, East Tennessee State University. Photo: James W. Sledge.*

10-10 NORA SPEYER. *Untitled.* 1983. Charcoal on paper, 30 × 24″. *Courtesy of Gross McCleaf Gallery, Philadelphia, PA. and Longpoint Gallery, Provincetown, MA. Photo: Chris Burke.*

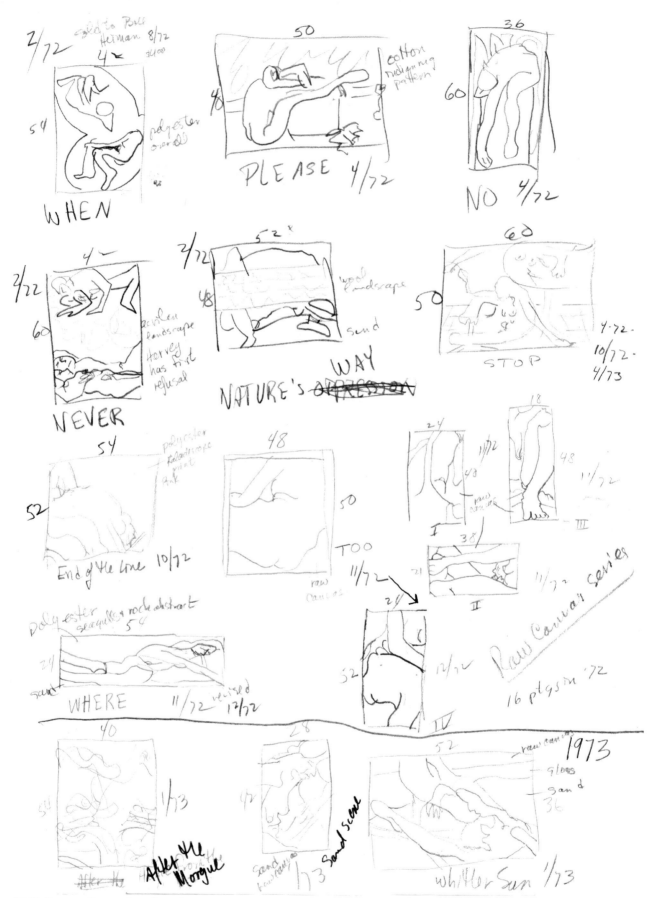

10-11 DEBORAH CURTISS. Page from sketchbook. 1972-1973. Graphite on paper, thumbnail sketches for paintings, 10¾ × 8". *Courtesy of the artist.*

A

B

C

D

10-12 Neil Welliver using a cartoon to transfer a drawing onto canvas: **A** perforating the tracing paper along the lines of the drawing; **B** pouncing the charcoal over the perforated lines; **C** transferred drawing (detail); **D** the completed painting. *Courtesy of the artist. Photos: Will Brown.*

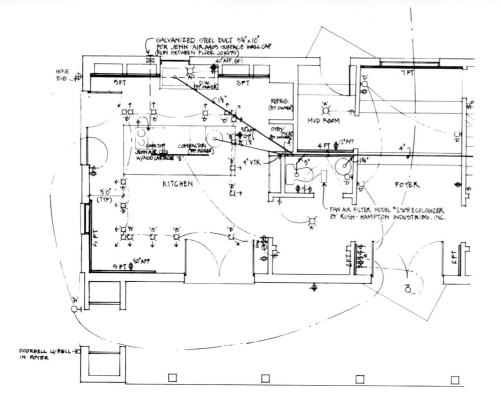

A MECHANICAL, ELECTRICAL, PLUMBING PLAN
1/4" = 1'-0"
SEE BASEMENT PLAN FOR ADDITIONAL M, P, E (DRAWING B/2)

10-13 MARGO LEACH. A mechanical drawing (blueprint) for a kitchen. *Courtesy of Margo Leach, architect, Philadelphia, PA.*

10-14 JOHN FAHNESTOCK. *Anamorphosed Head.* 1970.
Ink on paper, $9\frac{1}{2} \times 8''$. *Courtesy of the author.*

sizes and densities. A **contour drawing** is one comprised of outlines, pencil or pen, that delineate the edges of an object or form (**10-15**). A **hatched drawing** uses repeated lines to form shadows from the density of lines in straight, contour, and crossed patterns (**10-16**). A **chiaroscuro drawing** is tonal in that lights and darks have been developed in continuously blended, modulated gradations, ranging from white to black (**10-17**). Tonal drawings are most often made with graphite, charcoal, and/or chalk, but when made with ink they are known as **wash drawings** (**10-18**). A **monotype** is a cross between drawing and printmaking: one draws on glass with ink or paint, then places a piece of paper face down, and rubs the back to lift the image off the glass and onto the paper (**10-19**).

DRAWING FORMATS

The most prevalent format for drawing is that of paper. **Paper** is made from wood pulp, rags (natural fibers such as cotton, linen, and silk), synthetic materials or a

10-15 DEBORAH CURTISS. *Contour drawing.* 1977. Ink on paper, $5\frac{1}{2} \times 7''$. *Courtesy of the artist.*

10-16 OLIVER RODUMS. *Time Terrain H83.* Pen-and-ink on paper, 23 × 29″. *Courtesy of the artist.*

10-17 MANON CLERY. *Self-portrait: Movement Series #3.* Graphite on rag paper, 23 × 29″. *Courtesy of the artist, private collection.*

10-18 Student wash drawing. Ink on paper, 12 × 8″.

combination there of. Its fabrication is highly mechanized and involves various chemical and mechanical processes that affect its color, weight, texture, and finish (**10-20**).

Pulp papers become acidic, discoloring and/or turning brittle with age, which will affect the lifespan of a drawing. Pulp papers such as newsprint, kraft (brown wrapping paper), and bond papers are less expensive than acid-free 100-percent rag papers, and thus they are popular with beginning students. Once you gain a degree of proficiency and are making drawings worth saving, you will probably want to invest in either chemically treated acid-free pulp papers or naturally acid-free rag papers. Paper manufacturers are increasing the information regarding acidity of their papers, but unless you see it indicated, ask before buying.

Papers are available in a variety of colors and tones, textures, finishes, and weights (**10-21**). Softly colored papers are effective for pastel drawings because they can unify the colors more than will cold white paper. Mid-tone neutral (gray) papers are effective for use in charcoal and white-chalk drawings, again contributing to unity. Soft media such as charcoal and pastel require a paper with a "tooth," a rough texture that will hold onto the powdery pigments (**10-22**). These papers can come in a tiny grid configuration, known as

10-19 Tony Rosati. *Broken Tree.* 1983. Monotype, $17\frac{5}{8} \times 24''$. *Courtesy of the artist and Dolan/Maxwell Gallery, Philadelphia, PA.*

10-20 Paper manufacture. *Courtesy of Rising Paper Co., Housatonic, MA.*

10-21 Some drawing papers for artists. *Courtesy of the Rising Paper Co., Housatonic, MA.*

10-22 KÄTHE KOLLWITZ. *Self-portrait with Pencil.* 1933. Charcoal, 476 × 632mm. *Courtesy of the National Gallery of Art, Washington, DC. Rosenwald Collection.*

laid, or one that is more pebbly, **wove**. Pencil drawings are best on a medium-textured paper that is rough enough to hold the graphite but also smooth enough not to interrupt the continuity of the line and textures of the drawing marks (**10-23**). **Cold-pressed** papers are more textural.

Pen-and-ink drawings require a paper that is fairly smooth and not too absorbent, a **hot-pressed** paper. Producing watery washes in pen-and-ink drawing (**10-24**) calls for stretching and taping the paper to a firm board or surface to reduce warping. It must be wet all over and allowed to dry and shrink taut before beginning the drawing. This process is followed for watercolor also. Watercolor papers are heavy 100-percent rag, and highly textured.

Vellum, originally a calfskin cured and stretched to write and paint on, is now the name of a paper that has a similar smooth translucent quality; vellum is used in drawings for graphic, architectural, industrial, and fashion design. **Acetate** is a plastic film made from cellulose, a by-product of wood, that comes both clear and frosted. It can be drawn upon and is used in graphic design and photo-printing processes.

Tracing papers that have a high degree of transparency are available in both pulp and rag compositions. **Handmade** papers of many types offer visual interest and inspiration for creative visual statements (**10-25**).

The weight of paper given in pounds is not very helpful unless you know the size of the paper and have a calculator handy. The poundage refers to the weight of a ream (500 sheets), but because the cut size varies there is no standardization: a 60-pound paper may be lighter than a 40-pound paper. Check the feel of it for its appropriateness to your purpose.

10-23 JUDY STONE. *Waters of Babylon.* 1985. Graphite on paper, 32 × 24". *Courtesy of the artist. Photo: Eric Mitchell.*

10-24 NORA JAFFE. *Columnum.* Pen-and-ink on paper, 60 × 30". *Courtesy of the artist.*

10-25 MAUREEN ROBERTS. *Homage to the Land of the Rivers, Soft-ware Book #3* (open), and a selection of handmade papers and materials: 25% polypropylene, 25% chopped polyester fibers, and 50% cotton linters. *Courtesy of the artist.*

DRAWING MEDIA

Drawing media include pencils, sticks, and pen and ink. Pencils may have graphite- (erroneously called lead), charcoal-, conté-, or pastel-marking substances.

Graphite, also available in bars and powder, is a pure, natural carbon that is dark gray, has a metallic sheen that may be burnished (rubbed with a hard smooth object) for greater shine, and has a slightly greasy feel. Graphite pencils come in gradations from very hard, 12H, to very soft, 8B. The middle of this range, designated by the letters F or HB, is similar to an ordinary no. 2 pencil. **Ebony** pencils are thick soft graphite and manufactured carbon.

Charcoal, a carbon obtained from firing twigs in a kiln, is available in vine-shaped sticks, compressed into bars, and as a powder, as well as in pencil form. Charcoal comes in several degrees of softness and is capable of a rich black; it can be blended and rubbed to a variety of tones (**10-26**). **Chalk** is a natural mineral found in black, white, and reds. **Conté** crayons and pencils have a small amount of wax in them that makes them adhere better to the paper, but they do not erase well. Conté is available in black, sepia (dark brown), sanguine (rusty red), and white. **Lithographic** crayons and pencils are carbon, oil, and wax.

Pastels are pure powdered pigments of varying hues, tints, and shades, bound with a small amount of gum arabic into bars or sticks (**10-27**). Less expensive pastels contain noncoloring fillers and are not as brilliant in color. **Oil pastels** have oil added to pastel colors and are formed into sticks. Colors will not erase,

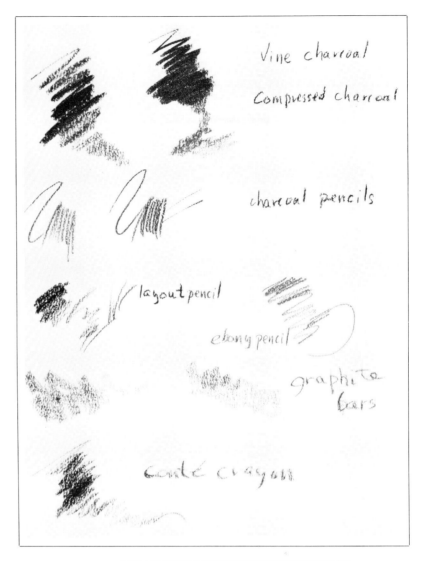

The handwritten labels on the image read:
Vine charcoal
Compressed charcoal
charcoal pencils
layout pencil
ebony pencil
graphite bars
conté crayon

10-26 A selection of drawing marks made with various pencils and crayons. *Photo: Michael McGuire.*

10-27 SHIRLEY FAKTOR. *Self-portrait I.* 1982. Pastel on paper, $25\frac{1}{2} \times 37\frac{1}{2}''$. *Courtesy of Brody's Gallery, Washington, DC.*

but they can be lifted and blended with a brush dipped in turpentine or mineral spirits. **Crayons** are pigments bound with wax and/or paraffin.

Ink is a fluid writing and drawing medium made from a variety of coloring substances and chemicals. **Drawing** or **India ink** is made especially for permanent drawings (**10-28**). **Chinese ink** is also permanent, but it is dried into cakes that are then put into solution by wetting with water and rubbing to get the desired gradation of black. **Japanese** or **Sumi** ink is similar. Less permanent, but not to be overlooked for their interesting graphic qualities, are ordinary ballpoint, nylon, and felt tipped pens.

DRAWING TOOLS

The effects of pencil and stick media can be altered with **erasers** that will lift or rub off the deposited marks. The kneaded rubber eraser leaves no residue and can be used repeatedly by kneading it with the fingers to a clean and effective lifting state. Art gum,

vinyl, and pink erasers are preferred by some people for different effects.

Stumps are rolled paper sticks that are effective in rubbing and blending tones and colors. **Chamois** (an especially soft goatskin) is a choice blending material; soft cloth, paper, or the fingertips can also be used.

Pens and brushes are used in conjunction with ink. **Pens** can be made from reeds, quills, and steel tips. Steel tips are manufactured in a variety of shapes, widths, and weights, and are attached to handles that may or may not contain small reservoirs for the ink. Those that do not hold their own ink must be dipped in the ink repeatedly. **Brushes** are made from animal hairs and synthetic bristles that are attached to a wooden or plastic handle by a metal ferrule. The finest brushes are made from sable, with most often a round shape tapering to a very fine point. They come in a broad range of sizes.

Silver point is a piece of six- to ten-gauge silver wire bound to a stick handle and used on a specially china-coated paper. The result is a delicate gray metallic line that is permanent (uncorrectable) and which oxidizes (tarnishes) in time to a deep gray (**10-29**).

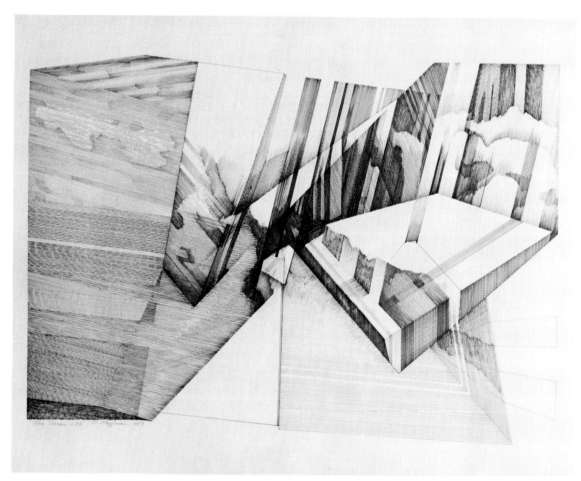

10-28 OLIVER RODUMS. *Time Terrain L83.* Pen-and-ink on paper, $22\frac{1}{2} \times 30"$. *Courtesy of the artist.*

10-29 NORA JAFFE. *Threnody for Sunshine #12.* 1981. Silverpoint on paper, 12″ × 9″. *Courtesy of the artist.*

DRAWING TECHNIQUES

Drawing techniques develop from the interaction of the visual creator with the format, medium, and tools used. There is a directness, an immediacy of gesture and feeling, that drawings can capture better than any other medium. Thus they tend to be more personal, more intimate.

Line drawings (**10-30**) are best made with pencils and pens that have a dependable point, whereas charcoal and pastels use techniques of blending and soft shadings of light and shadow or color (**10-31**). In developing technical facility we can learn much from the old masters. As a supplement to your drawing from real-life objects and spaces, take a sketchbook to a museum and copy, stroke by stroke, the drawings of a master. (Some museums have study rooms for this purpose.) Your awareness of technical possibilities will be enriched by this contact. And drawing masterworks of sculpture can also be a direct route to the spirit of genius. Who could get too much of that?

Developing technical facility is a process of discovery through experimentation and practice. Each of us has unique handwriting, and this ''personal signature'' will be evident in our drawings irrespective of medium.

CARE AND PRESERVATION OF DRAWINGS

Drawings from the soft media—graphite, charcoal, chalk, and pastel—will smear and rub off, and even shake off at the slightest provocation. Therefore they must be fixed with a spray **fixative**, a solution of natural or synthetic resin in a quick-drying solvent. Spray lightly in several separate coats holding the spray one to two feet away from the drawing for best results. The solvent is highly toxic, so be sure to use fixative in a well-ventilated place, and avoid inhaling the fumes.

Unframed drawings should either be stored flat in

10-30 HENRI MATISSE. *Yvonne Landsberg.* 1914. Pen-and-ink on paper, $25\frac{5}{8} \times 19\frac{7}{8}''$. *Collection, The Museum of Modern Art, New York. Alva Gimbel Fund.*

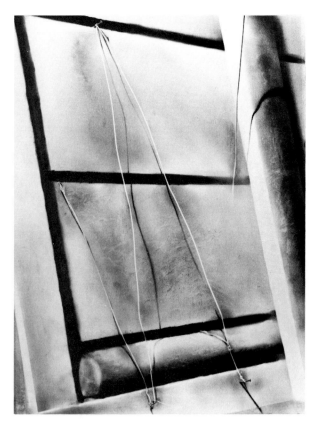

10-31 NONA HERSHEY. *Wall with Wires.* Graphite and pastel on paper, $30 \times 23''$. *Courtesy of the artist and Dolan/Maxwell Gallery, Philadelphia, PA.*

a box that contains them snuggly with glossy acid-free pages placed between each drawing, or be bound between pieces of firm board so that they will not slip and rub against one another.

When framing under glass, the mounting board and the mat board should both be acid-free, as should any tape used to affix the drawing to its mount. The mat center should be cut out to the size of the drawing to be revealed, and it should be thick enough so that the surface of the drawing does not come into contact with the glass. The backing board should be attached to the frame and sealed with a nondeteriorating cotton or linen tape.

SUMMARY

Drawing, as a discipline of visual literacy, is fundamental to both human nature and visual expression in all media. Its most common format is paper; its media are graphite, charcoal, chalk, pastel, crayon, and ink; its tools are drawing sticks, pencils, pens, brushes, erasers, and blending agents.

Learning to see through drawing is the entry to the magical world of transformative vision, a special appreciation and perception of the structure and interrelatedness of the objects and spaces that comprise the world around us.

FINE ARTS

11-1 Alice Aycock exhibit. *Courtesy of the Vanguard Gallery, Philadelphia, PA.*

In the **fine arts**—drawing, painting, printmaking, and sculpture—the visual statement maker both creates and solves visual problems. That is, in the fine arts the artist alone decides what is to be created and how. There is a synthesis of conscious intent with unconscious processes of self-expression. Art is made for the sake of art and not to serve any particular utilitarian purpose other than sharing one's visions, perceptions, and creativity.

The making of art objects in this spirit can include drawing, craftsmanship, excellence in design, the use of mechanical and electronic devices, and multimedia. So it is the absence of utility and the origin of the purpose with the artist that distinguish fine art disciplines from the classifications of chapters 12 through 15.

Persons who choose the fine arts as a professional commitment are often highly individualistic and have a deep inner necessity for the creation of original visual statements. They are willing to confront the unknown, and may even feel compelled to do so. Merely liking drawing, painting, printmaking, or sculpture is not enough to sustain an artist through the ups and downs, the questionings and lack of acknowledgment, that can arise in response to original creative endeavor.

Fortunately, these media lend themselves to avocational involvement. If you like doing them but don't have that burning need to paint or sculpt as if your life depended upon it, you still can create viable, meaningful works through part-time exploration of the medium of your choice. Drawing, of course, has been discussed in detail in chapter 10, so let's turn directly to painting, printmaking, and sculpture.

PAINTING

Painting is a process of magic: we apply colors suspended in a fluid medium to a surface in such a way as to create images or visual phenomena that transcend the material and substance of the paint itself (**11-2**). Therein lies painting's compelling, enticing, and seductive nature.

The art of painting offers an enormous number of technical options in producing visual effects, and it includes the rich reward of color in its infinite continuum. Painting is probably the least quantifiable or calculable of all visual media, and in its most magnificent form, is similar to composing music for a full-scale chorus and orchestra.

Illusion—a component in all two-dimensional pictorial media—is celebrated in painting with an abandon that embraces the full range from realistic

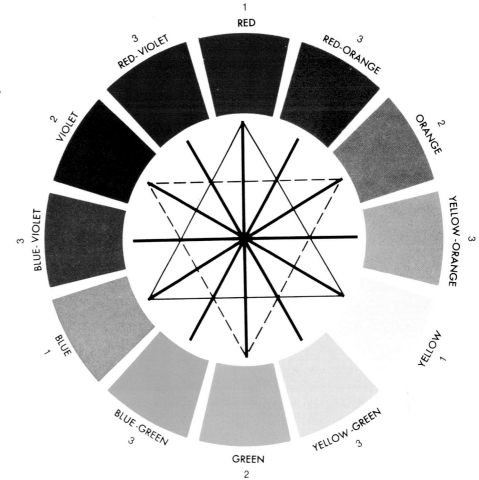

Colorplate 1A (chapter 4)
1 ———————— Primary color triad
2 ------------ Secondary color triad
   ———————— Complementary colors
3 Intermediate or tertiary colors
Reprinted by permission of Eastman Kodak Company

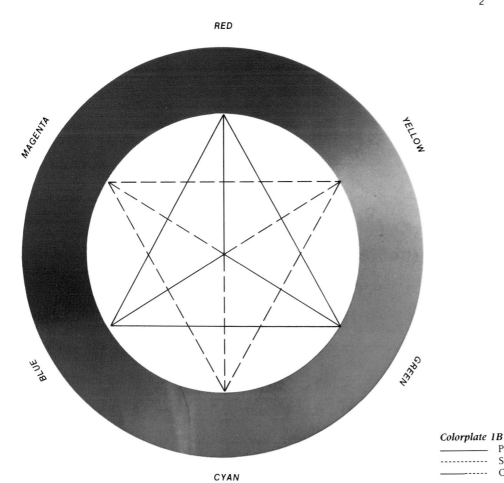

Colorplate 1B
———————— Primary color triad
------------ Secondary color triad
—·—·—·— Complementary colors

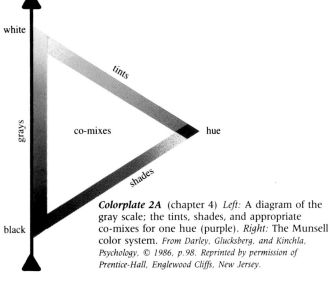

Colorplate 2A (chapter 4) *Left:* A diagram of the gray scale; the tints, shades, and appropriate co-mixes for one hue (purple). *Right:* The Munsell color system. *From Darley, Glucksberg, and Kinchla, Psychology, © 1986, p.98. Reprinted by permission of Prentice-Hall, Englewood Cliffs, New Jersey.*

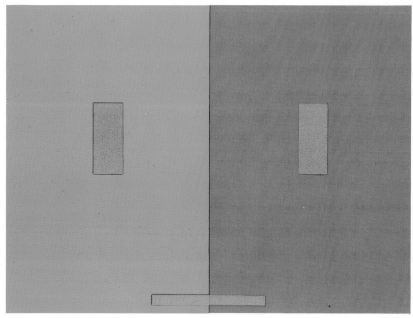

Colorplate 2B Simultaneous contrast—the same color has been used in the center of the two different surrounding colors.

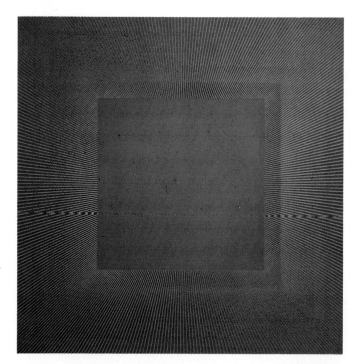

Colorplate 2C RICHARD ANUSZKIEWICZ. *Rainbow Squared Red Ocher.* 1981. Acrylic on canvas. *Collection of the Noyes Museum, Oceanville, NJ. Reproduced with permission from V. A. G. A., New York.*

YELLOW, MAGENTA, CYAN & BLACK

YELLOW PRINTER

MAGENTA PRINTER

CYAN PRINTER

BLACK PRINTER

Colorplate 3 (chapter 4) Example of four color separation. This section is enlarged to show printing dots. *Permission to reproduce this material from the 13th edition of* POCKET PAL® *was granted by International Paper Company.*

Colorplate 4 (chapter 6) Martha Armstrong. *Landscape with Yellow Dots.* 1983. Oil on canvas, 10¾ x 15¾". *Courtesy of Gross McLeaf Gallery, Philadelphia, PA.* Diagrams of the locations of the six major color families used.

Colorplate 5A (chapter 11) ELIZABETH MURRAY. *Return of the Sausages.* 1983-84. Oil on canvas, 92 x 80 x 6". *Collection of Jane and Gerald Katcher. Courtesy of the artist and Paula Cooper Gallery. Photo: Eeva-Inkeri.*

Colorplate 5B DEBORAH KOGAN. *Seminole Series #11.* 1984. Watercolor, gouache, drybrush, wetbrush, and sgraffito (scratching into surface), 22 x 29". *Courtesy of the artist and Rosenfeld Gallery, Philadelphia, PA.*

Colorplate 5C LOUISE GRASSIE. *Homage to Anaïs Nin.* 1977. Egg tempera and goldleaf on masonite, 37 x 50". *Courtesy of the artist and Rodger LaPelle Gallery, Philadelphia, PA.*

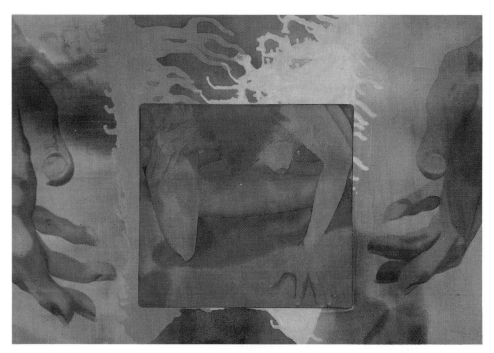

Colorplate 6A (chapter 11) DEBORAH
CURTISS. *Naps* (synapse series). Acrylic
polymer on two canvases, 22 x 24″ and
36 x 54″. Acrylic washes stained into
the canvas and opaque colors
containing iridescent mica powder.
Courtesy of the artist.

Colorplate 6B JAN C. BALTZELL. *Rabbit,
Run*. 1985. Oil on canvas, 56 x 46″.
*Courtesy of the artist and Gross McLeaf Gallery,
Philadelphia, PA.*

Colorplate 7A (chapter 11) LOIS JOHNSON. *Box Canyon*. 1983.
Offset lithograph, screenprint, edition 12, printed by the artist, 21
x 21". *Courtesy of the artist.*

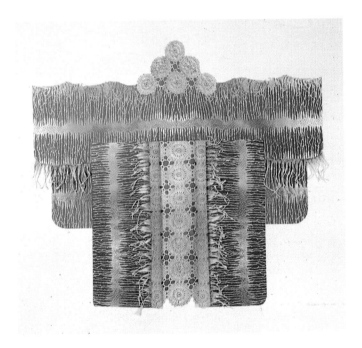

Colorplate 7B ENID MARK. *Imperial Object #III*. 1983.
Photo-lithograph from three metal plates printed on Arches paper
with collage of hand-colored fabric and lithographed Japan paper,
edition 4, 30 x 42". *Courtesy of the artist.*

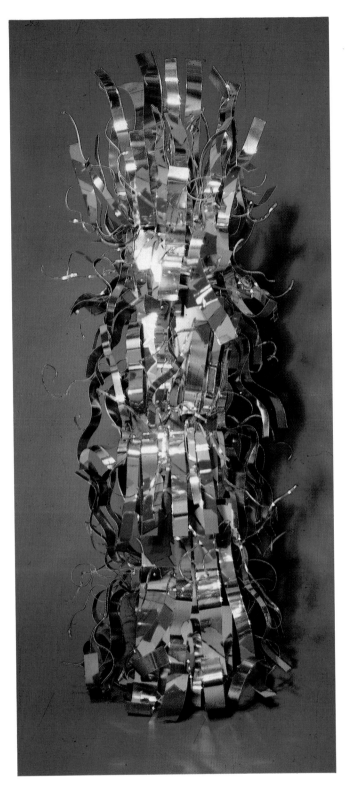

Colorplate 7C DOROTHY GILLESPIE. *A Royal Sentinel*. 1984. Enamel
on anodized aluminum, 72 x 28 x 28". *Courtesy of the artist. Photo:
Maynard Hicks.*

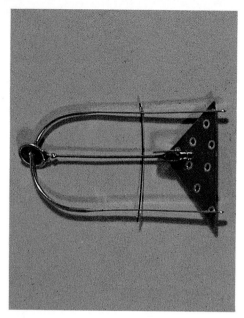

8A

8B

Colorplate 8A (chapter 12) DEGANIT SCHOCKEN. Brooch. 1985. Gold, $2\frac{1}{2}$ x $1\frac{1}{4}$ x $\frac{1}{4}$". *Courtesy of Helen Drutt Gallery, Philadelphia, PA.*

Colorplate 8B WILLIAM CARLSON. *Contrapuntal.* 1984. Blown, cast, and assembled glass, 16 x 12 x 6". *Collection of Jean and Hilbert Sosin. Courtesy of Snyderman Gallery, Philadelphia, PA. Photo: Susie Cushner.*

Colorplate 8C YVONNE BOBROWICZ. *Randomness and Order.* 1984. Wool, linen, monofilament, and rayon, 24 x 24". *Courtesy of the artist.*

Colorplate 8D STEVE GAMZA. *Bulging Vessel.* 1983. Raku, 8 x 10" diameter. *Courtesy of the artist and Works Gallery, Philadelphia, PA.*

Colorplate 8E GARRY KNOX BENNETT. Desk with Lamp. 1984. California Claro walnut, brass, polychrome, and copper and gold plate, 57 x 78 x 26". *Courtesy of Snyderman Gallery, Philadelphia, PA, private collection. Photo: Nikolay Zurik.*

8C

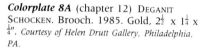

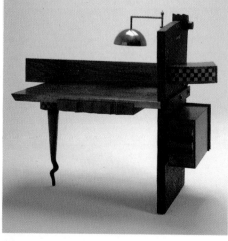

8D

8E

Colorplate 8F (chapter 15) SANDY SKOGLAND. *Maybe Babies.* 1983. Installation 10' 4" x 32' x 16' 2", sculptures cast epoxy resin approximately 3 x 2 x 1' each. Photograph: dye transfer print, edition 30, 30 x 40", © S. Skogland. *Courtesy of the artist and Castelli Graphics, New York.*

11-2 FRANCES M. COX. *DC in her Studio*. 1984. Photograph 6$\frac{1}{4}$ × 9″. Holding a container of wash calls for wearing a ski-mitten when working in an unheated attic studio. *Courtesy of the photographer and subject.*

representation through abstraction to total nonrepresentational celebration of the medium itself.

Because painting requires no expensive equipment and supplies are readily available in an affordable price range, it is a medium that is accessible to the novice. Yet its range of possibilities for continual discovery challenges the most advanced painters to a lifetime of exploration and expression.

Painting Formats

The format for painting is any relatively flat surface that will hold and support the paint. Known also as a *support* or *ground support*, the format may be paper; wood panel; a compressed wood product such as masonite; glass; plexiglass; or a fabric such as silk. But the most common format is linen or cotton canvas stretched over wood stretcher frames (**11-3**). Painting surfaces are usually rectangular, but round-, elliptical-, and compound-shaped canvases and panels have also been used to serve the purpose of the artist (colorplate **5A**). Interior and exterior walls can be a format for mural paintings.

Isolating the Format Some formats, such as acidic resinous wood, must be isolated so they will not threaten the stability of the painting medium. Other formats must be isolated from the corrupting influ-

ences of a medium, particularly oil paints that will, in time, rot unprimed canvas. The priming substance used is called a **ground**. Historically, a ground was comprised of several coats of animal-skin glue, to shrink and size the canvas, or of shellac to seal the wood. The sealer was followed by several coats of **gesso**, a combination of chalk, whiting, slaked plaster, and titanium pigment suspended in the glue. In some cases the primer or final coat would be flake white, an oil-based white lead. Because each coat had to dry before the next, it took several weeks to prime a panel or canvas. Today we have acrylic gesso that is available premixed. It can go directly on sealed wood or unsized canvas and requires only two coats that take only a few hours to dry.

Canvas is available commercially both primed and unprimed by the yard and/or stretched on wood stretchers (*see* **11-3 B**), or over cardboard. Sheets of primed canvas and canvas paper, which simulates the texture and surface of a primed canvas, are inexpensive formats for beginning painters in acrylics and oils.

Painting Mediums

There are three basic constituents of painting mediums: colored pigments, binders, and solvents. The binder/solvent combination is called a *vehicle* or

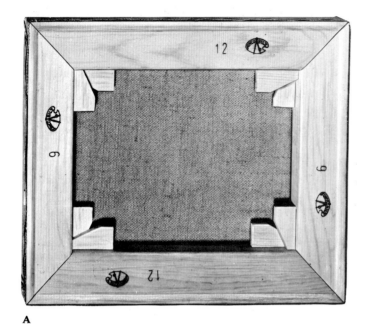

A

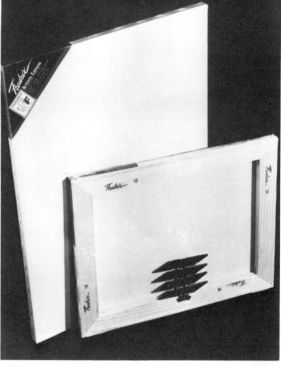

B

11-3 Canvas stretched on stretcher frames. **A** linen canvas. *Courtesy of Anco Wood Specialties, Inc., Glendale, NY;* **B** primed cotton canvas. *Courtesy of Fredrix Artis Canvas, Inc., Lawrenceville, GA.*

medium, and the plural for this specific use of the term is *mediums*.

Pigments, coloring agents, are derived from a variety of sources: animal, vegetable, mineral, and synthetic. Many of the animal and vegetable pigments are fugitive—impermanent, fading in light—and have been replaced by more reliable synthetic pigments derived from a variety of chemical mixtures. Pigments are purified and ground to a very fine powder before being either ground or suspended into a medium.

Binders are glue and gluelike substances that come from animal (egg, milk), vegetable (oil, gum), and synthetic (resins, acrylic polymer) sources. **Solvents** are thinning agents used to achieve a desired degree of fluidity for a given paint medium. Fluidity can range from a stiff gooey paste to a watery wash. Solvents come from minerals (mineral spirits, a petroleum by-product), vegetables (turpentine, distilled from the sap of live pine trees), and synthetics (toluene), but the most common solvent is water.

Aqueous Mediums Those painting mediums that are soluable by water are known as the **aqueous** or **water** mediums. They are differentiated by the binder, each of which has slightly different attributes. **Watercolors**, also known as *aquarelle*, are bound with gum arabic and are characterized by their transparent-translucent quality (**11-4**). **Gouache**, also bound with gum arabic, differs by the addition of white pigment, which gives a more opaque quality. Watercolor

and gouache paintings are usually done on 100-percent rag paper that comes in pads with taped edges to keep it from warping; or that has been presoaked, stretched, and taped to a board. Sable brushes and sponges are the preferred tools, and these mediums are particularly popular with illustrators because they are especially suitable for finely detailed work. **Dry brush** is a technique of squeezing or wiping out most of the paint from the brush until it separates into many fine lines (colorplate **5B**).

Tempera or **distemper**, pigments suspended in a rabbit-skin glue solution, are brilliant and flat, and they are often used for stage sets. They will crack, so they should be used on a relatively firm support such as paper backed with cardboard (**11-5**). **Egg tempera** is an ancient technique in which the yolk or whole egg is used as the binding agent. Egg will also **emulsify**—create a bond between water and oil—so different effects can be achieved with the addition of linseed oil, resin, wax, or gums to egg temperas. The colors are intense and luminous and can be buffed when dry with a soft cloth to achieve luster. Egg tempera should be used on a rigid support and is best kept to a small scale (colorplate **5C**). **Casein** is bound with a skim-milk by-product that has a strong, durable binding power. It is brittle and requires rigid support. The drying time with all aqueous mediums is quite fast, but can be extended by adding a few drops of glycerine to the vehicle.

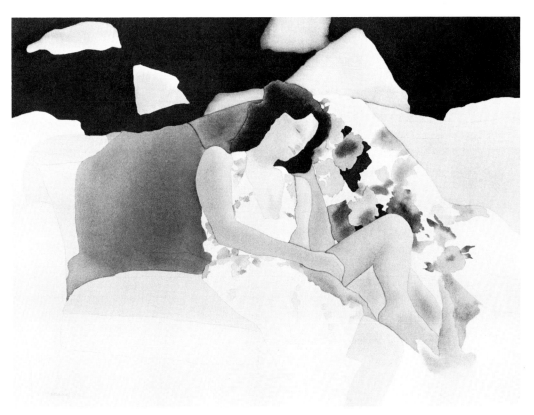

11-4 ELIZABETH OSBORNE. *Nava Against Blue Sea*. 1978. Watercolor, 23 × 29″. *Courtesy of the artist and Marian Locks Gallery, Philadelphia, PA.*

11-5 JACOB LAWRENCE. *Daybreak—A Time to Rest.* 1967. Tempera on hardboard, 30 × 24″. *Courtesy of the National Gallery of Art, Washington, DC. Gift of an Anonymous Donor.*

121

Acrylic polymer paints are bound with a synthetic resin, a milky plastic that dries to a tough, chemically inert clear film. Acrylics have tremendous versatility—from a thin wash that looks like watercolor to thick impasto that mimics oil paints. They can be used on all nonoily formats without priming because the binder itself is an excellent isolator (colorplate **6A**). Acrylics are less expensive than oils and require no toxic or flammable materials or solvents. As long as brushes are kept wet, they can be easily cleaned with soap and water.

Acrylic paints, depending upon thickness, dry quite rapidly, in less than an hour, so they can be recoated or covered fairly quickly. They have an even, flat covering power. Acrylics do not blend or glaze as well as oils, but drying retarders and gels have been developed to assist in these techniques. Acrylics cannot be used on oil-based grounds and don't adhere well to slick nonporous grounds, but on paper, canvas, fabrics, wood, plaster, or acetate a multitude of effects and interactions is possible.

Nonaqueous Mediums **Oil paints** have long been the monarch of paint mediums (colorplate **6B**). Pigments are ground into drying oils, most often linseed, that dry by a process of oxidation to a flexible and tough film. These oils, never chemically inert, are thus sensitive to variations in temperature and humidity. Drying time of oils varies greatly, from a few hours to a few weeks, depending upon the pigment, vehicle, and atmospheric conditions. **Alkyd**, a synthetic resin that has long been used in house paints, is now available in oil paints; it hastens drying time to about six hours.

Solvents used for thinning oil paints, wiping out areas of a still wet painting, and for cleaning brushes are turpentine and mineral spirits. Both are volatile, so must be used with good ventilation and away from flame. They are also skin irritants. Mixing mediums are available that are mixtures of driers, solvents, and varnish. Many of these give a buttery consistency to the paints that is pleasurable, but many are prone to discolor, turn brittle, crack, and flake with age. So research a mixing medium first.

An ancient and long-lasting form of painting is the **fresco**, which is made from pigments ground in water and applied to wet lime plaster (**11-6**). Frescoes dry to a waterproof film of crystalline carbonate of lime and have demonstrated their toughness by surviving from ancient Egypt and the eruption of Vesuvius in Pompeii. Lime-proof pigments are few, however, so the color range is limited.

Encaustic is the process of combining powdered pigments with beeswax and manipulating the wax

with hot tools and/or a heat lamp. Oil paints can be blended in, and turpentine can be used as a thinner.

Gold leaf, tissue-thin sheets of gold, can be applied to a prepared surface of bole, an iron oxide clay. It is especially compatible with egg tempera and can be used with acrylics (colorplate **5C**).

Painting Tools

Paints are most often applied with **brushes**. Sable brushes are best for water mediums and come in round and flat shapes in a range of sizes. They are also used for glazing in oils. Camel-, squirrel-, and ox-hair brushes are less expensive but don't compare in resiliency—maintaining a point. Natural bristle brushes of white hog's-hair are best for oil painting. They come in several shapes: *flats*—square ended; *brights*—square but shorter-bristled than flats; *rounds*—long, tubular, pointed; and *filberts*—round ended and fuller than flats (**11-7**). Because natural bristle brushes absorb water and become mushy and swollen when used with acrylics, nylon bristle brushes of the same shapes and sizes have been developed for use with acrylics. Care must be taken to keep all brushes clean: first clean in solvent or water to remove as much paint as possible, and then wash with warm water and soap. Rinse well, dry, and reshape. Store so the bristles are free of contact.

A **mahlstick** is a long, thin, flexible stick with a soft rounded tip that is placed on or beside the painting and held with the nonpainting hand to support the painting hand for careful, detailed work (**11-8**). **Palette** and **painting knives** are used for the mixing of paints on the **palette** (any surface used for that purpose) and for applying impasto to the painting. Like small spatulas or trowels, they come in a variety of shapes and sizes. Specifically, painting knives have thinner, more flexible blades and should not be used for scraping. The *palette* should be a nonabsorbent material such as glass or marble, or a porcelain tray or tabletop. Disposable coated-paper palettes are inexpensive and certainly expedite cleanup. With the more fluid aqueous media, china and metal mixing trays are available; plastic egg cartons, cups, and supermarket trays are thrifty disposable mixing surfaces. Sponges, absorbent rags, nonwoven wipes, and cheesecloth are good for a variety of procedures—mopping up, wiping out, softening edges, and paint application.

An **easel** is an adjustable frame for holding a painting in a vertical position while working on it (**11-9**). Easels can be purchased in a variety of sizes, shapes, and stabilities. For large works, artists often attach directly to a wall. The degree of stability to withstand the kind of action you give a painting will determine the kind you use.

11-6 Bernardino Luini. *Procris and the Unicorn*. Fresco. *Courtesy of the National Gallery of Art, Washington, DC. Samuel H. Kress Collection.*

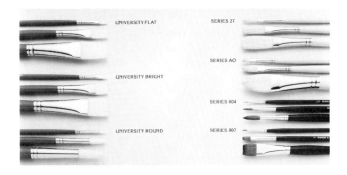

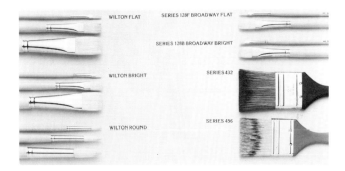

11-7 A selection of paint brushes. *Courtesy of Winsor and Newton, Secaucus, NJ.*

11-8 Brett Bigbee painting with a mahlstick. *Courtesy of the artist.*

11-9 An adjustable painter's easel. *Courtesy of Anco Wood Specialties, Inc., Glendale, NY.*

Painting Techniques

Painting is distinguished by its painterly quality, the use of brushstrokes and continuous areas of color. Within this realm there are limitless possibilities for visual response to technical considerations. It is possible to work wet with lots of blending and wandering of colors, to work in a dry and precise manner, and to use a thick textural impasto.

Direct painting is painting directly on the ground with full color and generally in one layer, although some overpainting might be included (**11-10**). **Indirect painting** is a multilayer procedure that can start with an **imprimatura**, a color wash of midtone upon white, to block out the basic organization of the painting. Then an **underpainting** in a monochromatic neutral color, usually tones of black or umber, is executed that develops the chiaroscuro values of the image. Once dry, the painting is **glazed** with thin, translucent colors (**11-11**). **Scumbling** is the

11-10 Nancy Clearwater Herman painting *directly* a landscape. *Courtesy of the artist.*

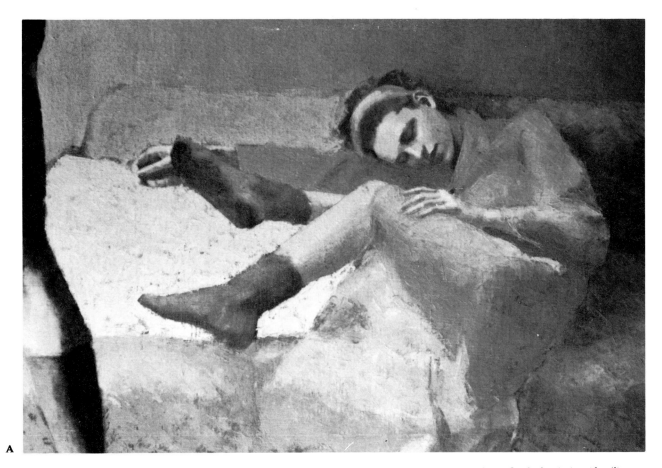

A

11-11 BRETT BIGBEE. *Ann Asleep on a Folded Futon.* Oil on canvas, 62 × 72″. **A** underpainting (detail); **B** finished painting (detail). *Courtesy of the artist.*

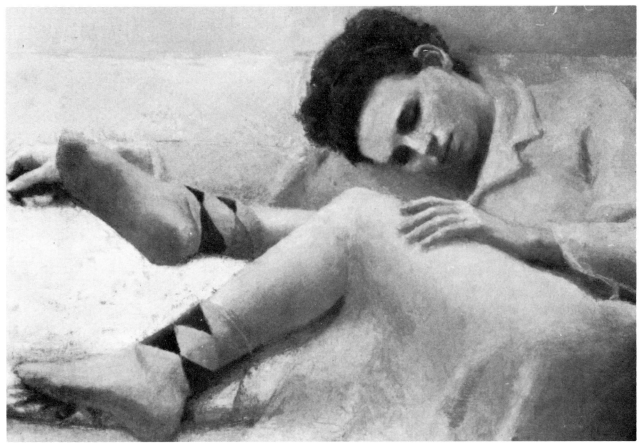

B

application of semiopaque light colors over a darker color, and thus the opposite of glazing. **Sgraffito** is incising into the texture of paint, often with the tip of the brush handle, to leave a line that exposes the ground surface or an undercoating of colors.

Techniques in paintings—little manipulations of the brush to get certain effects, to bring that spark of life with a highlight—are learned through doing. We are living at a time freer from formal technical rules and regulations than any other. It is a myth that you have to absorb all the techniques of the old masters before gaining the right to experiment and explore. By starting with the kinds of visual explorations that interest us most, we come to use traditional techniques as we need them. Then, like learning to ride a bicycle, we never forget them because they are a meaningful part of our vocabulary. Painting has far too many possibilities—including mixed media (chapter 15)—to be confined to the recipes and formulas of the past.

Summary

Painting is a process of applying colored pigments that have been suspended in a vehicle to a surface or ground in such a way as to transform that surface into something quite different: an image, a celebration of color, a symphony of meaning and feeling. It is a medium that is accessible to the novice and a challenge to the professional.

PRINTMAKING

Printmaking is the process of transferring an inked "master" surface to another surface to create multiple images or prints from a single work (**11-12**). As a fine art it utilizes the older methods of hand printing as differentiated from present-day mechanized and electronic processes. Mechanical printing is much faster, but lacks the hands-on involvement of the image maker. Printmaking may include photo imagery, but it differs from photomechanical reproduction techniques (chapter 14) in that much of the feeling of the artist and the process of printing remain in evidence.

Prints are made either directly by the artist or in collaboration with a master printer, one who has established him or herself as an expert in fine art printing. Fine art printmaking studios also make prints for artists who have established themselves in other media, such as painting and sculpture, and for artists who don't have the necessary equipment.

Prints have a broad variety of qualities and appearances due to the varying techniques employed in making them. *Printmaking* is a discipline that entails a great deal of technical process, of using tools, chemicals, and presses. Printmakers tend to have an affinity for the impact of ink on paper, the use of drawing qualities, and the indirectness of the process. This indirectness prevents arrival at quick answers and requires exploration, digging. It provides an opportunity to follow one's decision-making by recording that process with proofs at various stages of creation. These processes together with the making of many prints from the same image are the qualities that attract people to printmaking.

Printmaking Formats

Papers, both commercial and handmade, and fabrics are the principle formats for printmaking. One-hundred-percent rag papers that are specially suited for each of the different types of printing are commercially available. Silk and cotton are the best fabrics for printing. Synthetics are often not absorbent enough and result in uneven impressions, and the texture of wool presents a challenge that is best handled by experts. Some printmakers make their own papers for unique printing surfaces.

While in the process of developing a plate to be printed (a **plate** being the image-making master irrespective of the materials from which it is made), the artist **pulls** or makes a print to see how the plate is progressing toward the desired goal. These trial prints, or **artist's proofs**, are numbered consecutively as "state 1," "state 2," etc. Once the plate is ready for final printing, the artist decides the size of the **edition**, the number of prints to be pulled from that plate or series of plates (if it is to have several colors or techniques utilized). The artist may retain some of the first prints and number them "artist's proof 1," "2," and so on (*see* **7-5**). Thereafter the prints are numbered in a dual system. For example, "19/50" connotes that it is the nineteenth print in an edition of fifty ("ed. 50") (*see* **7-6**). Once the last print has been made, the artist may destroy or mutilate the plate and pull a **cancellation proof** to verify the end of the edition (*see* **7-7**).

Printmaking Media

Prints may be made with water- or oil-based inks, or be inkless. Inks prepared especially for printing must be used, and the various techniques require inks of differing consistencies. Printing inks are available in a broad range of colors, a range that can be extended by the printmaker's own mixtures.

11-12 Samuel J. Brown inspecting a state proof of his lithograph print. *Courtesy of Brandywine Workshop, Philadelphia, PA.*

Printmaking Tools

Most methods of making prints require a printing press. **Presses** come in varying sizes and capacities, but all consist of the same basic parts: a bed on which the plate lies face up, and a cylindrical drum on a track that can be rolled across the plate (or the plate under the drum) with variable pressure appropriate to the printing method (**11-13**). Drying racks are simple frame structures, some with shelves of screening, that will hold prints in contact-free positions until they are dry. Other tools vary with the techniques, so they are described below in company with the pertinent process.

Printmaking Techniques

There are four basic kinds of printing techniques: relief, intaglio, planographic (lithography), and stencil. Relief, intaglio, and lithograph prints are the reverse of the plate, whereas stencil and offset processes provide a "right-reading" (same as plate) print.

Relief printing is characterized by cutting away from a surface—with various shaped gouges (**11-14**)—the (negative) areas you don't wish to be inked. These include *woodcuts*, *wood engravings*, and *linocuts* (linoleum plate). **Woodcuts** often retain the quality of the grain of wood because it is easier and cleaner to cut

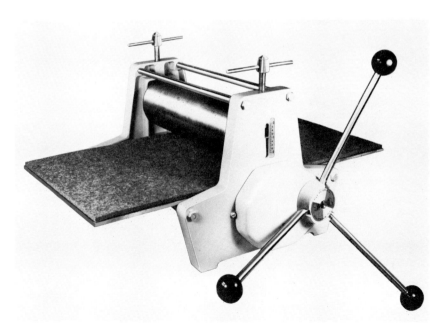

11-13 Fine Arts Printmaking Press for prints up to 12 × 14". *Courtesy of Dick Blick Co., Galesburg, IL.*

11-14 Printmaking gouges for wood and linocuts. *Courtesy of Loew-Cornell, Inc., Teaneck, NJ.*

with the grain than against it (**11-15**). The more uniform surfaces of linoleum and the end-grain used in wood engravings permit more fluid cutting in all directions. A **wood engraving** is mostly black with a white incised line (**11-16**).

The printing blocks or plates in relief techniques are inked by rolling a **brayer**, a hand-held roller with soft rubber or gelatin surface, over a small quantity of ink on a smooth nonporous surface until the brayer is uniformly coated with the ink. The brayer is then rolled repeatedly over the surface of the plate until it too has received a uniform coating of the ink. Paper is placed face down on the inked block and either run through a press or rubbed on the back side of the paper to *pull* the print. The block must be reinked for each print.

Intaglio (in-**tal**-yo, Italian meaning "cut in") prints are made from plates that have been incised with a variety of processes. Ink is rubbed into those lines, and paper that has been soaked in water and backed with soft blankets is run through the press at

11-15 HESTER STINNETTI. *Timbering* (ed. 10). Woodcut, 20 × 24″. *Courtesy of the artist and Dolan/Maxwell Gallery, Philadelphia, PA.*

11-16 CLARE LEIGHTON. *Limbing* (ed. 100). Wood engraving, $8\frac{1}{2}$ × 12″. *Courtesy of Dolan/Maxwell Gallery, Philadelphia, PA.*

high pressure. The pliable paper is pressed down into the lines and lifts the ink out in the reverse image of the plate. **Etchings** are created by covering the plate, usually zinc or copper, with a waxy acid-resistant ground known as the **resist**. One draws into the ground with a needle that exposes the plate in a series of highly personal drawing lines. The plate is then immersed in an acid bath—for which you will need special trays and ventilation—and left in until the desired depth of etch, *bite* has been achieved. The ground is removed with a solvent, and the plate is inked by rubbing a stiff etching ink into the etched lines. The excess is rubbed off the surface of the plate, and the print is pulled (**11-17**). **Aquatint** is a variation of etching that will give broad areas of tone. A powdered resin is sprinkled over the area to be aquatinted and melted slightly on a low heat hotplate so it will adhere. The remaining parts of the aquatint plate are covered with resist and, once dry, put in the acid bath. The longer the aquatint is in the acid, the darker the areas will print (**11-18**).

In an **engraving**, lines are drawn into a metal plate with a sharp tool called a **burin** or **graver** (**11-19**). An exacting technique, engraving gives sharper lines than an etching. Tonal areas can be created with **mezzotint**, a process of abrading and roughing up the plate surface with patterned and textured *rockers* so ink will adhere to it (**11-20**). **Dry-point** engravings are made by scratching into the surface of a plate with a sharp tool that raises a burr along the side of the scratched line. This burr holds the ink instead of the groove as in an engraving. Engravings, mezzotints, and dry-point engravings are inked and printed in the same manner as an etching.

Planographic printing is printing from a flat surface in which the printing and nonprinting areas are on the same level but are separated by differences in substances that either hold or resist the ink. **Lithography**, which was invented in the Industrial Revolution, in its mechanized form radically transformed visual communication. Limestone slabs or metal plates are used as a drawing surface for a greasy *litho* pencil,

11-17 TONY ROSATI. *Near Hilltop.*
1983. Etching, artist's proof, 3 ×
5". *Courtesy of the artist and Dolan/
Maxwell Gallery, Philadelphia, PA.*

11-19 Etching and engraving tools. *Courtesy of Loew-Cornell, Inc.,
Teaneck, NJ.*

11-18 PIERRE COLLIN. *Maurepas XIV.* 1983. Etching and aquatint, $62\frac{1}{2}$ ×
$28\frac{1}{2}$". *Courtesy of Brody's Gallery, Washington, DC. Photo: Edward Owen.*

11-20A Richard Hricko. *Mantle.* 1984. Etching and mezzotint, artist's proof, $14\frac{1}{2} \times 17\frac{1}{2}''$. *Courtesy of the artist and Dolan/Maxwell Gallery, Philadelphia, PA.*

11-20B Look closely at this detail of the above etching to see the mechanically-even mezzotint markings.

crayon, or ink called *tusche*. A nitric acid solution is applied to litho-stones; areas not drawn upon resist ink while those partially covered resist only to the degree that they do not coat the stone. Thus a broad range of tonal variation and the gestural marks of drawing remain much in evidence. The stone is kept wet with water, and the surface inked with a brayer in a manner similar to inking relief plates. The oil-based ink adheres to the drawing and is resisted by the wet bare stone. Paper is placed face down on the plate and pulled through the press. (**11-21**).

In **stencil** printing, ink-resistant materials or films are cut into shapes where no ink is to be transferred to the paper or fabric. Stencils include **serigraphy**, also known as **silkscreen**. The stencil is cut from a special film and affixed with a solvent to a very fine piece of silk (or most likely Dacron) that is tightly stretched over a frame (**11-22**). This frame, usually wood, also serves as a container for the silkscreen ink, which is very gooey. The frame with the silkscreen and stencil is placed on top of the paper or fabric. The ink is placed along one end of the frame, and a squeegee, the full width of the frame, is drawn to pull the ink across the screen in one single, even movement. The ink passes through the silk (or Dacron) screen to all areas not blocked by the stencil (**11-23**). The frame is lifted slightly to free the paper, another is put in its place, and as many prints as desired can be made in quite rapid succession. Silkscreen has reached the mass market in recent years with the popularity of printed

11-21 KÄTHE KOLLWITZ. *Death Seizing a Child*. 1934. Lithograph, 756 × 530mm. *Courtesy of the National Gallery of Art, Washington, DC., Rosenwald Collection.*

11-22 Silkscreen printing on fabric. *Courtesy of the Fabric Workshop, Philadelphia, PA.*

11-23 CATHERINE KERNAN. *Traversal II.* 1984. Serigraph print, artist's proof, 16 × 22". *Courtesy of the artist and Dolan/Maxwell Gallery, Philadelphia, PA.*

11-24 Fabric printed at the Fabric Workshop, Philadelphia, PA.

11-26 MERLE SPANDORFER. *W. Algoe Translator.* Inkless intaglio, also known as a blind embossing print, 40 × 30″. *Courtesy of the artist.*

T-shirts. There are special textile inks for fabrics (**11-24**).

Miscellaneous printmaking processes include **collography**, prints made from a surface that has been built in the manner of a collage (collé is French for "glue"). Papers, shaped cardboard, string, and various found objects can be glued to a backing surface. The whole "plate" can be inked or not, and run through the press with a moist piece of paper that will pick up both the texture and any ink (**11-25**). With or without ink, the raised areas of the print are what is

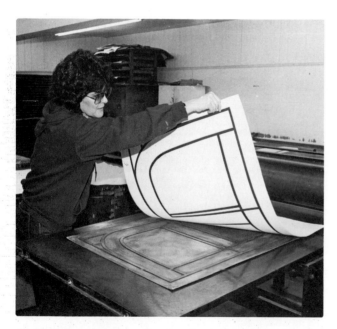

11-25 Merle Spandorfer pulling *E Series Black*, collograph, 40 × 30″, from plate of pasted cardboard. *Courtesy of the artist.*

known as **embossed**. Embossed papers with creative images and designs can also be formed from a variety of plates: they can be etched in the traditional manner but not inked, they can employ a plastic plate that has been carved, or they can exploit whatever methods artists devise. Such prints are known as **inkless intaglios** (**11-26**).

Transfer prints are similar to monotypes (chapter 10) in that ink is applied to a nonporous surface and the paper is placed upon it face down. But transfers are different from a monotype in that the ink is dispersed with a brayer. Another paper containing the master image is placed on top of the paper that rests on the ink, and the master is redrawn, pressing the bottom paper to pick up ink under the drawn line (**11-27**).

The intaglio and planographic plates are available with photo-sensitive resists and stencils so that photo imagery is available as an integral part of printmaking processes (colorplate **7A**). Many printmakers today are combining media and new techniques in unique and challenging ways (colorplate **7B**).

11-27 MERLE SPANDORFER. *Eruption.* Transfer print (also known as a transfer drawing), 22 × 30. *Courtesy of the artist.*

Summary

Printmaking is a process of making multiple copies from one image. A discipline with many technical challenges, perhaps the biggest challenge of printmaking is to create images that are worth repeating.

SCULPTURE

11-28 Sculpting with modeling clay. *Photo: Prentice-Hall.*

Sculpture differs from the disciplines of drawing, painting, and printmaking in that it pertains to actual three-dimensional forms and spaces rather than illusory or implied forms and spaces. (**11-28**). Except for conceptual sculpture (chapter 15), sculpture is concrete, real, solid, tactile; it has mass, weight, substance, and presence.

Once made only from clay, stone, wood, and metal, sculpture has been a discipline fraught with tradition and ideas of proper form. Today it embraces a staggering range of possibilities. Every form of matter is available for the sculptor to rethink, utilize, manipulate, and exploit in any manner to suit his or her vision.

People who make sculpture do so because of the pleasure derived from working with their hands and with tools and equipment. Some have an inclination for thinking big, working over long periods from conceptualization through development and fabrication to realization. Such large projects may entail the assistance of other people and of industrial fabrication shops and equipment. At the other end of the spectrum, intimate manipulations of clay or small-scale constructions can be meaningful paths to immediate self-expression.

In this section we will look at the more standard approaches to creating sculpture, while the more radical, multimedia formats are considered in chapter 15. Chapter 12 contains information on clay, glass, fibers, metal, and wood that is also relevant for sculpture.

Sculpture Formats

The *form* of any given sculpture is itself the format. Thus it may be round or jagged, miniature or monumental, heavy metal or lightweight plastic, open (penetrated by space) or closed. Its substance is *matter*, that of which any physical object is composed. As in all three-dimensional visual statements, matter and form are inseparable (**11-29**).

Sculpture Media

Clay, stone, wood, metal, and plastics are the primary categories of sculpture media. **Clay**, a decomposed state of rock and water, is found naturally in the environment deposited in the earth and in water beds. It is workable when moist, dries by evaporation to a hard brittle state, and vitrifies (becomes glass-hard), when fired to temperatures between 1100°F and

11-30 MARY FRANK. *Lovers.* 1973-74. Terracotta, 62 × 33 × 19″. *Courtesy of Zabriskie Gallery, New York. Private collection.*

11-29 LOUISE BOURGEOIS. *Blind Man's Buff.* 1984. Marble, 26 × 35 × 25″. *Courtesy Robert Miller Gallery, New York. Photo; Allan Finkelman.*

2600°F. Clay sculpture is often called **terra cotta**, (Italian for ''baked earth'') (**11-30**). Oil-based clay (Plastilina, Plasticene) is easily manipulable but never hardens, so it is used primarily as a preparatory process to make the forms for works to be cast in another medium. Plaster, cement, wax, wood, and mixed media can be used to sculpt forms for casting.

Stone is also found in the natural environment and comes in three basic qualities. **Sedimentary** stone (limestone, sandstone) is relatively soft and was formed by minerals deposited by glacial activity and/or the chemical and physical reactions of water erosion (**11-31**). **Igneous** stone (granite, basalt) is solid and dense, and resulted from fire or volcanic action. **Metamorphic** stone (marble, soapstone) is the finest textured, and it was once sedimentary or igneous rock that was transformed by geological occurrences of immense heat, pressure, and chemical reaction (**11-32**).

Synthetic stone is made from varying mixtures of cement, plasters, aggregates of sand, marble chips, vermiculite, and other materials. It can be mixed and built with when still moist, or allowed to harden in a block to be carved (**11-33**).

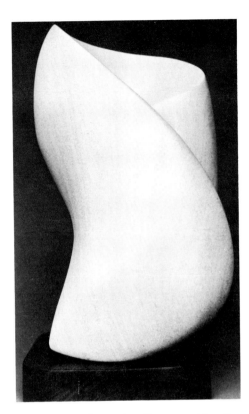

11-31 JEAN DOWNEY. *Waltz.* Cordova limestone, 12 × 7 × 6″. *Courtesy of the artist.*

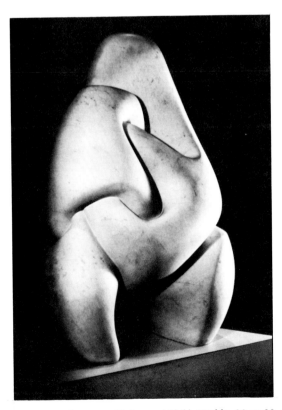

11-32 JILL SABLOSKY. *Mother and Child.* Marble, 30 × 20 × 14″. *Collection, Hilton Hotel, Allentown, PA, gift of Philip I. Berman. Courtesy of the artist.*

11-33 JAMES J. LLOYD. *Morpheus.* 1983. Direct buildup of synthetic stone material over a welded steel and foam armature, 9′ × 4′ × 20″. *Courtesy of the artist.*

Wood, which comes in a variety of grain patterns and colors, has a natural fibrous texture that is compact and strong. Many woods are readily available. Soft, easy to carve woods are cedar, poplar, spruce, white pine; medium-hard woods are apple, cherry, birch, butterwood; and hard are ash, maple, oak, and walnut, to name a few of the more common (**11-34**). (See also woodcraft in chapter 12.)

Many **metals**, both in their pure form and in alloys (combinations), are used in sculpture (**11-35**). Most frequently used are aluminum (colorplate **7C**); bronze—various combinations of copper, lead, tin, and zinc—(*See* **11-48**); steel for large-scale works; and precious metals such as gold, silver, and platinum for small-scale works. Metals are available in a broad range of formats: ingots (solid blocks), sheets, wire, rods, tubes, filings, powder, and scrap. (See metalcraft, chapter 12.)

Plastics are a synthetic material made from various combinations of carbon and other basic chemical elements. With more than twenty different kinds available, they have expanded the options for sculptors. Plastics may be molded and cast, calendered into sheets, extruded into threads and rods, machined, laminated, coated, and used as a coating on other materials. **Thermoplastics** can be heated and reheated to change their shapes. **Thermosetting plastics** are formed under heat, but once cool they cannot be reheated to be reformed (they'll scorch, melt, shrink, or do something else undesirable). Depending upon their attributes, plastics are available in a variety of shapes and sizes: blocks, sheets, tubes, rods, powder, fibers, and liquid. Some are clear while others are milky—translucent to opaque. Many can be tinted and colored (**11-36**).

Sculpture Tools and Equipment

The tools for making sculpture are numerous beyond any possible count. Some of them are unique to the medium, while many others, especially power tools, have been developed for the more commercial purposes of construction and manufacture and are adopted by sculptors to suit their needs. One's ability to express oneself with sculpture is in direct relationship to the tools and work space one has available.

11-34 MARY FRANK. *Untitled (reclining woman 2 parts).* C. 1963. Wood, $24\frac{1}{2} \times 34 \times 23''$. *Courtesy of Zabriskie Gallery, New York. Photo: Richard DiLiberto.*

11-35 MARJA VALLILIA. *Harbor.* 1983. Cast iron and steel, 28 × 43 × 31''. *Courtesy of Zabriskie Gallery, New York.*

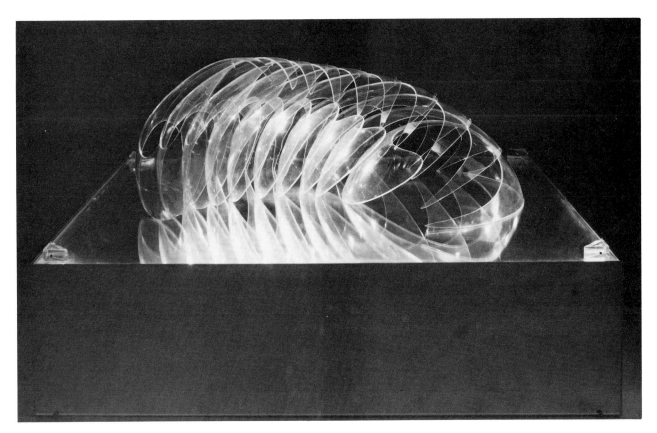

11-36 DEBORAH DEMOULPIED. *Palamos.* 1965-67. Molded Plexiglas.
Courtesy of the Hirshhorn Museum and Sculpture Garden, Smithsonian Institution, Washington, DC.

11-37 Robert Woodward texturing aluminum with power disk tool. *Photo: Susan Rosenberg.*

Modeling For modeling with clay or wax, special modeling and texturing tools are available made from wire, metal, wood, plastic, or a combination thereof (**11-38**). Since clay and wax have little resilience or tensile strength, they are best supported by an **armature**, a structural device built to hold the medium in the desired shape. Armatures are also used under plaster, cement, papier maché, or synthetic modeled forms. They can be made out of a broad range of materials: wire, screening, hardware cloth, chicken wire, plywood, masonite, wood, pipes and pipe fittings, and styrofoam. Modeled sculptures are most often cast in bronze or polyester resins for the final object.

Carving Carving wood, stone, or hardened plaster and cement is aided by mallets, hammers, chisels, gouges, picks, files, rasps, scrapers, and sandpaper (**11-39**). Electric drill and bits, grinders, routers, and air hammers are a few of the power tools that might be used.

Metalworking For working with metals that may be shaped and formed in a variety of ways, some of the tools one might need are cutters, hammers, forging tools, riveters, welding equipment (**11-40**), soldering irons, as well as wrenches, screw drivers, and clamps (**11-41**).

Plastics Tools and equipment for working with plastics may include all of the above as well as a hot-wire cutter and equipment for mixing, pouring, heating, and forming.

Sculpture Techniques

In traditional sculpture there were two basic techniques, additive and subtractive. **Additive** refers to modeling and building up with clay while **subtractive** refers to carving, taking away. Early in this century *construction* was added as a sculptural technique. **Constructed** or **constructivist** (also called **techtonic**) sculpture is assembled from a number of discrete preshaped parts, usually of one material (**11-42**). In its earliest forms, it was of plastic or metal sheets that were assembled by glue, wires, nuts and bolts, rivets, etc. Since then, techniques for making sculpture have expanded tremendously, and most are now a combination of additive and subtractive, and direct and indirect methods (**11-43**).

Two preliminary procedures that are commonly used in making sculpture are *drawings* and *maquettes*. By anticipating the actual sculpting process, they can greatly reduce the occurrence of costly errors. Informal sketches, whether pencil on paper or of modeling clay,

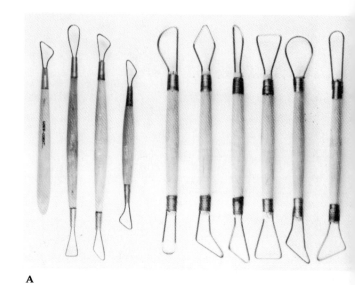

A

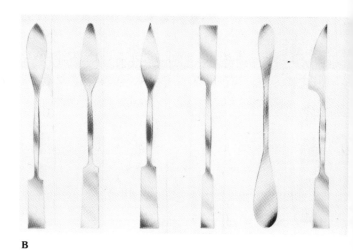

B

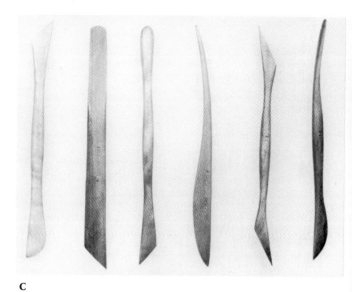

C

11-38 Clay modeling tools: **A** wire tools; **B** metal tools; **C** wood tools. *Courtesy of Loew-Cornell, Inc., Teaneck NJ.*

11-39 Sculpture carving tools made by Jill Sablosky. From left to right: chisel (subia), hammer, claw or tooth chisels, bush hammers, flat-edged chisels and finishing tools, and scrapers and finishing tools. *Photo: Jack Deitsch.*

11-40 Studio of Andrew Harper: arc welding in process with oxygen-acetylene welding/cutting apparatus in background. *Courtesy of the artist.*

11-41 ANN SPERRY. *The Garden of Delights.* 1980. Welded and painted steel, $7\frac{1}{2}' \times 142' \times 32'$. Installation at Wards Island, NY, sponsored by Artists Representing Environmental Arts (A.R.E.A.), New York. *Courtesy of the artist, collection of the University of Nebraska, Lincoln, NE.*

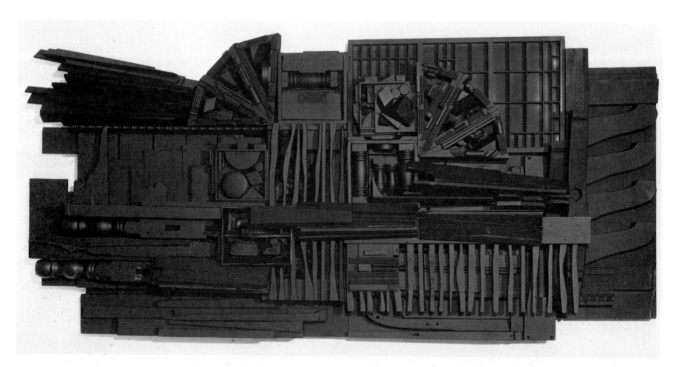

11-42 LOUISE NEVELSON. *Rain Forest Garden.* Black painted wood, $44 \times 95 \times 11''$. *Courtesy of The Pace Gallery, New York.*

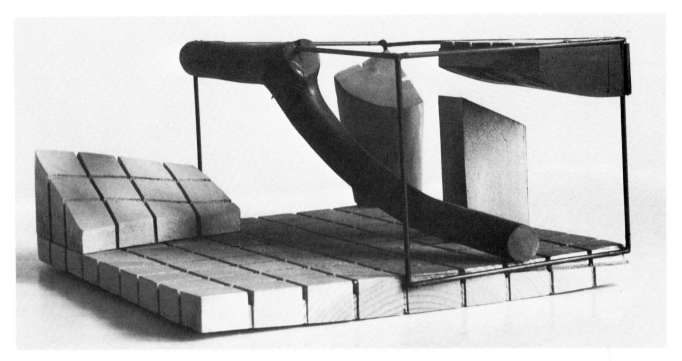

11-43 Margot de Wit. *Environment II.* Wood and metal; carved, welded, and constructed; 5 × 9 × 9". *Courtesy of the artist.*

can be sources for ideas and/or formats for working out design concepts and expression. Cartoons can be developed from several angles and transferred to blocks of wood or stone. A **maquette** is a scale model made from the same or closely related materials as the proposed finished work. Making a maquette can reveal trouble spots and provide a forum for working out technical requirements and procedures (**11-44**).

Modeling, Moldmaking, and Casting **Modeling** entails the manipulation of pliable matter such as clay, plaster, cement, wax, or plastics into the desired sculptural form. A mold may be made of the form so that a more permanent medium such as bronze, clay, or plastic may be poured into it to create a *cast* sculpture. Cast sculptures may also originate with constructed and/or carved materials such as wood, metal, stone, plastic foam, fiber-reinforced polyester resin, and found objects. The sculptural form to be cast is sometimes called a **pattern**, a term borrowed from industrial design (**11-45**).

Once the sculpted pattern attains the desired form, a **mold** is made from materials suitable to the purpose. These may be plaster, sand, silicone, or latex rubber. The pattern is removed from the mold and often destroyed in the process, and the mold is reassembled and supported to receive the casting material (**11-46**). Molten metal or liquified clay are poured into the mold and allowed to cool or harden (**11-47**). With clay the still-liquid center is poured off to be reused. With metal a **core mold** can be made so that the cast-

ing will also be hollow. Melted or liquid plastics are brushed into the mold and laminated in layers with a fiberglass reinforcing material.

The mold is removed and the sculpture is given finishing touches such as a **patina**, a method of coloration, and a protective coating such as wax on metal (**11-48**); it is fired and glazed if clay; and polished if plastic. The casting of metal sculptures is done in a **foundry** that is equipped with furnaces, moldmaking equipment, hoists, carts, as well as tongs, safety equipment such as heat-insulated suits, helmets with visors, respirators, and gloves. If the mold is of such a composition that it can be reused, a casting may be done in an edition of several identical pieces. The casts of an edition are numbered, for example, "2/6" connoting the second cast in an edition of six.

Carving Techniques for carving vary according to the grain and density of the medium. Plaster, cement, and synthetic stone have no grain and can be cut away with less risk and more control. Hammer and chisels are used for deep cuts while files, rasps, and scrapers work down the surface into the desired shape.

When carving wood or stone, sensitivity to the grain is extremely important: an "overhit" can cause a whole section to break away. For extremely hard stone such as marble or granite, electric-powered drills, grinders, and routers speed rough carving (**11-49**). The piece is then finished with files, scrapers, and sandpaper.

11-44 ARLENE LOVE: *Jacob Wrestling with the Angel*, maquette, cold cast bronze (epoxy bound bronze grindings), 21 × 15 × 7″. *Courtesy of the artist.*

B

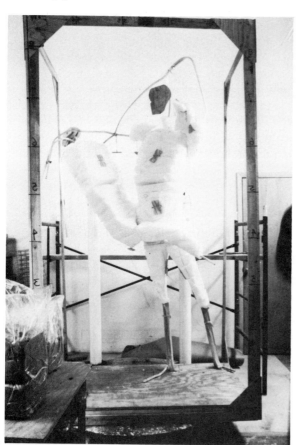

A

11-45 ARLENE LOVE: the making of *Jacob Wrestling with the Angel*, **A** the steel and aluminum armature filled out with styrofoam; **B** putting clay on the styrofoam; **C** finishing the modeling process. *Courtesy of the artist.*

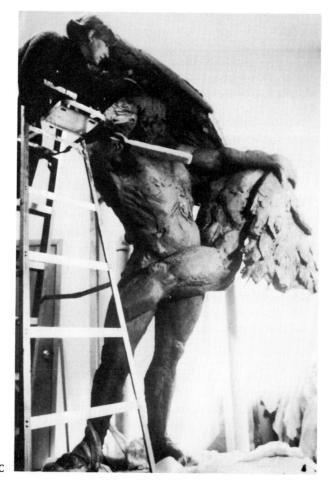

C

11-46 ARLENE LOVE: the mold-making of *Jacob Wrestling with the Angel,* **A** first coats of plaster applied to the bottom sections; **B** a lumber super-structure being affixed to each part of the mold; **C** sections of the mold lying out to dry. *Courtesy of the artist.*

11-46 **B**

11-46 **C**

11-47 ARLENE LOVE: the casting of *Jacob Wrestling with the Angel,* **A** the top section mold; **B** grinding off the seams of the lower section. *Courtesy of the artist.*   **B**

146

11-48 ARLENE LOVE. *Jacob Wrestling with the Angel.* 1984. Bronze, 10′ high. *Courtesy of the artist, collection University of Scranton, Scranton, PA.*

11-49 Jill Sablosky working in her studio with power grinder on marble. *Courtesy of the artist. Photo: Jack Deitch.*

Constructing **Constructing** entails two primary processes: *cutting* and *joining*. Materials, whether metal, wood, or plastics, are cut into shapes and joined together by a variety of processes. Cutting may be accomplished by hand and power saws, scissor-type cutters, knives, hot wires for plastics, and laser cutters for metals and plastics. The shapes may also be bent, molded, and otherwise altered through a variety of techniques appropriate to the medium. They then are joined by glue, fusion, and/or hardware.

Different materials, or different layers of the same material, may be *laminated* with glue or heat and pressure. Laminated forms can be built to a dimensional block and carved in ways similar to carving solid pieces of wood (**11-50**).

Polyester resins reinforced with fiberglass is a ver-satile and strong construction technique. Fiberglass serves as a reinforcing material and is available in thicknesses that range from very thin pliable veils to heavier woven cloths. The resin comes in a thick liquid form and requires a catalyst to harden. Until hardened, the resin and catalyst are toxic.

Miscellaneous Sculpture Options

In recent years the following materials and techniques have gained recognition and attracted practitioners. **Soft sculpture** is built from fabrics or soft plastics that have been cut and sewn into shapes and draped or stuffed with kapok, synthetic fibers, or polyfoam (**11-51**). Neon and fluorescent lighting elements have been shaped and configured into sculptural presentations (**11-52**). **Kinetic sculpture** has

11-50 Gabriel Kohn. *Nantucket (Equatorial Trap)*. 1960. Laminated wood construction, $28\frac{1}{4} \times 35\frac{1}{2} \times 23\frac{3}{4}$". *Courtesy of Hirshhorn Museum and Sculpture Garden, Smithsonian Institution, Washington, DC.*

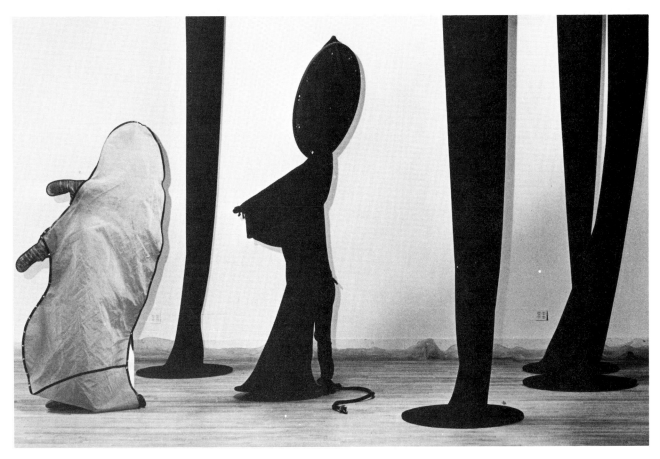

11-51 Woofy Bubbles a.k.a. Christopher Hodge. *In Search of the Woo.* Soft-sculpture and soft-sculpture costume and biological farce performance piece; black stretch cotton knit, hula hoops, plastic tubing, lamé, nylon, vinyl, PVC mesh, leather, elastic, and fasteners; 14 × 20 × 35′ × 1 hour performance space and time. *Courtesy of the artist and collaborators. Photo: Thomas Moore.*

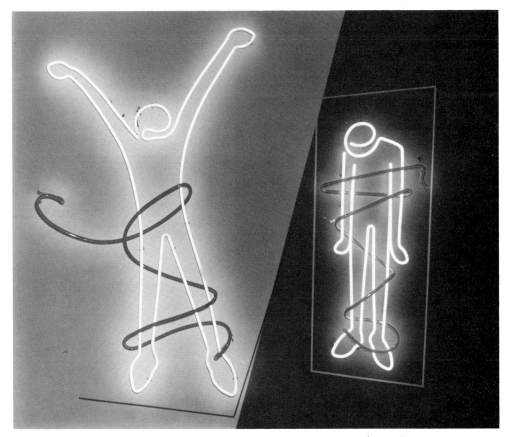

11-52 Alice Lees. *Breaking Through.* 1984. Kinetic neon on painted panel, $67\frac{1}{2}$ × $81\frac{1}{2}''$. *Courtesy of Wallace Wentworth Gallery, Washington, DC. Photo: Breger & Assoc.*

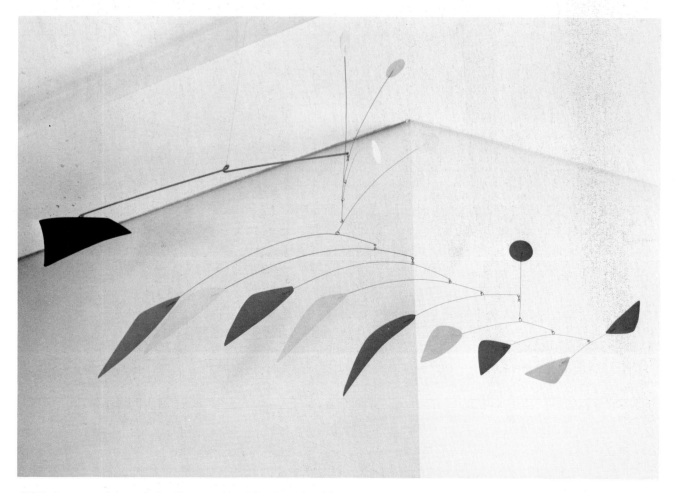

11-53 Alexander Calder. *Spring Blossoms.* 1965. Painted metal and heavy wire, 52 × 102". *Collection Museum of Art, The Pennsylvania State University.*

moving parts, either by the influence of touch and air currents (**11-53**), or by installed motors. Other innovative sculptural activities can be found in chapters 14 and 15.

Summary

As the three-dimensional fine art discipline, sculpture offers a rich variety of options for visual expression. The basic materials are clay, stone, wood, metal, and plastic, but any form of matter may be drawn into the service of one's vision for eclectic and meaningful articulation.

FINE ARTS SUMMARY

The fine arts are drawing, painting, printmaking, and sculpture. In these disciplines, the visual statement maker is at complete freedom to create whatever images and forms he or she wishes. At its most profound, conscious intent of visual organization and craftsmanship are fused with unconscious expression of feeling, beingness, and inner necessity in such ways as to engage both the maker **and** the viewer visually, emotionally, and intellectually.

CRAFTS

12-1 Installation of Rudolf Staffel porcelain exhibit at Helen Drutt Gallery, Philadelphia, PA. *Courtesy of Helen Drutt English.*

Devoting a chapter to crafts allows us to pay homage to a tradition dating back to the stone age and at the same time to herald the extraordinary metamorphosis that is taking place in the craft media today. This change entails the explosive expansion of craftmaking into forms of visual expression that go far beyond the utilitarian purpose of handcrafts of the past. Yet, while we look at the new directions and what they have produced in recent years, we must also recognize that most often people are attracted to crafts because of the functional nature of the objects created.

Handcrafted objects such as domestic utensils, clothing, jewelry, and furniture are, at their best, made with the spirit and creativity associated with the fine arts. Their principle materials are clay, glass, fibers, metals, plastics, and wood.

Craftsmanship is a high degree of, and love for, dexterity and technical skill in handling the materials of one's discipline. It entails patience and perfectionism in the search for excellence in the design and finish of visual statements, and is relevant to all visual media.

Craftspeople engage in self-expression, originality, excellence in design, the use of mechanical and electronic devices, and probably have the earliest history of multimedia creations. Moreover, they use drawings to conceptualize and plan their objects. So it is the making of functional objects that distinguishes the crafts from the other media described in Part V.

The distinction between a craft object and a work of fine art, for example, sculpture, can be unclear. Some craftspeople make monumental works that have little or no utility and so are celebrations of the object as form (**12-2**). Others make works of such exquisite originality and creativity that, especially with fragile ceramics, they are used only for display (**12-3**).

We will look at the various crafts as they are distinguished by their materials. All have accessibility for a beginner, but because of the equipment required for their making and completion, many of the handcrafts are best learned from experienced craftworkers.

Conception and method receive a good workout in the handcrafts. Processes can be so absorbing that one can lose sight of the visual qualities of what is being made. As with all visual statement making, critical visual assessment must be an ongoing aspect of the process of making crafted objects.

CERAMICS

Ceramics involves the making of objects with clay that is fired to become permanently hard (**12-4**). This includes sculptural forms (as indicated in chapter 11),

12-3 Rudolf H. Staffel. *Bowl.* 1969-70. Porcelain ceramic, $5\frac{1}{2}$ × $9\frac{1}{2}''$ diameter. *Courtesy of the Philadelphia Museum of Art, gift of the Philadelphia Chapter, National Home Fashions League. Photo: Will Brown.*

tiles, vessels, and pottery. Ceramicists find deep satisfaction in working with the elemental earthiness of clay, the ''hands-in'' as well as ''hands-on'' feel of its moist pliability. They constantly test and push the medium, but in many ways they must submit to its limitations. Ceramics is fraught with uncertainty, risk, and intrinsic demands that require attentiveness and a

12-2 Magdalena Abakanowicz. *Lady.* Sisal natural weaving, handwoven tapestry, 9'10" × 9'2". *Courtesy of Jacques Baruch Gallery, Chicago, IL.*

12-4 William Daley. *Tri-D-Out.* 1983. Unglazed stoneware, 18 × 19 × 21". *Courtesy Helen Drutt Gallery, Philadelphia, PA. Photo: Charlotte Daley.*

tenderness for tiny yet significant decisions. The medium undergoes a radical transformation from wet and mushy to dry and hard. But the meditative aspects of forming clay into shapes, and the ritual of firing and removing finished pieces from the kiln, can provide spiritual rewards that balance the many technical challenges.

Ceramic Formats

The formats of ceramics and pottery are the structures of the created object. These may be classified as pots and tableware, tiles and bricks, and the full range of sculptural figures and abstractions.

Ceramic Media

The medium of clay comes from two basic sources. **Residual** clay is found where it was formed; **sedimentary** clay has been carried by wind and water and deposited in a new location. **Earthenware**, low-fire clays, are coarse surface shale and clays; they are red or tan and remain porous after firing (**12-5**). **Stoneware** clays require a higher firing temperature; are denser than earthenware; may be gray, tan, brown, red, or white; and are waterproof upon firing (**12-5B**). **Porcelain** contains a high degree of **kaolin**, a very pure fine white clay, and is a high-fire clay (*see* **12-3**).

Glazes are mixtures of silica, fluxes, and alumina, with various coloring agents and other chemicals. They are ground into a fine powder, mixed with water, and applied to fired pots for waterproofing and decoration. Upon firing they vitrify (for they are a form of glass) and can be transparent, translucent, or opaque; glossy or dull, clear or colored, bright or subtle depending upon the chemicals that are used. Many glazes are toxic: gloves and a respirator mask should be worn when handling.

Tools for Ceramics

Clay must be **wedged**—kneaded and slammed onto an absorbent surface (usually a hardy cloth such as canvas)—to remove excess moisture and all air bubbles. Once wedged and in a workable consistency between wet and dry, clay may be formed by hand, with a wheel, with the application of modeling tools, and by molding.

A **potter's wheel** is a disk, usually metal, mounted on a central rotating shaft and moved either by kicking an attached disk or lever at foot level, or by an electric motor also operated with the foot on a rheostatted switch (**12-6**). **Modeling tools** made from wire, metal, wood, plastic, or a combination thereof, are available, and are the same as those for clay sculpture. **Sponges** are used to apply or reduce moisture.

Once the pot is formed, it is allowed to dry on a drying shelf. The dry **greenware** is then fired in a **kiln**, a closed, controlled furnace fueled by gas, electricity, oil, or wood. Once fired to a minimum of 1700°F, it reaches the **bisque** state. If you live in the country, primitive firing techniques can be followed; they include homebuilt ovens from dung cakes, stones, or bricks—sometimes in a pit—and firing with wood, sawdust, leaves, or dung as fuel.

A second hotter firing is required for glazing.

12-5 Oddy Curtiss. **A** *Raku Pot.* 1985. White clay fired to 1800°F, $2\frac{1}{2}$ " × $2\frac{1}{2}$" diameter. **B** *Handbuilt Pot.* 1985. Brown clay, fired in oxidation kiln to 2180°F, $2\frac{1}{2}$ × $1\frac{3}{4}$ × $1\frac{3}{4}$". *Courtesy of the artist.*

12-6 Elizabeth Dailey using a potter's wheel to trim a coffee mug before adding the handle. *Courtesy of the Clay Studio, Philadelphia, PA.*

Ceramics Techniques

Handbuilt ceramics (*see* **12-5**) can be: **pinched:** pinched, pulled, molded entirely by hand; **coiled:** clay rolled into snakelike strands coiled round and round to form a pot, each coil being pinched or smoothed together; and **slab-formed:** clay rolled to uniform thickness with a rolling-pin, cut into shapes, and fused with **slurry**, smooth wet clay the consistency of thick cream, (**12-7**).

Wheel-formed or **thrown** pots are shaped by placing a ball of clay in the center of a potter's wheel, turning the wheel, and holding and manipulating the clay as it turns (**12-8**). Once placed, the clay is **centered** or made even; it is then **opened** in the center to form a cylinder, the sides are **pulled** up and **shaped** by an interaction between the potter's hands and the nature of the clay. It is an intimate process: one learns by many trials before getting the feel of it; we discover techniques through applying the subtleties of touch that alter the form. Modeling tools may be applied as well as one's hands in this shaping/throwing process.

Molded pottery is a method for producing duplicates of a desirable pot. Molds are made of plaster or bisqued clay, and **slip**—a liquid state of the clay—is poured into them. When a skin of the desired thickness has formed, the excess is poured off. The pot is allowed to dry in the air and then fired in the kiln. After the bisque firing (**12-9**) the pot may be finished by glazing and/or with a number of decorative and finishing techniques.

Raku is a Japanese firing method that entails taking a red-hot glazed pot from the kiln (using long tongs) and placing it in a pit in the ground or in a steel can or drum that has been filled with dry leaves, straw, or sawdust. These ignite and give the pot its uneven charred appearance (colorplate **8D**).

12-7 Elizabeth Dailey working on a slab method handbuilt red stoneware façade wall hanging. *Courtesy of the Clay Studio, Philadelphia, PA.*

12-8 Janice Merendino demonstrating wheel throwing technique. *Courtesy of the Clay Studio, Philadelphia, PA.*

Tilemaking is a slab process where tiles of uniform shape are made and decorated for application with mortar to a wall, floor, or objects. When the tiles are very small and used pictorially, the technique is **mosaic**. Mosaics can also include pieces of glass.

Summary

Ceramics involves making objects with clay. They may be handbuilt, sculpted, molded, or formed on a wheel. Clay is fired to a permanent hardness, but ceramic objects remain breakable. Finishing and sealing with glazes requires a second firing.

GLASS

Glass is the fusion of inorganic materials through the application of intense heat and then rapid cooling—to a hard, rigid state before crystals can form. When in a hot, molten state, glass can be blown into shapes, attenuated by stretching, flameblown into fibers (source of fiberglass), folded, pulled, twisted, clipped into a variety of shapes, and fused with other glass objects (colorplate **8B**).

Glass can be transparent, translucent, or opaque, and it can take any color from the spectrum. Glassblowing and forming involve a lot of work. There is something primitive about the glass studio: its dirt floor, dark dingy interior, and elemental fire; and magical pure energy, hot glass, transformation. A glassblower can feel godlike in breathing life into this fundamentally inert substance.

Glass Formats

Vessels, windows, and whatever shapes and forms a sculptor can imagine, both representational and abstract, arc the formats of works madc in glass.

Glass Media

Glass is the earliest known synthetic material, synthesized most often from a mixture of **silica**, an ingredient of common sand, **soda ash**, a sodium oxide that functions as a *flux* (flowing agent), and **lime**, calcium oxide that functions as a stabilizer. Glass is tinted and colored by adding small amounts of metallic oxides such as copper, silver, or cobalt.

Glass Tools

Depending upon the way glass is handled, studio requirements will vary. Working with **stained glass** to make windows, essentially a two-dimensional for-

12-9 Bisqued and glazed stoneware pots awaiting final firing. *Courtesy of the Clay Studio, Philadelphia, PA.*

mat, calls for facilities to cool the glass in flat sheets and to join it by fusion or with lead strips. **Glass-forming** uses molds and casting procedures outlined in the sculpture section of chapter 11. **Glass-blowing** requires blow pipes, a specially designed bench, and various molds and tools for handling, shaping, and finishing the blown piece (**12-10**).

Working with glass requires a furnace or two for heating the glass, an annealing oven to control its cooling, various tweezers, tongs, and jacks to grab and hold the hot glass; files, shears, and cutters for cutting it; and grinding wheels for smoothing and polishing.

Glass Techniques

Stained glass entails working with either handmade colored or painted glass or commercially available colored glass. Sheets of the glass are cut into shapes that will fit together to form a predesigned image or abstract design. They are held together with strips of malleable lead (**12-11**).

A glassblower gathers molten glass on the end of a *blowpipe* by dipping it into hot glass repeatedly until enough glass has been built up to create the form desired. The outer skin is cooled by turning the gathered glass either into shaping forms (usually carved wooden blocks), or in the air. Air is blown into the glass through the blowpipe to expand it. Blocks and hand tools are used to create the desired shape. When this has been accomplished, the glasswork is allowed to cool slowly in an annealing oven. The cold piece can still be worked by grinding and polishing, and it can be decorated with glass enamels, lusters, metal plating, or by etching or sandblasting.

Summary

Glass as a creative visual medium offers a special highlight to our visual vocabulary. As well as being shaped, formed, and blown for its own expression, it can be used as a dynamic accent in works of other media.

12-10 Roland Jahn gathering glass to be blown at the glass furnace in his studio. *Courtesy of the artist. Photo: Alexander Limont.*

12-11 NARCISSUS QUAGLIATA. *Portrait of Suzuki Roshi.* 1980-82.
Stained glass, 6 × 4′. *Collection of Metropolitan Museum of Art, New York.
Courtesy of the artist and Snyderman Gallery, Philadelphia, PA.*

FIBERS

Fiber arts is a collective term that includes works created both from natural and synthetic threads and from any pliable material, fibrous or otherwise. Texture, softness, flexibility, and versatility are the distinguishing characteristics of fiber media.

Persons who choose to work with fibrous materials explore a medium with a vast range of options for engagement and expression. The traditional handcraft processes of knitting or crocheting garments, of weaving and coloring fabrics, and of stitching them together for clothing and domestic needs, continues unabated. Since the industrialization of these processes, however, *designers* (chapter 13) today design for looms and knitting machines for commercial production. In recent decades, fiber arts have offered an alternative to fine arts as a medium of original expression (**12-12**).

In fiber arts one builds a surface or structure from tiny threads, like lines, that trace and document the creation of the entire piece. From the tiny fibers from which the threads are spun, through interlocking, weaving, knotting, and/or stitching, creations of substantive texture and form can evolve.

Fiber Formats

Fibers and pliable materials may be combined to form fabric, cloth, garments, vessels, and original sculptured forms. These shapes and forms may be two- or three-dimensional (**12-13**).

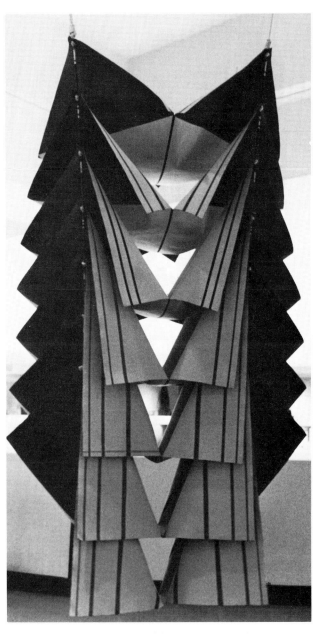

12-12 PAMELA BECKER. *Hanging Tower VII.* Painted and stitched canvas, 5′ high. *Courtesy of the artist and Works Gallery, Philadelphia, PA.*

12-13 CLAIRE ZEISLER. *Free Standing Yellow.* 1968. Black jute, yellow and black wool, 48½ × 48″. *Courtesy of Helen Drutt Gallery, Philadelphia, PA.*

Fiber Media

Natural fibers come from animal fur: wool from sheep, alpaca from llama, cashmere from mountain goat, silk from the silkworm; and from plants: cotton; linen from flax; and rayon from cellulose, a wood by-product. The tiny fibers are spun into a **thread** or **yarn** of various density and thickness. **Synthetic fibers** such as nylon or polyester are formed from carbon and other elements; they are the fibrous form of related plastics. Synthetic fibers likewise can be spun into threads and yarns. **Monofilament** is technically not a fiber but, as its name implies, one continuous synthetic strand that has been extruded rather than spun (colorplate **8C**). **Paper**, made from wood and natural fibers, can be extruded into yarnlike strands for interlocking. Paper particles can also be cast into molds and glued to create images or forms (**12-14**).

Nonfibrous pliable materials include *leather*—the treated hide of animals—and *synthetic sheeting* such as vinyl and polyurethane.

Fiber Tools

Tools for creating and handling fibers and pliable materials are many: **spinning wheels** for twisting fibers into threads or yarn; **looms** and all their accompanying gear of harnesses, heddles, beaters, shuttles, bobbins, spools, winders, for weaving threads, yarn, and other materials into fabrics and hangings; **needles** for knitting and sewing, **hooks** for crocheting and lacemaking; **vats** for dyeing, **racks** and screens for drying, facilities for melting and applying wax for batiking; machines for sewing, twisting, looping, and coiling; cutting implements; and any tools, devices, or machines that are relevant to achieving a fiber artist's goals.

Fiber Techniques

Techniques for creating with fibers and pliable materials include *interlocking, dyeing,* and *stitching.*

Interlocking Weaving, knitting, crocheting, netting, lacemaking, felting, looping, coiling, twining, braiding, and knotting are all **interlocking** techniques by which threads can be combined to form fabrics, garments, and ropes.

Weaving entails the interlacing of threads at right angles to one another; it must be accomplished on a loom that holds the lengthwise yarns, the **warp**, in tension. Filler threads or yarn known as the **woof** or **weft** are woven between alternating warp threads. **Tapestry** is a pictorial form of weaving where the warp threads have been obscured by heavier weft threads of irregular lengths that conform to an image or design (**12-15**).

Knitting employs spike-shaped needles to wrap and loop a single strand of yarn into a continuously interlocking knit. **Crocheting** is similarly performed, but with a hook. **Netting** and **lacemaking** are intricate methods of twisting and looping threads to create a pattern. **Coiling, twining,** and **braiding** are methods for creating thick strands of fibers such as ropes (*see* **12-13**). **Macramé** is a process of tying knots to create patterns and nets for decorative purposes. But **knotting** can also be employed in many creative ways to achieve sculptural forms (**12-16**). **Felting** or **matting** is combining unspun fibers into a flat mass by the application of moisture, heat, and compression. **Emballage** is a process of twisting, tying, and knotting fibrous materials into amorphous ball-like shapes (**12-17**).

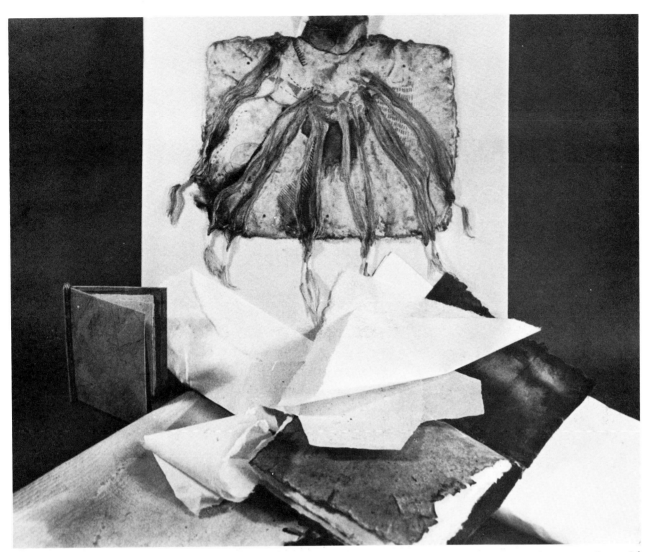

12-14 MAUREEN ROBERTS. *Canyon Walls #2, Maquette for Ladies Room, Soft-ware Book #3,* and a selection of handmade papers and materials: 25% polypropylene, 25% chopped polyester fibers, and 50% cotton linters. *Courtesy of the artist.*

12-15 ADELA AKERS. *High Tide.* A radial tapestry weave used to create dimensional forms. *Courtesy of Helen Drutt Gallery, Philadelphia, PA.*

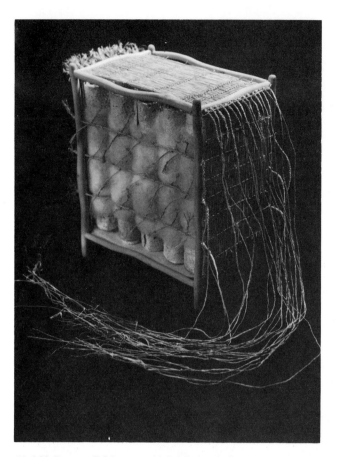

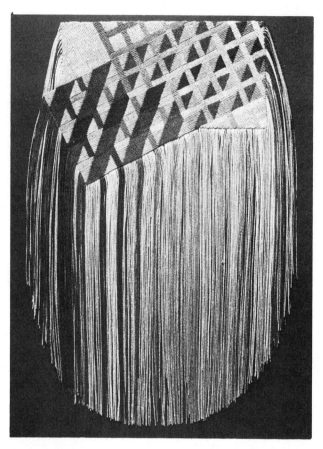

12-16A DOMINIC DIMARE. *Untitled. Collection of Robert Pfannebecker.Courtesy of Helen Drutt Gallery, Philadelphia, PA.*

12-16B DIANE ITTER. *Summer Lattice.* 1980. Knotting/linen, 8 × 6″ (knotted area). *Private collection. Courtesy of Helen Drutt Gallery, Philadelphia, PA.*

12-17 MAGDALENA ABAKANOWICZ. *Embryology.* Installation, fiber sculpture. *Courtesy of the Museum of Contemporary Art, Chicago, IL.*

Dyeing **Dyes** are pigments of great intensity that are mixed with water and a chemical wetting agent so as to penetrate the natural fibers. **Dyeing**, the process of coloring fibers, may be done at any stage of the fabric-making process. Fibers may be dyed before being spun, after they are spun, and after they have been woven. (Synthetic fibers are colored when they are made due to the industrial techniques they require to take on color.) **Tie-dyeing** is a process of tying and knotting pieces of fabric together very tightly so that the dye will not penetrate evenly, thus leaving abstract patterns. **Batik** is a process of wax resist, in which melted beeswax is selectively applied in designs to a woven fabric. The dye will penetrate only the unwaxed fibers. Pictorial imagery is possible by painting with dyes (**12-18**). **Ikat** is a process of resist dyeing threads with planned bands of color before weaving so that they create a pattern in the woven form.

Stitching **Stitching** can both join and decorate. In its joining function it is the primary method for putting together—sewing pieces of cut fabric, leather, or any pliable materials—to create a form. The form is usually a garment, but may also be a soft sculpture or other creative endeavor. **Stitchery** as an expressive medium and as decoration includes *embroidery, needlepoint, crewel,* and many other imaginative stitchmaking

12-18 GAYLE FRAAS and DUNCAN W. SLADE. *Couch in Stonington.* 1983. Painted and quilted textiles, 24 × 24". *Courtesy of the artists and the Works Gallery, Philadelphia, PA.*

12-19 Nancy Clearwater Herman. *Peacock Halleluja.* 1984. Quilted satin and cotton. 60 × 60″. *Courtesy of the artist.*

procedures. Examples of stitching that is both decorative and joining are *smocking* and *quilting* (**12-19**).

Related Media

Printing on fabrics with printmaking techniques (**12-20**); costume and clothing design, wearable art; chair caning and basketry; papier-maché, and collage/assemblage are some of the media and techniques that interface with fiber processes, all of which offer viable means for visual expression.

Summary

Fiber arts offer many distinct techniques that can be used separately or combined to create visual statements with fibrous and pliable materials. These include the interlocking of threads, the stitching together and decorating of pliable materials, and the dyeing and printing of fabrics. Two- and three-dimensional formats are possible, as are pictorial images and nonrepresentational designs. Objects created with fibrous materials may range from utilitarian garments or floor coverings to creative expressions of environmental art (chapter 15).

METALS AND JEWELRY

Jewelry and **metalsmithing** are closely aligned because of their shared medium of metals (colorplate **8A**). Jewelry, however, is often a mixed medium that includes precious and semiprecious stones and a variety of other substances. Working with precious metals is exacting. It requires a high degree of manual dexterity, attentiveness to detail, tenacity, and persistence.

Metals are valued for their survivability: they are never exhausted but can be found and reformed over and over again. In working with metal one experiences its transformation, its change from solid to liquid to new solid. Heating, hammering, pulling, winding, etching, polishing, and fusing are a few of the manipulations that alter and reshape metals.

Metalcraft and Jewelry Formats

Jewelry formats include headpieces, earrings, necklaces, pendants and collars (**12-21**), tie clasps,

12-20 JUDY RIFKA. *Museum Wallpaper* 1983, being printed at the Fabric Workshop, Philadelphia, PA.

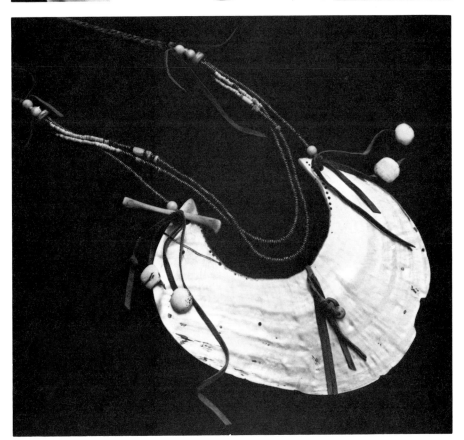

12-21 JUDY CORLETTE. *Tattooed. Necklace.* Conch shell (New Guinea), copper (Kenya), conch buttons (Nepal), bird bone, leather strips, Pre-Columbian shell beads, 18 × 8". *Courtesy of the artist and Works Gallery, Philadelphia, PA. Private collection. Photo: Carolyn Jones.*

buttons and studs, pins and brooches, armbands and bracelets; cufflinks, rings, belts and buckles, anklets and shoe ornaments. Bowls, platters, tumblers, goblets, tableware, tools such as letter openers and razors, and accessories such as money clips and card cases are some of the formats that a metalworker might work in (**12-22**).

Metalcraft Media

The most common metals used are gold, silver, pewter, copper, brass, bronze, aluminum, stainless steel, and titanium. Jewelry and body ornamentation might incorporate shells, leather, fibers, woods, plastics, feathers, bone, ceramics, and seeds, as well as stones, whether precious gems or otherwise.

Metalcraft Tools

Because jewelry and metalcraft are on a small scale, a metalworking studio needn't take much room (**12-23**). But the quantity and variety of tools and equipment it might contain is enormous. These will include hand tools such as hammers, tweezers, and

A

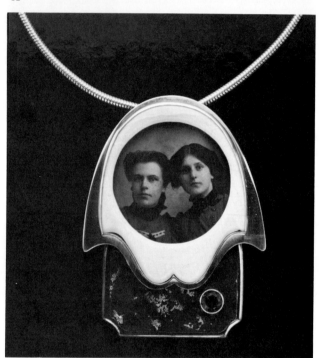

B

12-23 BARBARA SATTERFIELD. **A** jewelry-making studio 11 × 13'; and **B** *Atlantic City Sisters.* Pendant of antique photograph, carved ivory, sterling silver, rusted iron from Atlantic City bathhouse lock, faceted citrine, and copper, 3 × 2". *Courtesy of the artist. Photos: Peter Handler.*

12-22 SUSAN HAMLET. *Bowl Series #6.* 1985. Hastelloy, aluminum, bronze, stainless steel, plastic, rubber, $16\frac{1}{2}$ × $13\frac{1}{2}$" diameter. *Courtesy of Helen Drutt Gallery, Philadelphia, PA.*

screw drivers; an anvil, scrapers, a vise, pliers, and punches for marking; rasps, files, clamps, gravers for engraving, burnishers, and chisels. Electric tools may include a drill, a drop hammer to stamp out designs, a soldering iron; electroforming and electrolytic equipment; machines for bending, flattening, buffing, and polishing; kilns for annealing (restoring metal to a malleable state), for enameling (fusing glass to metals), and for fusing metals to metal. Gas-fueled torches and burners for fusing, annealing, and heating metal are also standard workbench equipment.

Metalcraft Techniques

Metals are known for their high formability. At room temperature, they may be shaped by hammering, cutting, pulling, or pressing. **Repoussé** is hammering metal to raise or emboss an area, while **chasing** is hammering to form a recessed area. Heating metals will allow them to be bent, fused, laminated, welded, and cast into molds.

Granules of glass can be heated and fused onto metal, a process known as **enameling**. A method for controlling where the glass is deposited is **cloisonné**, in which thin metal wires are fused to a base in intricate designs. Different colors are placed throughout the design and fused by heat in the kiln (**12-24**).

These are just a few of the possible techniques of metalworking.

Summary

Various metals are used in the making of jewelry, utensils, and small sculptures. Metalcraft and jewelrymaking are closely related disciplines that require meticulous care in the handling of materials and details, but which can have breathtaking visual reward in their finest forms.

WOOD

Vessels, furniture, decorative objects, and cabinetry are the products of woodcraft. Woodcraft is closely affiliated with industrial design for furniture, with architecture and interior design for restoration and cabinetry, and with sculpture for personal expression (colorplate **8E**).

The smell of a woodshop is like no other. The look and feel of wood, its warmth of tone and varying grain, its moderate temperature to the touch, its organic unpredictability and grace, make it a deeply rewarding medium with which to work. A woodworker is dedicated to excellence in the design and finish of the crafted object. Woodcraft differs in emphasis from the technical nuts-and-bolts of most high school shop programs. As one woodworker told me, "I had the typical woodshop background, but I got a summer job with a woodcraftsman, who awakened me to the excitement and limitlessness of *design*. It was like seeing in technicolor for the first time!"

Woodcraft Formats

Formats in woodcraft are the form of the object itself, whether it be a chair, table, bowl, cabinet, or abstract sculpture.

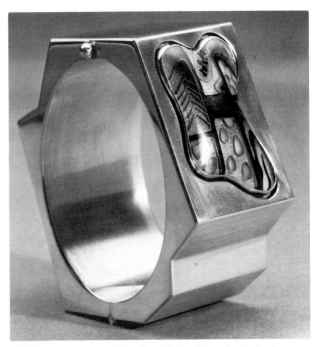

12-24 COLETTE. *Hinged Bracelet with Two Enamels #1.* Sterling silver with 24k gold bezels, cloisonne wire, and two enamels, $1\frac{3}{8}$ × $2\frac{1}{2}''$ diameter. *Courtesy of the artist and Works Gallery, Philadelphia, PA.*

Woodcraft Media

All kinds of available wood may be crafted. They may have varying grains, textures, colors: from soft pine to hard oak, light poplar to dark ebony, even-grained cherry to dramatically modulated paldau or zebrawood.

Woodcraft Tools

Hand tools for wood include saws, hammers, chisels, planes, jigs, vises, clamps, gouges, and so forth. Power tools are central to woodworking: saws of many types, a lathe for turning and shaping, drill presses, sanders, jointers, a planer, and a router (**12-25**). A balance between confident handling and respect for power tools is utterly necessary. Overconfidence can result in carelessness and accidents, while fear of using power tools can limit your expression.

Woodcraft Techniques

It takes several years to master the craft of woodworking, and perhaps longer to get the medium to respond to one's visions and feelings. The material is expensive, so one develops conceptualizing and drawing skills as part of the craft. Rough sketches of a proposed object evolve to more and more detailed

12-25 Robert B. Worth working with power tools in his studio. *Courtesy of the artist.*

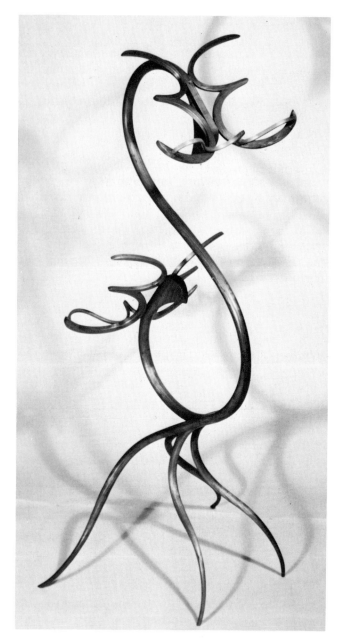

12-26 ROBERT B. WORTH. *Double Rack Music Stand.* Bent and laminated cherry, 57 × 24 × 24". *Courtesy of the artist.*

sketches. Then perspective drawings from several points of view are made in which the proportions of the object are consistent. A **rendering**, a descriptive drawing of the anticipated outcome, may be drawn and colored. Full-scale working drawings with step-by-step *specifications* and paper *patterns* for the pieces to be cut are the next step. A *scale model* or *maquette* might be made from inexpensive styrofoam or plywood to work dimensionally in preparation for cutting the wood and assembling the final work.

The pattern is applied; the selected wood is cut. The wood may be shaped with planers or bent with moisture before being joined together by the appropriate technique. These include a combination of glue, hardware, and **jointing** principles such as *dovetailing, hole and peg, tongue and groove, finger joints,* or *lock miters.*

Once securely joined, the work may be decorated with *routed* grooves and carvings or *inlays.* Sanding removes any roughness, and oil, laquer, or a synthetic sealant give a glowing finish.

Lamination is a technique of gluing together layers of wood so that its tensile strength will be increased. Laminates are more resistant to splitting, breaking, or warping (**12-26**). **Plywood** is a laminate where the grains of the plies are at right angles to one another. Plywood can be given a top surface of a choice wood, known as a **veneer**, a 1/28-inch thick slice. This provides strength, stability, and mass, and cuts costs. Handcrafted laminated wood of contrasting grains and colors can offer a broad expansion of design and esthetic potential (**12-27**).

Summary

Creating beautifully crafted works with wood requires patience, dedication to the medium, and respect for tools and methods. Original works made of wood have a special presence in our lives (**12-28**).

RELATED AND MISCELLANEOUS CRAFTS

Decorative arts refers to handcrafted objects designed by a craftsperson to be produced in quantity.

12-27 WILLIAM KEYSER. *Coffee Table with Discs.* 1978. Elm slab top; maple, cherry, walnut laminate base, $18\frac{1}{4} \times 69 \times 22''$. *Courtesy of the artist and Snyderman Gallery, Philadelphia, PA. Collection of the artist.*

12-28 ROSANNE SOMERSON. *Conference Table with Windows.* 1983. Bubinga, curly maple, glass, inlay purfling, anodized aluminum, delrin, $29\frac{1}{2} \times 48''$ diameter. *Courtesy of Snyderman Gallery, Philadelphia, PA. Collection of Robert Kaufman. Photo: Susie Cushner.*

When the esthetic quality is high these works may receive recognition by collectors, galleries, and museums.

Bookbinding, papermaking, maskmaking, beading, and leather tooling are just a few of the many craft possibilities available to us. Others are **collage**—the making of designs or images by gluing cut, torn, or found papers; **decoupage**—the application of such papers to an object with glue and sealing with varnish or shellac; and **papier-mâché**—the pressing of glue-soaked papers to an armature. In the hands of people with a creative visual sensibility, these media are as capable as any other of esthetic significance.

CRAFTS SUMMARY

All of the craft media are exercises in delayed gratification. The basic materials are rough, unformed, often quite unattractive. Through patience and devoted work, these materials are grappled with, pulled, pushed, hammered, cut, thrown, and put through no end of manipulations toward becoming unique, exquisite handcrafted objects. Clay, glass, fibers, metals, wood, paper, and plastics are the primary materials that can accompany us on our quest for visual literacy.

DESIGN

13-1 Environmental design and graphic design were an integral part of a product design exhibit at the Whitney Museum of American Art, New York, in 1985. *Courtesy of Venturi, Rauch and Scott Brown, Philadelphia, PA. Photo: Tom Bernard.*

In the **design** disciplines the problems to be solved are most often provided by individuals and circumstances other than the designer. The **designer** is an *expert* who solves the visual-spatial, product, and visual-communication requirements for clients of many backgrounds and needs. Because of the services and expertise they render as architects, illustrators, interior designers, industrial designers, and graphic and fashion designers, they are among the most commercially viable of visual statement makers. Despite their tremendous contributions to our daily lives, however, designers are most often anonymous. The products they design are almost never signed and are usually executed or produced by others such as builders, printers, and manufacturers. The obligations and imperatives of the design disciplines are so specialized that, in most cases, a minimum of four years of rigorous professional training is required. Years of hands-on, trial and error, experiential designing and making under the guidance and challenge of professional teachers and practitioners is imperative in becoming a designer (**13-1**).

Drawing ability is essential to designers. All ideas, preparatory sketches, and plans are graphically realized. Professional designers are able to synthesize self expression and originality within the specifics of their design idiom. The best may develop a signature and make a contribution to the visual vocabulary of the discipline and of the culture. Craftsmanship is critical to design. The process of design is exacting and requires precision and responsibility on the part of its practitioners. Designers employ mechanical and electronic devices in their work. In addition to traditional photographic processes, **computer-aided design** (CAD) has radically altered and expedited both the design process and the way designers think about and conceptualize objects and spaces (**13-2**). Computer literacy is imperative for designers today. The design disciplines are intrinsically multimedia. So it is the origin of the problem with the client, and the execution or production of the designed object by persons other than the designer, that distinguish the design disciplines from the visual media discussed in the other chapters of part V.

Because the design disciplines are client oriented, all designers need to have good verbal, social and interpersonal skills. Freelance designers may work alone, but they still must make contacts for jobs—a process that requires confidence and perseverence. Until one acquires contracts for ongoing work, one must look for the next job as soon as another is accepted. The ability to keep perspective in the face of rejection is not everyone's forté, and such personal factors must be considered in making a professional commitment to the highly competitive design fields. Another personal factor is that designers have a responsibility not only to their own ideals and/or their

13-2 Printout from Computer Aided Design (CAD). *Courtesy of Space Data Group, Philadelphia, PA.*

client's needs, but also to the common social and environmental good of all.

Before describing the different disciplines, let's look at the formats, media, tools, and techniques that are shared by designers.

Design Formats

Formats vary in design disciplines from the paper of the preliminary sketches and plans (**13-3**) to the shape and form of the produced object (**13-4**). Tracing paper, both inexpensive rolls and quality vellum, is frequently used by designers of all disciplines.

Design Media

The procedures of design utilize all drawing media plus those of model and prototype construction: wood, cardboard, cork, plastics, fabrics, glass, metal, glue, etc. (*see* **13-12**). Design plans may be reproduced by photographic and electrographic methods (**13-5**).

Design Tools

Most designers work on a **drafting table** or **board** that can be adjusted in height and slant (**13-6**). A T-square, rulers, French curves, templates, mechanical-drawing implements such as pens and compasses, and many other drawing tools—including layout pencils and felt-tipped marking pens—are found in a designer's studio. Computer-aided design (CAD), with its graphic and transformational capabilities, is the tool of the present. It expedites conceptualization by offering, in moments, many possible solutions to a design problem, and its printout capability replaces much time-consuming drafting (**13-7**).

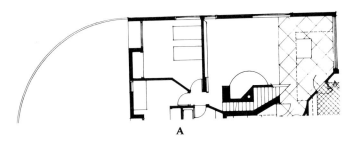

A

B

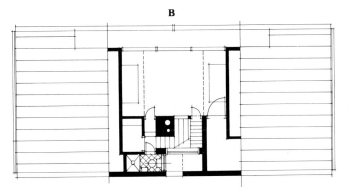

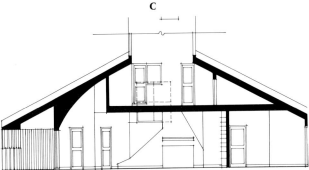

C

13-3 ROBERT VENTURI. *Vanna Venturi House.* 1964. Philadelphia, PA: **A** first floor and **B** second floor floorplans, **C** section drawing. *Courtesy of Venturi & Rauch, Philadelphia, PA.*

13-4 ROBERT VENTURI. *Vanna Venturi House.* 1964. Philadelphia, PA, front and rear views. *Courtesy of Venturi & Rauch, Philadelphia, PA. Photos: Rollin LaFrance.*

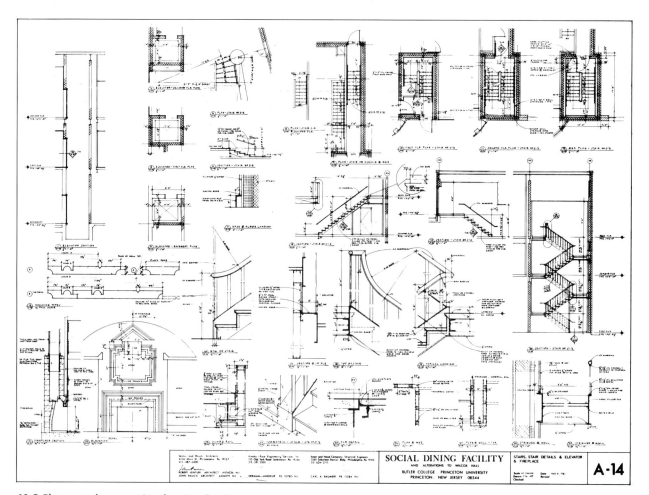

13-5 Photostatted construction drawings for alterations to Wu Hall, Butler College, Princeton University. *Courtesy of Venturi, Rauch and Scott Brown, Philadelphia, PA.*

13-6 An adjustable drafting table. *Courtesy of Anco Wood Specialties, Inc., Glendale, NY.*

13-7 CAD in use. *Courtesy of Space Data Group, Philadelphia, PA.*

Design Techniques

Drawing, both freehand and mechanical, dominates the design disciplines. Paste-up and construction techniques are used in layouts for graphic design and in model building for environmental and industrial design.

ENVIRONMENTAL DESIGN

Environmental design is a collective term that pertains to the design of any three-dimensional area or space. It includes architecture, landscape architecture, interior design, aspects of urban and regional planning, stage-set design, and exhibit design.

Architecture

Architecture, the design of buildings and structures, is a synthesis of art and engineering: a combination of function, space, materials, and esthetics. Its purpose is to enclose space to shelter human beings in such a way as to support human needs, behaviors, activities, products, and pets; and also to provide a visually and functionally pleasing environment. At its most sublime, architecture is a synthesis of poetry and reality.

Buildings are made from a broad range of natural and synthetic materials and have a variety of sizes, shapes, functions, and appearances (**13-8**). Architec-

ture is a highly responsible discipline, and its practitioners are licensed by examination to determine their readiness to design with reliability. Buildings must be structurally sound, a contribution to the safety, health, and well-being of the people who inhabit and use them. An architect is committed not only to the client, but also to the community, to the land, to the people, and to the region.

The Post-modernist movement in architecture is attempting to integrate human needs, both physical and psychological, with the modification of the natural and built environment that we have inherited from the successes and failures of the past. Astuteness is required to do this authentically—with homage to the intrinsic nature of both materials and human behavior.

Architects dream and conceptualize design and environmental possibilities as an ongoing part of their art. Through this process, together with their study of the works of others, they develop a mental reservoir of design ideas. They meet with clients to ascertain, as completely as possible, the requirements and vision of the client. They then do some informal sketches of the proposed building and its specifications (**13-9**). When agreement has been reached with the client on the design, mechanical drawings, known as the **schematic design**, are made on tracing paper. These include floor plans, elevations, site drawings, and section drawings; they contain, through symbols and labels, all the design specifications (**13-10**). Reproduced and collated, they are together known as the

13-8 Aerial view of Philadelphia. *Courtesy of The Captured Image, Norwood, PA.*

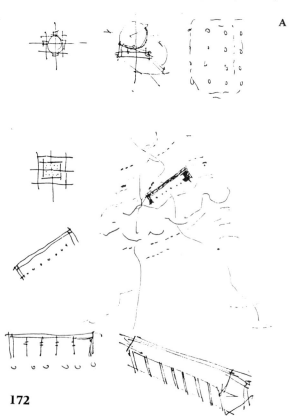

A

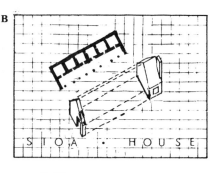

B

STOA · HOUSE

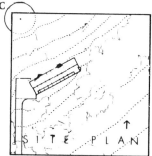

C

SITE PLAN

13-9 Margo Leach. Sketches and plans for Leach House:
A informal idea sketches; **B** plan of a stoa, an ancient Greek
plan; **C** site plan. *Courtesy of the architect, Philadelphia, PA.*

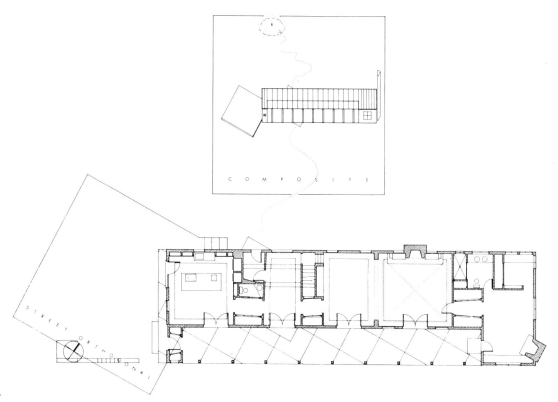

A

13-10 MARGO LEACH. **A** Floor plan and **B** wall construction drawing for Leach House. *Courtesy of the architect, Philadelphia, PA.*

B

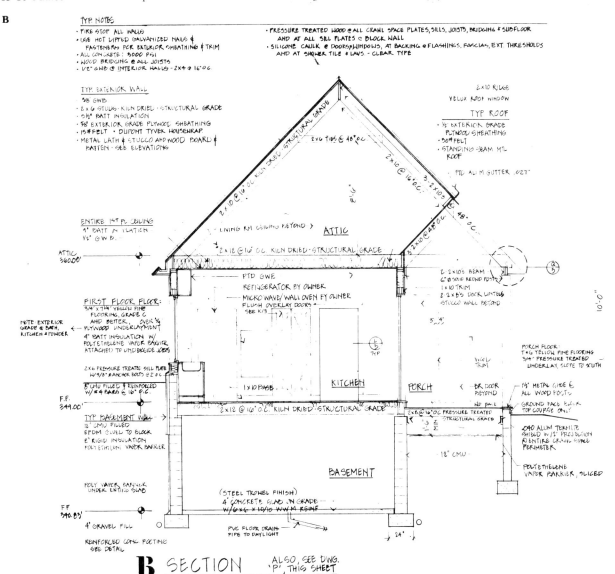

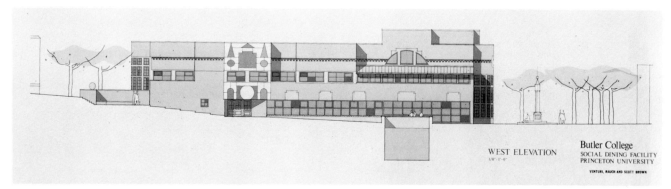

13-11 VENTURI, RAUCH and SCOTT BROWN. Rendering West Elevation, Wu Hall. 1983. Butler College, Princeton University Princeton, NJ. *Courtesy of Venturi, Rauch and Scott Brown, Philadelphia, PA.*

construction design document. This document is followed by the contractor and all who participate in the construction process. A **rendering** (**13-11**), an illustration of how the building will look when completed, and a **scale model/maquette** may also be made by the architect for the client (**13-12**).

From this point on the architect works not only as a designer, but as the client's representative and as a **coordinator** who calls upon the expertise and cooperation of others: civil, electrical, mechanical, and structural engineers; interior designers, landscape architects; urban and regional planners, and construction managers (**13-13**).

Few of an architect's designs reach completion. Books and exhibits offer architects the opportunity to share with others, as conceptual art, the plans that for one reason or another have not reached fruition.

Requirements upon architects have expanded to herculean proportions with the population growth of the twentieth century. Thus the discipline has divided into several subspecialties: interior design, landscape architecture, and city and regional planning. Independent architects continue to respond to individual commercial and residential needs (**13-14**), but larger developments are handled by architectural design firms that have architects, engineers, interior designers, landscape architects, and city and regional planners on the staff. An administrative staff, often headed by an experienced architect, coordinates the projects.

Interior Design

Interior design is a specialized branch of architecture that is concerned with the function, esthetics, character, and psychological impact of interior spaces (**13-15**). Interior designers are trained to interface with

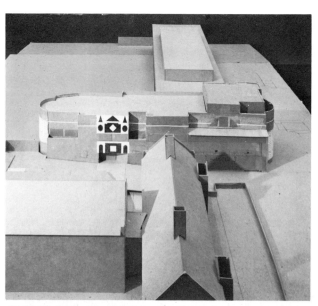

13-12 Model for Wu Hall, Princeton University. *Courtesy of Venturi, Rauch and Scott Brown, Philadelphia, PA.*

13-13 VENTURI, RAUCH and SCOTT BROWN. Wu Hall. 1983. Butler College, Princeton University, Princeton, NJ. *Courtesy of Venturi, Rauch and Scott Brown, Philadelphia, PA.*

13-14 MARGO LEACH. Leach House. *Courtesy of the architect.*

13-15 VENTURI and RAUCH. Dining area of Vanna Venturi House.
1964. Philadelphia, PA. *Courtesy of Venturi and Rauch, Philadelphia, PA.*

175

the architect's intent and the whole envelope of the interior space. The discipline includes **interior decoration**, the esthetic concern for color, materials, wall and floor coverings, window treatment, furniture, and lighting. But interior design also entails a course of study that encompasses behavioral psychology, rigorous training in architectural principles, building materials and construction, and mechanical and electrical systems. Interior designers work on a contractual basis, and many use the designation, ASID (American Society of Interior Designers) (**13-16**). A licensing procedure is under consideration.

Landscape Architecture

Landscape architects are usually responsible for the sites of architectural development, the use of open spaces, and the ecological protection of the surrounding land. Awareness has grown that we cannot go on developing land and using its resources without imperiling the human race. As with all design, a landscape architect brings together diverse elements and systems in such ways as to create a harmonious whole.

Urban and Regional Planning

In the **urban** and **regional planning** disciplines, design and visual esthetics play a significant role. Planners are also concerned with access, transportation and flow patterns, economics of a region, ecologically responsible land use, and impacts upon human social behavior. Planners work in concert with other people and groups to improve the quality of life for the ever-increasing multitude of people in the world (**13-17**).

Miscellaneous Related Disciplines

The dividing lines between the above disciplines and graphic and industrial design are indistinct. Persons trained in one medium may gravitate to another due to a combination of circumstances and personal proclivities. This interaction has yielded specialists in theater design, exhibit design, lighting design, industrial fabric design, furniture and construction system design, and so forth.

Summary

Environmental design disciplines are interactive. Architecture, interior design, landscape architecture, city and regional planning endeavor to integrate visual esthetics and engineering with the challenges of the human condition, working toward the improvement and enrichment of the world in which we live.

GRAPHIC DESIGN

Graphic design is an umbrella term under which all visual statements that combine words and images are collected. Thus it includes advertising, information design, package design, commercial art, typography, printing/reproduction; and illustration (**13-18**).

Often confused with graphic design is the collective term, *graphic arts*, that includes any medium which uses lines, marks, or characters on a two-dimensional surface: these can include drawings, prints, sometimes painting, as well as the graphic design media.

13-16 Two views of a business (contract) interior design. *Courtesy of Venturi, Rauch and Scott Brown, Philadelphia, PA.*

A

B

13-17 Philadelphia's Penn Center in **A** 1950, and **B** 1985. The Suburban Station Building on the right and the roof tops of City Hall on the lower left appear in both photographs. *Courtesy of Philadelphia City Planning Commission. Photo: A. K. Strohl.*

Media arts, another collective term in common use, sometimes refers only to the electronic and broadcast media of radio, video/television, film, tapes, records, and disks. But it can also include any form of communication utilized by the fast-growing information industry: books, maps, newspapers, magazines, posters, and photographs.

Yet another collective term is *surface design*, which includes textile, paper and wallpaper design, package design, and so forth.

Irrespective of how a graphic designer defines or describes what she or he does, graphic design is proba-

bly the most visually literate of all visual disciplines. Graphic designers deliberately make visual statements that are to be *read* and *comprehended*. Word and image are used conjunctively, reinforcing each other to leave no doubt about the *intent* or *content* of the visual statement. This clarity is both the discipline's appeal and its effectiveness as a tool of information and persuasion (**13-19, 13-20**).

There is probably no group that is more cognizant of widespread visual illiteracy than people in the advertising business. They know more about human

13-18 Rob Larsen. *Art Attack.* Pen-and-ink on paper, $8\frac{1}{2} \times 17''$. *Courtesy of the artist.*

THE
SECRET'S
Out!

13-19 Graphic design: promotional materials. *Courtesy of Prentice-Hall, Inc., Englewood Cliffs, NJ.*

But there's still more you should know about—

Last January we released news of a secret formula that we've been developing for quite some time now—*the solution to your need for a text that stresses biological chemistry*—the formula Boikess + Breslauer + Edelson.

Among other things, we talked about our authors' highly regarded reputations—two internationally-known chemistry authors and educators (Boikess + Breslauer) and one of America's leading science writers (Edelson).

And we talked about their comprehensible and lucid writing style, and how the text was formed around the needs of students who are interested in a broad range of allied health related disciplines.

Now we'd like to reiterate some points and elaborate on others, and to tell you about the enormous supplements package available to you when you adopt this new text: ELEMENTS OF CHEMISTRY: General, Organic, and Biological.

ELEMENTS OF
CHEMISTRY
GENERAL, ORGANIC, AND BIOLOGICAL

ROBERT BOIKESS
Rutgers, The State University of New Jersey

KENNETH J. BRESLAUER
Rutgers, The State University of New Jersey

EDWARD EDELSON
The New York Daily News

Did they say stereopedagogy?

Indeed. ELEMENTS OF CHEMISTRY features a tightly bonded, three-tiered sectional sequence that first presents a survey of general and organic chemistry that prepares your students for the final presentation of biological chemistry.

Continuously driving toward the ultimate goal—*that students acquire the background and skills needed to understand biological chemistry*—each section builds on what has been presented earlier.

And, in keeping with that goal, ELEMENTS OF CHEMISTRY presents and explains chemical principles in a manner that is directly related to health, the environment, and other areas of immediate concern to your students:
• analyzes the **chemical changes associated with life processes** and the practical needs of the laboratory.
• presents such **up-to-date applications as genetic engineering** and **nuclear medicine.**
• surveys several of the **most important classes of organic compounds,** using material selected to lead toward the study of biological chemistry.
• emphasizes **medical, industrial, and environmental applications of chemistry** to meet your students' varied interests and needs.

Some topics of special concern—

Overall, the topical coverage in ELEMENTS OF CHEMISTRY, with its relevance for your applied health students, is unchallengeable. Rather than burdening you with an excessive list, we've assembled a few important topics of special concern. . .

Atomic and molecular structure:

A microscopic look at the atom and the elements kicks off the General Chemistry sec-

tion, the foundation for the study of biological chemistry.

Here you'll find deft explanations of such topics as **periodicity** and its relationship to orbitals; **subatomic particles;** and the **natural abundances of isotopes.**

Of particular interest to you and your students are the straightforward and uncluttered definitions and facts concerning the atom's make-up. This concise, logical, and simple approach leads in neatly to the concept of a **mole** and **Avogadro's number,** which is presented as a *"unit of amount."*

Stereochemistry:

Devoting an entire chapter to stereochemistry, the authors impart a crystal clear understanding of **three-dimensional chemical structure.**

The authors have selected examples that help students develop an appreciation for the correlation between three-dimensional structure and biological activity—a major theme in the biological chemistry section.

Nutrition:

Featuring an excellent choice of examples (e.g., high caloric value of ethanol, comparison of fat types), Health, Diet, and the Environment (Ch. 28) contains important information which students in health related areas need to know.

The authors describe **nutritional requirements for good health,** the relationship of **diet to both weight control and behavior,** and the **effect of environmental pollutants** on our well-being.

And, just to remind you—

• presents the factor-label method of problem solving throughout, a method that students easily master.
• generates and retains interest with careful interaction of principles and descriptive material throughout.

• uses the **functional group approach** to organic chemistry at just the right level.
• features an overview of **metabolic pathways** with an emphasis on overall function rather than specific reactions.
• emphasizes how our **health and body chemistry** are influenced by our **diet and environment.**
• presents the **biochemical basis** for physiological disorders.
• features "**Chemistry at Work**" essays on topics of current interest, all related to the chemistry presented in that chapter.

Comprehension catalysts—

• an **opening photograph** that symbolizes chapter content.
• **chapter previews** that place the subject in context.
• highlighted **key terms** and **important concepts.**
• numerous **solved examples,** with end-of-chapter exercises for quick reinforcements—answers appear in the appendix.
• detailed end-of-chapter **summaries** of concepts and terms.

In all, there are **50 additional photographs,** more than **1200 end-of-chapter exercises,** more than **400 illustrations,** numerous **tables** and **charts,** and an extensive **glossary** for easy reference.

We've let you in on a secret . . .

. . .now it's up to you—

Take a few moments to look over the sample pages, the enormous supplements package, and the *complete* Table of Contents. We feel confident you'll like what you see.

We've let you in on our secret. Now we're inviting you to take advantage of it. Request your examination copy of ELEMENTS OF CHEMISTRY *today!*

3

13-20 ARLENE and MICHAEL McGUIRE. Anthony Orlando Recital Advertisement. 1977. 17 × 14″. *Courtesy of McGuire & McGuire, Jenkintown, PA.*

This book was set in Meridien,
a face designed by Adrian Frutiger in 1957
and first cast by Deberny and Peignot.
The display type was set in Eurostyle with Meridien initial caps.

Designed by Lisa A. Domínguez
Cover underpainting by Deborah Curtiss
Manufacturing buyer: Ray Keating

13-21 Colophon for *Introduction to Visual Literacy.*

13-22 Sign design by a graphic designer. *Courtesy of Gregory Benson, photographer.*

psychology, how to cut through our defenses to get a message across effectively, than any other profession. Add graphic design, mix well, and commercialism reaches ever higher levels of financial success.

Graphic designers also develop corporate communication and identity through the design of logos, letterheads, brochures, and other promotional literature. They design posters, books, magazines, newspapers, catalogues (**13-21**); exhibits, television and film graphics; and signs for transportation and commerce (**13-22**).

People who are attracted to and successful in graphic design share some specific attributes:

Intelligence, curiosity, desire to participate in information exchange
Visual adeptness for exploring communication alternatives that range over diverse media, codes, and techniques
Manual dexterity, attentiveness to detail, love for order and codification into patterns and concise images
Willingness to subjugate one's own inspiration to the purpose and needs of the client; to have work evaluated in terms of the marketplace rather than for its originality
Possession of a good liberal arts background; can interact with clients of many different interests; tend to be more generalists than specialists

Social adroitness and psychological astuteness for working collaboratively with colleagues and clients who have many different interests and values.

Often the material provided by a client is vague, dull, inadequate, and unsuitable for visual expression. The designer must take this material and provide clarity, interest, and pertinence through an interaction of words, visual symbols, and representations. Graphic designers must communicate in order to succeed, anticipating their audience's needs and reactions. Whether their designs are informative, persuasive, interesting, direct, witty, shocking, or arresting; they must be, above all, relevant and comprehensible.

In their visual statements graphic designers employ all design theory and principles (chapters 3 through 7), calligraphy (the art of hand-lettering), type, illustrations, and photographs. Increasingly they are using computer graphics to generate imagery (chapter 14). Whatever components are used, they are combined into a **layout** that consists of **copy**, the verbal text, and **visuals**, any form of images (**13-23**).

Typography and Printing Media

Both graphic designers and typographers must be knowledgeable about the various typefaces available and the methods for printing. Designers may create

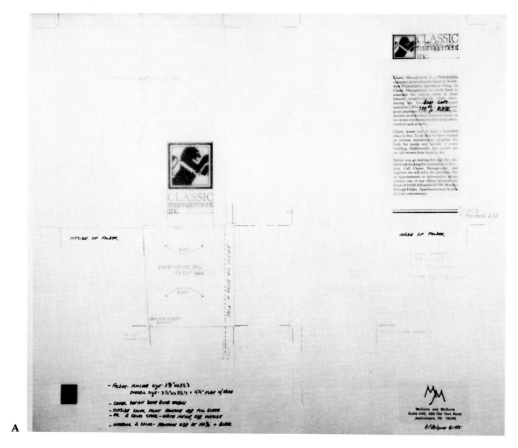

A

13-23 ARLENE MCGUIRE. Layout mechanical: **A** with, and **B** without overlay tissue. 1985. 18 × 24″.
Courtesy of McGuire & McGuire, Jenkintown, PA. Photos: Michael McGuire.

B

their own typeface or select type and layout copy from the many previously designed typefaces. The **typographer** sets the type for printing, and the **printer** prints the combined copy/visuals. Typefaces and sizes, known as **font**, are of many designs, and include variations

in proportion	condensed to extended
in weight	light to **bold**
in slant	*italic* to roman to backslant

and combinations thereof. Additionally, typefaces may have **serifs**, those little decorative tails on type such as this or be sans ("without") serif. Serifs give letter forms interesting shapes and grace. They serve to help us see groups of letters as words and, because most serifs are horizontal, they facilitate the eye in keeping to one line. As a result, serif type can be much easier to read. Appropriate use of **upper case** letters (CAPITALS) and **lower case** letters, together with the spacing between lines (the **leading**), also contribute to readability of a text. Sans serif may look clean and neat on a page, but because of its reduced connectiveness, it can be visually fatiguing to read. It is thus not appropriate for text copy.

Printing processes vary. **Letterpress**, printing from a raised surface, began with the invention of movable type in the fifteenth century. It was superceded by **lithography**, printing from a planographic surface, invented during the Industrial Revolution. Development of photosensitive printing plates, **photo off-set**, during the late nineteenth century created a fast and clear method of printing (**13-24**). Today

13-24 Close-up of one step in web printing process. *Courtesy of Cameron Graphic Arts, Somerset Technologies, Inc.*

most typesetting is computerized, producing a "type-set" copy on special photographic paper. This copy is photographed, producing a negative which is, in turn, used to produce the printing plate. **Electrographic** printing is valued for its "instantaneousness" and used primarily for small printings (*see* chapter 14). When it becomes cost-effective, nonimpact computerized electrographic printing, already in existence, will replace offset lithography.

Illustration

Whether in the form of original drawings, prints, paintings, or photographs, **illustration** is an integral part of graphic design. Color and abstract shapes can bring interest and dynamics to a graphic design, but illustrated images of recognizable subjects done with varied color, tone, and style immeasurably enrich the print media (**13-25**).

Illustrators have excellent analytical and descriptive drawing skills, which they are able to apply to a broad range of subjects chosen by clients (**13-26**).

13-26 PONDER GOEMBEL. *Weightwatcher Snacks.* Pen-and-ink with pencil on paper, $4'' \times 5\frac{1}{4}''$. *Courtesy of the artist.*

Drawing in all media; painting (often with aqueous mediums and drybrush and airbrush techniques) (**13-27**); all printmaking methods; and mixed media such as collage, three-dimensional assemblage, and photomontage are employed by illustrators. The key issue is that the work reproduce well (**13-28**).

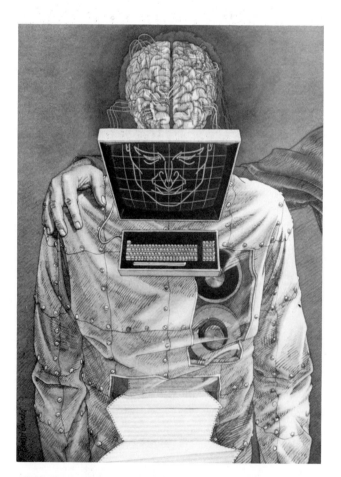

13-25 PONDER GOEMBEL. *Untitled.* Sepia ink and acrylic wash on watercolor paper, $14\frac{1}{2} \times 10\frac{1}{2}''$. *Courtesy of the artist.*

13-27 Airbrushes. *Courtesy of Badger Air-Brush Co., Franklin, IL.*

Illustrations must garner attention and be accessible to the intended audience. Illustrating is a highly competitive field, and most work is freelance because, in general, the print media prefer variety. Thus, to succeed as a freelance illustrator, pragmatic business acumen and drive are important skills to possess. Illustrators who obtain ongoing positions usually have graphic design skills, or can illustrate fashion, medical, or scientific topics (**13-29**).

Summary

Graphic design includes all combinations of word and image that are for the purpose of verbal/visual communication. It has a broad range of applications, especially to the business world and the information industry. Calligraphy, typography, illustration, printing/reproduction, and photography and computer graphics (chapter 14) are all interactive with graphic design endeavors.

INDUSTRIAL DESIGN

Industrial design is a relative newcomer to the visual arts field. (**13-30**). Industrially mass-produced items were initially designed for function alone. But in 1929,

13-28 MICHAEL McGUIRE. *Hunter, Costumier.* 1982. Dress form, hunter's jacket and hiking boots, fabrics, satchel, and various accoutrements of his trade, 5′ × 3′ × 2′. *Courtesy of Photohandwork, McGuire & McGuire, Jenkintown, PA.*

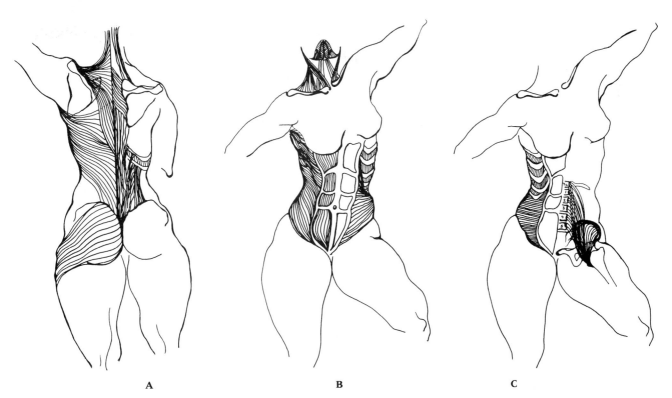

| A | B | C |

13-29 IRENE DOWD. Illustrations from *Taking Root to Fly*, pp. 32-33 © Irene Dowd, reproduced with permission. **A** Muscles of the back, **B** abdominal and anterior neck muscles, and **C** transversus abdominus and iliopsoas muscles. *Courtesy of Irene Dowd, neuromuscular trainer, author, and illustrator.*

13-30 An electric automobile. *Courtesy Electric Auto Corporation.*

13-32 VectaContract. *Gibilterra Series.* Designed and mass-produced furniture. *Courtesy VectaContract.*

Raymond Loewy galvanized the manufacturing world by designing a copying machine that was visually arresting as well as functional. Today **industrial design** refers to the design of all mass-produced, three-dimensional objects, whether they are industrial, domestic, artistic, recreational, educational, religious, edible, or disposable (**13-31**). (The only exception is clothing design which is discussed below.)

Furniture, lighting, toys; machines such as dishwashers, typewriters, lawnmowers; vehicles such as airplanes, cars, ships; equipment such as stereos, video

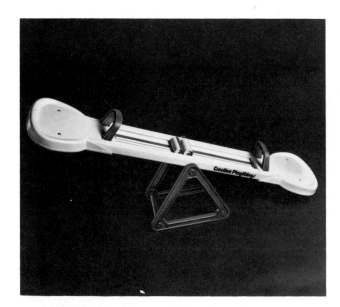

13-31 Creative Playthings. *See Sam Rollway. Courtesy Creative Playthings, CBS Toys.*

systems, and computers have had the input of industrial designers. Some are trained as engineers—aeronautic, structural, acoustical—who approach a project from the standpoint of function and technology. If esthetics and human engineering have been given integrated attention, it is probably because an industrial designer—one trained to think and "problem solve" humanistically, esthetically, functionally, and commercially—has created the design (**13-32**).

Industrial designers have versatile abilities: they can distill a need, define the problem to be solved, research and analyze similar products, synthesize a solution; implement the design both in terms of drawings and maquettes; critique the design; and present and sell it to others. To be effective they also need to know about materials, manufacturing processes, and where to get economic and marketing information. It is a highly complex and creative process in which intuition and empathy with potential users of the product are integrated with the practical and functional realities of product development. The computer (chapter 14) plays a significant role both in expediting the design process and in the manufacture of products. Because of the vast array of products, industrial designers often develop a specialty and work in a design firm where expertise can be combined and shared.

Summary

Products shaped by industrial designers are omnipresent in our lives. They include the chair we are sitting on, the vehicle we took to get where we are, the packages for the food we most recently ate, and the television we're going to watch later.

13-33 Fashion design studio. *Courtesy of The California Institute of the Arts, Valencia, CA.*

CLOTHING DESIGN

The range of possibilities for creative endeavor in clothing design is wide, from basic utilitarian clothing to high fashion, from costume design for the performing arts to art-to-wear (**13-34**).

Irrespective of the focus, **clothing designers** have an interest in the human body, how it moves, and how garments will fit and move with the body. In a sense, clothing is a form of sculpture with the body as armature (**13-35**). Clothing designers also have an interest in the look, feel, and performance of fabrics.

While most of a designer's work is at the drawing board or computer, training includes learning to make patterns, assemble garments; learning about fabrics, textures, colors, and design principles; and using and designing for the machines of clothing manufacture. Clothing design is a highly competitive field that requires motivation, perseverance, interpersonal savvy, and devotion to the medium.

Highly creative individuals may place an emphasis on original one-of-a-kind designs, often fabricated by themselves for costumes and art-to-wear. Creating **costumes** for theater and dance calls for the expertise of a clothing designer who has a high degree of imagination, knowledge of clothing history, and a passion for theater and dance. There is no limit on creativity in making **art-to-wear** which interfaces with the art and craft of fibers and body ornamentation (*see* chapter 12).

Summary

The clothes you are wearing, from your hat to your shoes, have been designed, probably by from six to ten or more different designers. A complex array of decisions regarding styles, shapes, design, fabrics, col-

13-34. LILY YEH. *Philadendrum Kimono.* 1984. Silkscreen on fabric, 54 × 27". *Courtesy of the artist and the Fabric Workshop, Philadelphia, PA.*

13-35 JANE STEINSNYDER AND MARIE VITALE FOR CASSOWARY. *African Dress.* Cotton oxford cloth with Afghanistan patchwork applique yoke; inspired by design from Sierra Leone. *Courtesy of Cassowary, Philadelphia, PA.*

13-36 Which art and design disciplines were engaged to create the objects pictured in this photograph? *Courtesy of Prentice-Hall.*

ors, sizes, manufacture, and distribution participated in getting those garments to you. You engaged in a visual design process when you selected them to wear together.

DESIGN SUMMARY

The design disciplines include many fields: space planning—architecture, interior design, landscape architecture, exhibit and stage design; product design—industrial and clothing design; and graphic design—advertising, package design, illustration, and typography (**13-36**). These highly commercial disciplines require practitioners to have professional visual and technical training, computer literacy, verbal and interpersonal skills, and business acumen.

Design affects the quality of our lives in direct and ubiquitous ways. As visual literates we are able to assess objects, spaces, and information by their humanistic, esthetic, and functional design merits, rather than solely by their popular appeal.

MECHANICAL AND ELECTRONIC MEDIA

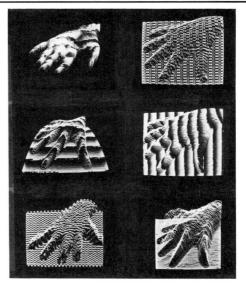

14-1 WOODY VASULKA. *Hybrid Hand Study.* 1983. Computer digitized image altered by Scan Processor, an analog device; size variable. *Courtesy of the artist.*

Mechanical and **electronic** methods of visual image making include the use of all kinds of still and movie cameras, computers (**14-1**), and electrographic processes.

Lenses and principles of the camera have been used since before the Renaissance. It was the discovery of light-sensitive chemicals and the development of photosensitive film in the nineteenth century that permitted mechanical imagemaking and reproduction. For over 100 years visual communication has accelerated and expanded with relentless developments in imagemaking and transmittal (**14-2**). At the beginning of the twentieth century hand-cranked movie cameras and motion pictures were introduced. Many of the mechanical aspects of still and movie cameras have been improved upon or replaced by electronic devices, so that strictly mechanical cameras are no longer produced (**14-3**).

The basis of video and television is the electronic communication of visual images through small screened dots of light of varying intensities. Electrographic printing processes, such as Xerox, transmit images through static electricity, heat, and magnetic charge. The application of images to disks and tapes for computer graphics and video is also an electromagnetic process. Lasers are used in visual statement making both as a visual phenomenon and as a process to create holograms. The distinguishing characteristics of the visual disciplines itemized in this chapter center around their use of *light* and *energy*.

With this chapter we return to media accessible to the beginning visual statement maker. Cameras are designed so that even children can use them: Instamatics require no more skill than pointing at the subject and pressing a button.* Similarly super-8 movie and video cameras are simple enough to be used by almost anyone. The personal computer has brought computer graphics into the home, and imagemaking with an electrographic printer is as accessible as a copier.

People who possess mechanical and technological aptitude are particularly attracted to the media described in this chapter. But successful visual communicators in mechanical and electronic media have also developed their visual perception and esthetic sensibility, qualities that enrich all visual art.

One of the most compelling attractions to making images with mechanical and electronic means is the opportunity to see the whole image emerge or be produced so quickly. Immediate feedback is so rewarding that engagement with these media can become addictive. It can also be a non-seeing, thoughtless spewing forth of visual rubbish. Therefore, the primary chal-

---

*Because looking through a view-finder to compose a photograph is an excellent way to learn about composition and design principles— and because most students have access to a camera—photographic assignments (using commercial processing) can be a valuable contribution to any design curriculum.

14-2 Editing room, Downtown Community Television Center, New York. *Courtesy of AIVF via Robin White, Media Alliance, New York.*

14-3 Video still camera. *Courtesy Sony Corporation of America.*

lenge is to invest our visual awareness, literacy, and substance as a whole person in the process of making significant and selective photographs, videotapes, computer graphics, or electrographic prints.

PHOTOGRAPHY

Photography is the process of recording optical images on a light-sensitive surface that is developed by chemical action. Photosensitive films and papers must be kept in the dark, selectively exposed to light so that only the desired image is retained, and chemically treated to develop the latent image and stop the photo-sensitivity (**14-4**).

Photography Formats

The principal formats for photography are light-sensitive paper, ranging in size from miniscule to wall-sized murals, and film transparencies. Transparencies are most commonly in a 2 in.-by-2 in. slide format, but they can also be much larger; they are dis-

played via a diffused light source. Other formats, such as printing plates, are used as part of printing processes.

Photography Media

Photosensitive chemicals vary, but the most common is a silver bromide compound suspended evenly in gelatin and applied to either a transparent film or to paper. In the case of black-and-white film there is a single layer; for color film there are three layers, treated to be sensitive to blue, green, and red. The actual color of the developed film is formed by dyes suspended in the gelatin interlayers of the film that are activated by the developing process.

Film is available with either negative or positive responses to light. In black-and-white and color-print film it is **negative**; when they are printed onto paper the tones and colors will be reversed and come out duplicating the original subject. With color-slide film (and black-and-white movie or slide film) the film is a **direct positive**.

14-4 Frances M. Cox. *True Inspiration.* 1984. Photograph, $5\frac{1}{4}$ × 8″. *Courtesy of the artist.*

Photography Tools

A **camera** (Italian for "room") is in principle a light-locked chamber that will keep the film in total darkness except when light is allowed in through the lens and aperture. The size of the **aperture** (opening) and the **speed**, or length of time it is open, are determined by an adjustable **shutter** that is activated by pressing a **shutter release** button. Surrounding the aperture is the **lens**, which can be adjusted to focus the image on the film.

Most cameras today have a built-in **focusing apparatus** and a **light meter** powered by a small battery. When looking through the **view finder** to line up your desired photograph, various indicators will appear that measure light and focus (**14-5**).

Once you have shot a roll of film it will need to be developed. (**Self-developing** Polaroid cameras develop and deliver a photographic print in seconds for black-and-white and in a few minutes for color.) You can send film to commercial processors or engage in the cost-saving and potentially creative process of developing and printing your own film. For this a **darkroom** is required, and many amateur as well as professional photographers have set up their own darkrooms in a bathroom, kitchen, or basement (**14-6**). Running water and dark are the basic requirements. Developing equipment consists of specially designed canisters and chemicals for film, and trays to hold the chemicals for developing enlarged photographic prints. An **enlarger** is required to cast the negative image onto the desired size photographic print

paper. **Safelights** that will not activate photosensitive film or papers, usually red or orange, allow you to see what you are doing. A thermometer that attaches to your water supply and a timer for timing exposures are also needed.

Beyond this basic equipment there are many possibilities: an array of lenses (telephoto, wide-angle, fish-eye) and filters to use with your camera; a tripod on which to mount the camera for steadiness; contact printers and enlargers of varying capabilities; and equipment for drying film and prints, mounting prints to backing boards, and for storage of film, slides, and prints.

The **video-still camera**, first used by photojournalists to cover the 1984 Summer Olympic Games, is now commercially available. Images are recorded onto a magnetic disk or tape and are transmitted electronically to a video monitor and/or to a thermal dye printer. The video-still camera is designed to interface with computer graphics, electrographic printing, and electronic transmittal (see **14-3**).

Photography Techniques

There are many approaches with photography beyond the mere documentation of a scene or event. Successful photographs don't occur by chance as much as by conscious seeing. *Assess the whole frame* of the photograph before releasing the shutter. One first determines whether the whole frame is free of extraneous, distracting elements (**14-7**), then whether it is

14-5 A 35mm camera. *Courtesy of Nikon.*

14-6 BENEDICT TISA. A home darkroom. *Courtesy of the photographer.*

14-7 Unseeing photography can result in bloopers. *Courtesy of a generous but anonymous photographer.*

well composed in terms of underlying structure. (Is the picture's major vertical image in alignment with the vertical edge of the frame? Are shadows enhancing or confusing the image?) This *whole field* assessment greatly improves the quality of photographs, and with practice takes only a few seconds.

From this point, the range of creative possibilities is endless. Lighting, color, vantage point, focus, subject, content, visual organization can all be used with subtle nuance toward the development of your unique vision and personal expression (**14-8**).

In the creative realm of the darkroom, different chemicals, procedures, and timing can alter images to create a more personal statement. If you have ever seen a photograph develop, you know what a thrill it is to see the image slowly emerge from a blank sheet of paper. Even the most seasoned photographers continue to experience it as miraculous.

The best path toward continued growth in photography is a course of study where you can learn from others and expand your visual vocabulary. Professional training is required for the many commercial applications of photography.

Nonsilver Processes   Prior to the development of silver printing, a number of chemicals and processes were used that today are not practical for mass-produced photography; but they have remained of interest to creative photographers, printmakers, and painters. Most common of these are cyanotype and gum bichromate printing (**14-9**). They require a **contact negative** (the same size as the final image) but it needn't be from a photographic source—drawings on acetate can be used.

FILMMAKING

Filmmaking, the making of movies, is a form of visual expression that spans a broad gamut from the amateur home movie to professional spectacle; from simple documentation to complex story telling. It is seldom a solitary activity—even with home movies there are participants in the action. With more elaborate film projects, actors, lighting and sound crews, directors, producers, and filming staffs are just the beginning of a collective endeavor (**14-10**).

Filmmaking engages the dimension of time, so a filmmaker needs to have a sense of timing as well as visual-spatial sensibility. An independent filmmaker should also acquire a number of other qualities: the ability to organize people and events, to explain intentions clearly, and to raise funding and promote distribution. Perhaps most important, she or he needs to be highly motivated, disciplined, practical, and in touch with that compelling necessity to interact with the medium.

Film Format

Whether we use super-8, 16 mm, or the strictly professional 70 mm, the format is transparent film,

14-8 Ilse Bing. *Self-Portrait in Mirror.* 1931. Photograph, $7\frac{1}{2} \times 8\frac{3}{4}''$.
Courtesy of Zabriskie Gallery, New York.

14-9 SARAH VAN KEUREN. *Mountain of Bedspreads*. 1982. Cyanotype and gum bichromate print, $8\frac{1}{4} \times 11\frac{1}{2}''$. *Courtesy of the artist.*

14-10 Production crew at ''Choose Life'' rally in Central Park, New York, June 1982. *Courtesy of Media Generation, Haverhill, MA via AIVF and Robin White, Media Alliance, New York.*

black-and-white or color, enlarged and projected onto a screen so that it may be seen by a number of people at one viewing.

Film Medium

Except for its difference in size and the fact that it is a direct positive film, the film for movies is also made from silver bromide crystals suspended in gelatin and affixed to transparent plastic. It is developed with procedures similar to developing photo film.

Filmmaking Tools

A movie camera has a battery-operated motor that moves the film past the aperture at twenty-four frames per second, and it has a timing mechanism that opens and closes the shutter in synchrony with the film's movement to expose each frame while it is stationary. A spring-held trigger starts and ends shooting, a slow-motion button (which actually increases the speed at which the film passes), and a light meter are standard features. Most 8 mm cameras take rolls of film that last around three minutes; 16 mm lasts twelve to fourteen minutes. Many movie cameras have a **zoom lens** that allows the operator to move in closer to a subject without actually moving the camera, and some have a device that fades in and fades out for changing scenes. A tripod is necessary to maintain steadiness in handling.

Filmmaking Studio   Our first films are probably shot out-of-doors with available light but, as we develop new ideas, artificial lighting may become preferable. The filmmaking studio can be a makeshift setup for a single film, or it can be elaborate, with special lighting, tracks and booms, backdrops and scenery, and so forth.

Crucial to a creative filmmaker is an **editing machine** on which film can be cut and **spliced** (reattached) so as to rearrange, shorten or lengthen the film at will, and to create continuity and wholeness. As a highly plastic and flexible medium, it is in the editing studio that a filmmaker gives further attention to detail, creates the desired emotional, rhythmic, and dynamic aspects of image and time, and sets the sequential mood and presence of the film as a whole. Simple hand-operated editors are inexpensive; they provide a tool for home-movie makers to create thoughtful and visually meaningful films. More com-

plex editors can handle both film and sound simultaneously.

For films 16 mm and larger, sound is an integral aspect of filmmaking. Developed awareness of the interaction of sound and light waves is one of the most profound challenges of the medium for the filmmaker. Formal procedures similar to the sequencing of images are employed and built upon in designing the soundtrack. A **sound studio** entails a complex array of equipment that is usually overseen by a sound engineer. Filmmakers can rent time in the studio and hire sound mixers to participate in creating the soundtrack (**14-11**).

Most movie film is sent to a laboratory for processing and reproducing. A projector and screen are needed for viewing the film.

Filmmaking Techniques

Films are made to serve a number of purposes—personal, creative, commercial, political—but in each the technique is essentially the same: to expose the film selectively to staged or spontaneous events. The primary component in film is the *content*. Visuals, such as nuances of movement, pacing, use of angles, fades, zooms, and all of the unique aspects of the filmmaker's personal visual consciousness will affect content.

Independent filmmakers can be highly inventive in the use of subjects, lighting, techniques, sequencing, in order to provide films that are provocative, challenging, thrilling, and delightful. Professional and commercial **cinematographers**, who may use both film and/or video, have extensive training to come to terms with the many vicissitudes of these rich and variable media.

Animation   **Animation** is a synthetic process of constructing movies and **film shorts** one frame at a time from drawings, paintings, computer-generated images, collages, or assemblages of a variety of materials (**14-12**). Each frame of the movie film is exposed separately, and between takes, slight modifications are made to the imagery (**14-13**). When the film is developed and shown at a speed of twenty-four frames per second, the characters in the series of images seem to move about, change expressions, and engage in action. Animation is used in the creation of commercials and TV station-identification spots as well as the cartoons familiar to Saturday morning TV viewers. Traditionally, one artist makes the images while another shoots and edits the animated film. Today a number of filmmakers are doing both with creative and interesting results (**14-14**).

14-11 Sound studio for video and film. *Courtesy of the Sound Shop, New York.*

14-12 GEORGE GRIFFIN is shown working with the story board setup for *Thicket. Distributed by the Museum of Modern Art, New York. Courtesy of the artist.*

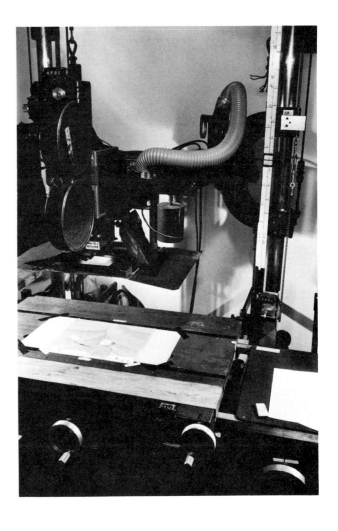

14-13 An animation camera and set-up. *Courtesy of George Griffin, New York.*

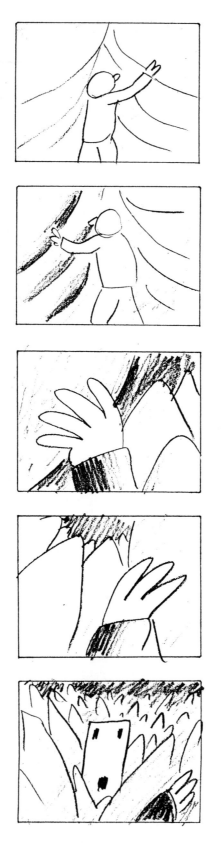

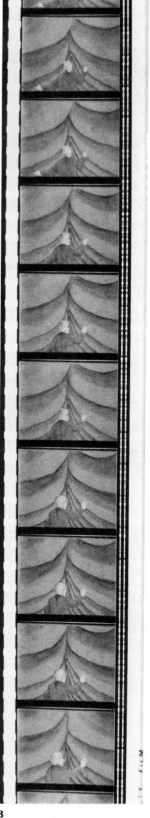

A

B

14-14 GEORGE GRIFFIN. Steps in making the animated film, *Thicket.* **A** preliminary sketches of story; **B** a filmstrip. *Distributed by the Museum of Modern Art, New York. Courtesy of the artist.*

14-15 Julie Harrison. *Correspondance.* 1985. Video, 4½ minutes. *Courtesy of the artist. Photo: Robert Kleyn.*

VIDEO

Video is a process of recording images on electromagnetic tape or disk in the form of miniscule bits of information, dots of varying intensities that register color and value and, often, sound. The information so recorded is played back on a video casette deck and displayed on a **monitor**, a cathode ray tube similar to a television screen (**14-15**).

Video is used in a variety of ways, from unedited footage on TV newscasts to artist-created expressions. Because video editing requires a complex electronic transfer process to a blank tape, a videographer interested in narrative works must visualize the story, anticipating sequencing and progressive continuity prior to shooting. With editing equipment, however, many alterations can be made. The images can be masked or matted, speeded up or slowed down, reduced or enlarged, colonized into one area of the screen, superimposed with other images or graphic designs, and distorted in a variety of ways. These techniques of editing and altering, which can interface with computers, entail a kind of play and manipulation that creative people thrive on. Thus, artists active in other disci-

plines have been attracted to video as an extension of their visual vocabulary and expression (**14-16**).

The video cameras and cassette recorders widely available to consumers use half-inch tape and can record or play up to eight hours, depending upon power supply and quality desired. Once recorded, the images are immediately available to be played on a video cassette receiver for display on a monitor or television screen. Industrial/commercial video cameras use a ¾-inch cassette tape for a higher quality (**14-17**). Video cameras may be equipped with microphones and sound-recording systems. Sound can be **recorded live**, simultaneously with shooting, or overlaid later.

Instantaneous reproduction is one of the most desirable attributes of video. A tiny monitor on the video camera can be watched while shooting, or used for immediate replay. The medium's technology offers options to filmmakers as well; and with transfer and copying equipment the two media can be interfaced to take advantage of the unique qualities of each: the ease of editing film and the ease of altering imagery in video. A recent commercial development, for example, enables old black-and-white films to be turned into color films. They are first transferred to video, then programmed to make different objects in a scene cer-

197

14-16 DARA BIRNBAUM. *Damnation of Faust*. Video installation, Stedelijk Museum, Amsterdam, Holland. *Courtesy AIVF via Robin White, Media Alliance, New York.*

14-17 Television video camera. *Courtesy of Michael Owen, MICA TV, New York.*

tain colors; those colors are overlaid with the light and dark values on the tape, and the colored tape is transferred back onto color film, which is processed and projected.

In the hands of someone with visual sensibility and creative ideas, video can be a dynamic manifestation of visual statement making. In the hands of someone less creative, the results can be technically amazing but visually chaotic or boring.

Television Television is comprised of transmitted video images that are received by the cathode ray tube in our TV sets. Most broadcast video tapes are in a one-inch wide, reel-to-reel format, but many earlier tapes were two inches wide. Because of easier handling, three-quarter inch and sometimes half-inch cassette cameras are used for on-the-spot news reporting.

Television is a team process, for it takes a minimum of ten people to produce a one-minute spot. A TV production team might include a director, camerapeople, sound engineers, editors, costume and set designers, and makeup artists (**14-18**).

As a quintessential means of mass visual communication, television has the distinction of being derided as a wasteland that rarely acknowledges the importance of visual organization and substantive visual expression. There seems to be a fear in the industry that if we use TV in more visually sophisticated ways, it would be elitist and not as commercially viable. Visually aware and sensitive broadcasting needn't be didactic, precious, or prescriptive. It can celebrate, be evocative, and reinforce the news or a dramatic plot (**14-19**).

14-18 Video Workshop, Downtown Community Television Center, New York. *Courtesy AIVF via Robin White, Media Alliance, New York.*

14-19 Television production. *Courtesy of Michael Owen, MICA TV, New York.*

COMPUTER GRAPHICS

Computer technology is revolutionizing our lives, and visual creation is one of the areas that is significantly affected. **Computer graphics** and computer-generated visual systems represent more than a tool to expedite design. They offer new ways of thinking and perceiving, a new vocabulary, and new modes for visual expression (**14-20**). While the print and electronic media are most immediately affected, all aspects of visual arts and communication are reflecting computer influence (**14-21**). For example, television advertisements and station logos that use computer-formed and transformed images and texts are common. And the computer term "user-friendly" is now used in environmental and product design as well.

One of the exciting aspects of computer-generated visual experience is that its practitioners are freely sharing and using the concepts and programs developed by each other instead of creating unique niches of expression. This sharing and communication increases options, generates variety, and expedites the development of new uses and manifestations of computerized concepts and imagery.

Computer Graphics Formats

In **soft-copy**, the image is on the monitor screen. In **hard-copy** it may be:

Committed to a video tape or disk, which may be replayed, altered, or reproduced as a time-oriented work (*see* **14-16**)

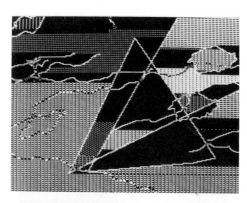
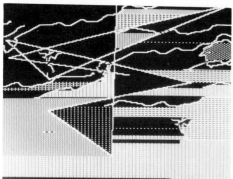
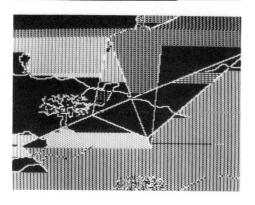
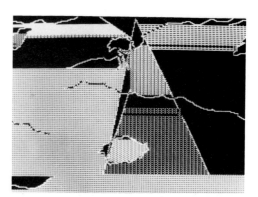
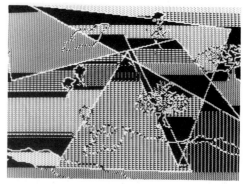

14-20 THOMAS PORETT. *Softlands.* 1985. A disk-based program that continuously creates mediated landscapes (dot-matrix prints). *Courtesy of the artist.*

14-21 FRED DANZIGER. *Eagle Thought*. 1985. Acrylic paint and computer ink-jet print on board and paper, 14″ × 14″. *Courtesy of Rodger LaPelle Gallery, Philadelphia, PA.*

Printed out with a dot-matrix printer or an ink-jet (color) printer onto paper for a two-dimensional work (*see* **14-20**)

Printed onto a printing plate (a tough plastic film) for reproduction (two-dimensional)

Produced in materials and shapes as determined by **CAM** (computer-aided manufacture) for three-dimensional objects (*see* **14-22**)

Combinations of the above.

For example one could create a conceptual 3-D form. Then, with computerized commands, one could walk around it, into it, over it, turn it inside out, fly with it, alter it, transform it, and request a printout of a particularly interesting configuration of it. Or the monitor could be a "gallery" in which a viewer could interact with a program of either real or conceptual works of art, and by giving appropriate commands, view the programmed works in any of several different ways.

Computer Graphics Media

The media in which computer-generated imagery may be manifest are many. Video and print media on paper are the most common and readily available. CAM hard-copy capabilities exist, but as they employ highly sophisticated robotic technology; they are cost-effective at present only in high-volume commer-

cial or industrial production. A few prototype sculptures have been so created (**14-22**).

Computer Graphics Tools

A personal computer graphics system, known as the **hardware**, consists of a **computer**, which has memory and a keyboard to type commands; a **monitor** (cathode ray screen or liquid crystal viewer) on which one sees what is going on; one or two **tape** or **disk drives**; a drawing implement known as a **joy stick** or a **mouse**; and appropriate printers.

Software is disks or tapes that contain information; that is, **programs** that set up the computer and give it commands to do certain operations. These usually refer to the format, the layout of information in specific locations of the dot matrix, which is the fundamental structure of the system of imagemaking. Programs can be purchased ready-made or created by you when you've learned how.

Computer Graphics Techniques

Any designer can draw on the monitor screen using the joy stick or mouse to form a desired image. Corrections are instantaneous, and computer-aided

14-22 ROB FISHER. *Skyharp*. 1985-86 work in progress. Stainless steel aircraft cable and polished rod, bead chain, and folded plates silk-screened in multiple colors, 14 × 18 × 4'. The *Skyharp* series is based on the use of computer graphics and computer-aided design. The computer also outputs construction data from which the work is fabricated to exacting dimensions. *Photograph courtesy of the artist.*

design programs can transform that information to give three-dimensional representation. The designer can thereby work out all aspects of the design and, when appropriate, have the image either committed to disk for further use or printed out on paper for submission with a proposal.

Some programs for personal computers allow you to make a contour drawing and then put it through a sequence of transformations. When you see a configuration you especially like you can commit it to a disk, either as a single item or as a sequence, or make a single image in a print format. You have to move quickly for once the sequencing moves on, unless the program has a reverse command, it is gone forever.

Creativity with computer graphics reaches a higher level of interest and challenge when you learn to create your own programs, as many creators of glitzy computerized entertainment videos have demonstrated. Some original works of fine art have been created and exhibited (**14-23**), but curators and the public tend to be wary. It is not easy to leave the time-honored and valued touch of the human hand, the struggle of the human eye, for electronically pro-

duced imagery. Therefore computer graphics have been more readily accepted for their commercial applications; fine artists today, however, are beginning to use computers as a tool for expression.

ELECTROGRAPHIC PRINTING

Electrographic printing, commonly known as Xeroxing, after the company that first developed it, is a combination of heat, static electricty, and magnetic charge that transfers an image onto a sheet of paper in a matter of seconds. Its technology has achieved clear and faithful reproduction. In the hands of visually aware individuals, it can be the source of striking visual statements.

Different colored inks, known as **toners**, are available and, through the use of the four-color separation process, full-color registration and reproduction are possible. Artists tend to gravitate toward unique creations of spontaneously overlaid images and colors. Anything, objects as well as images on paper, can be placed on the glass (**14-24**). The immediate feedback of the produced image supports experimentation and

202

14-23 THOMAS PORETT. From the series, *Icons/Idols*, 1984. Collage from found images, video digitized, and color ink-jet printed, 11 × 11". *Courtesy of the artist.*

development of ideas. The copier can also be used as a tool for working out compositions to be executed in other media (**14-25**).

Enterprising artists gain access to electrographic copiers when and where they can—perhaps after-hours at a business. It is also possible to rent, lease, or buy a copier for personal use.

MISCELLANEOUS ELECTRONIC MEDIA

Electronic Art

Electronic art can include any use of light, sound, video, and mechanizations. Light sculptors have created works and environments with fluorescent lights, neon lights (*see* **11-52**), and lasers (*see* illus. **I**). Others have worked with abstract patterns on cathode ray tubes using oscilloscopes and computerized programs (*see* **9-16**, **14-15**, and **14-16**).

14-24 CATHERINE JANSON. *Erika.* 1983. Xerography on cloth, fabric collage and stitchery, 6' × 4'. *Courtesy of the artist.*

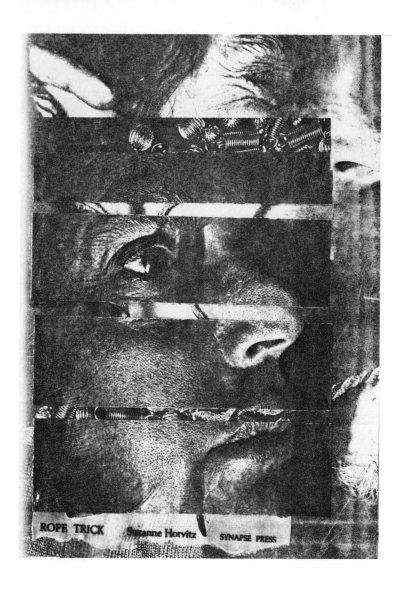

14-25 SUZANNE REESE HORVITZ. *Rope Trick.* Xerographic collage for book page. *Synapse Press, Philadelphia, reproduced with permission. Courtesy of the artist.*

14-26 DOUG MILLER. Two holograms. *Courtesy of the artist and Holographic Design, Philadelphia, PA.*

Holography

Probably the most unique entry into the visual vocabulary is the hologram. **Holography** is an imaging technique wherein lightwaves reflecting off a solid object or scene are recorded, using laser light, onto a light-sensitive emulsion (film). The resulting **hologram** is a projected image that has all the three-dimensional characteristics of the original object or scene. When looking at a hologram, the 3-D image seems actually to be suspended in space; but when you reach to touch a hologram, nothing is there—it is only light waves (**14-26**).

In the early 1970s excitement about holography led to exhaustive study to extend the technology of this radical form of imagemaking. Holographic motion pictures have been made and holographic television may be a reality in the not-too-distant future. Problems of resolution—the tendency for the image to fade or be eroded around the edges depending upon the angle of viewing—and of transmission are yet to be resolved.

White light holograms, those that can be viewed under ordinary light, diffract light into the spectrum, giving a rainbow appearance that doesn't necessarily follow the actual coloration of the object.

Holographic embossing is a process by which holograms are transferred onto mylar or plastic film to achieve specific localized colors. These "prints" have been commercially used and are available in jewelry, plastic decorative stickers, and more recently in holographic photographs. Because of the spectral quality of the color, they are visually intense and aggressive. Time will tell whether and how this mode of visual expression will be integrated into the broader visual vocabulary.

A laboratory studio for making holograms can be an expensive proposition, but the technology and techniques are accessible to the motivated visual statement maker. Some art schools, colleges, and universities have holographic studios.

SUMMARY

The mechanical and electronic media for visual statement making include photography; filmmaking; video/television; computer graphics; electrographic printing; holography; and electronic uses of light, sound, and mechanisms. In these disciplines mechanical and technological processes provide contexts for visual inquiry in which visual literacy is important and highly desired.

Multimedia and Intermedia

15-1 Susan Rosenberg. *Reflections at the Exploratorium.* 1982. Video image. *Courtesy of the artist.*

Multimedia, the combination of two or more media in a visual statement, is not new: architecture is intrinsically multimedia, the sculpture of ancient Greece was painted (polychromed), and handcrafted tools and vessels from the dawn of history have combined clay, metal, leather, and wood (**15-2**).

Intermedia usually connotes the use of electronic media in the procedures of visual art expression and display. It may include slide, video, or film presentations, as well as lighting, sound, and mechanisms (**15-1, 15-3**).

The deliberateness of presentation is what distinguishes multimedia and intermedia works today. They entail unexpected combinations of visual techniques drawn from many disciplines, including some normally considered outside the realm of visual arts and communication. These presentations are made in galleries, museums, concert halls, and **alternative spaces**, a collective term to designate some place other than an art gallery. An alternative space might be a firehouse, a restaurant, or an abandoned school (**15-4**). Multimedia and intermedia events might take place in the water, on a street, in a valley, in the air, on a coastline, or in a park (**15-5**).

Names given to presentations of a multimedia nature have been *assemblage, happening, conceptual art, environmental art, earth art, performance art,* and *collective art.* The motivations have been many, not the least of which is to break away from tradition and the conventional. Thus reaction against the known is a strong

15-2 Anonymous. *Sioux Porcupine Quilled Pouch.* Nineteenth century. Hide, quills, beads, feathers, and tin; approx. 10 × 15″. *Courtesy of The University Museum, Philadelphia, PA.*

15-3 Chevron Corp. *Creativity—The Human Resource* is an exhibit that utilizes computers for active discovery and creation in conjunction with conventional displays. *Courtesy of the Pacific Science Center, Seattle, WA.*

motivating factor. Because of the lack of connection to former modes of visual inquiry and expression, such directions seem at first anarchistic, but we know from history that such experiments are eventually absorbed into the collective visual vocabulary, enriching everyone whether or not they succeed or endure as great art.

ASSEMBLAGE

Assemblage is a three-dimensional collage, a combination of nonrelated materials and objects into a visual statement. It is different from assembled, constructivist sculpture in its free range of materials stretching from found objects, trash, junk, debris, and garbage to created, deliberately sculpted and shaped forms (**15-6**). Assemblages may also include words, recorded sound, lighting, mechanisms, and smells.

ENVIRONMENTAL ART

Any sculpture large enough to be entered or walked into can be said to have environmental qualities. Those assembled specifically for the purpose of creating a unique environment are known as **environmental art**. Environmental art (colorplate **8F**) can have an ambiance that is clear and composed or cluttered like an abandoned attic. Persons who create environments tend to delight in the unexpected, in the deliberately confounding and perplexing. They thus endeavor to stimulate a chain of thought, a mode of thinking, that is new, unfamiliar. Some environmental art invites the participation of viewers to bring new objects and to take something home as a memento. Others invite sitting and contemplation (**15-7**).

Environmental works that have been assembled spontaneously in a gallery will probably never be seen again. After the exhibition's end they are disassembled and the materials discarded or put to some other use. Plans, photographs, and verbal descriptions remain as documentation of the creation (**15-8**).

CONCEPTUAL ART

The contemplative aspects of environmental art, and its ultimate disposal, contributed to the emergence of conceptual art. **Conceptual art** challenges the idea of art objects as a consumer product: the artist posits ideas, frames propositions, and analyzes the projected

15-4A Public School #1 in Queens has been used since 1976 as a place for artists to work and exhibit. *Photo: Thomas Struth.* **B** KIM JONES. Performance 1985 at P.S. #1. *Photo: Anne Turyn. Both photos courtesy of the Institute for Art and Urban Resources, Inc., P.S. #1, Long Island City, NY.*

15-5 VITO ACCONCI. *Face of the Earth.* 1984. Astroturf over wood, 30″ × 20′ × 16′. Installation at The Quadrangle, Springfield, MA. *Courtesy of Carpenter + Hochman Gallery, New York.*

15-6 PATRICIA NIX. *Anatomy of Lower Egypt.* 1983. Paper, zebra skin, wood, metal, plastic, and oil paint; 26 × 28 × 2½″. *Courtesy of the artist and Baumgartner Galleries, Washington, DC. Photo: Otto E. Nelson.*

15-7 ALICE AYCOCK. *I Have Tried To Imagine The Kind Of City You And I Could Live In As King And Queen: The House Of The Stoics.* 1984. Painted wood and steel construction, 32' × 11'9" × 13'6". Permanently installed in Miyazaki-Mura, Japan. *Courtesy of the artist.*

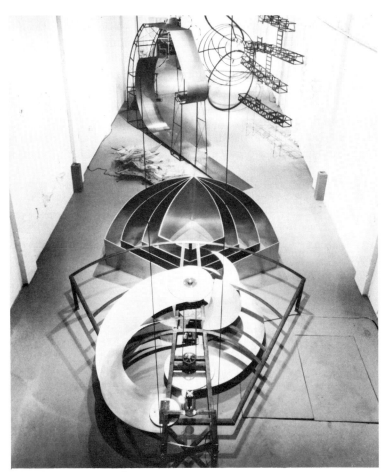

15-8 ALICE AYCOCK. *The Thousand and One Nights in the Mansion of Bliss.* 1983. Temporary installation at Protetch McNeil Gallery, New York. *Courtesy of the artist. Photo: Wolfgang Staehle.*

results. This process challenges traditional esthetic values in its elimination or ephemeralization of the art object. Works of conceptual art are most often manifest as sketches with verbal descriptions and proposals that may or may not be executed (**15-9**). Conceptual art emphasizes the decision-making process of the creator, the train of thought that leads to the proposal. Play, humor, the ridiculous, and fantasy can be freely indulged.

HAPPENINGS

Environmental art was also important in the development of **happenings**, affairs in which an audience is invited to witness a collage of nonrelated events. Happenings often take place in a made-for-the-event environment where the audience walks through to see staged events, or sits in folding chairs to see confounding and outrageous actions take place interac-

15-9 JODY PINTO. *Finger Span: For Climbers' Rock.* 1985. Proposal for bridge of Cor-ten steel and Cor-ten mesh steel, 75′ × 8′ × 4′. Commissioned by Fairmount Park Art Association, Philadelphia, to be completed in 1986. *Courtesy of the artist and Hal Bromm Gallery, New York.*

15-10 ELAINE CRIVELLI. *Downward Ascent.* 1984. Environmental installation and performance work: painted wood, lighting, and spun and dyed wool fiber, 25′ × 50′ × 65′. Performance by Seminole Works Dance Company at The Painted Bride Arts Center, Philadelphia, PA. *Courtesy of the artist.*

tively with the environment. The sequence of events might be planned, but the actual happening is a once-only occurrence that is shaped to a significant degree by chance and circumstance. The audience can take part in the activities. Everything within the time and space frame set by the creator is part of the work—its visual, temporal, interactive, and experiential phenomena.

PERFORMANCE ART

Performance art is less involved with chance and is a more-designed event. The creator is usually responsible for everything: the scenery/environment, props, costumes, lighting, and sound, as well as the performance of the work. This art, a synthesis of visual and performing arts, is similar to happenings in that it is often nonnarrative and fragmented, more allusive than specific (**15-10**).

COLLECTIVE ART

Happenings and performance art often entail the creative energies of several people, all of whom contribute to the work's form and outcome. From time to time artists come together to create works on a theme, to make a political response, or to gain creative energy from one another. **Collective art** is an umbrella term that designates that a number of persons have collaborated on a visual statement or event (**15-11**).

EARTH ART

Earth art is environmental art that engages the earth in some kind of transformation (**15-12**). Patterns may be plowed in a field and planted with contrasting crops, or a field of grain at harvest time might be plowed with a design. Rocks may be piled to form designs, holes may be dug, mountains made, or coastlines wrapped. It is an encounter with the real world, a movement away from artifice and illusion toward grappling with earth-shaping equipment; a transformation of concept into a dialogue with the substance of geology, archeology, evolution, and organic processes of creation and decay. It may entail a concern for ecosystems, a willingness to work within nature's great pattern. As art objects, these endeavors tend to be in remote places, so most are known through documentation by photographs and descriptions (**15-13**).

Space art offers inspiration and challenge for visual creators too. The technologies of astronomy and space flight have enticed artists to create ''signal art,'' an artistic conjecture about a universal imagery that might bring response from life beyond our solar system (**15-14**). There is no containing the imagination on this subject.

15-11 The Dinner Party. 197
A collaborative project of 40
persons coordinated by Judy
Chicago; 48' on each side of
triangle, mixed media, prima
china paint on porcelain, fibe
and needlework. *Courtesy of
Through the Flower Corp., Benicia,
Photo: Michael Alexander.*

15-12 NANCY HOLT. *Waterwork*
1983-84. 6″ galvanized steel
pipe, 8″ clay channel pipe,
concrete, steel, and water; 20
70′ × 130′. Gallaudet Colleg
Washington, DC. *Courtesy of the
artist.*

15-13 JODY PINTO. *Split Tongue
Pier.* 1980. Spruce timber, 48'
2' × 2″ thick planks on varyir
height pilings. Temporarily
installed at Swarthmore Colleg
Swarthmore, PA. *Courtesy of the
artist and Hal Bromm Gallery, New
York.* *Photo: Drew Vaden.*

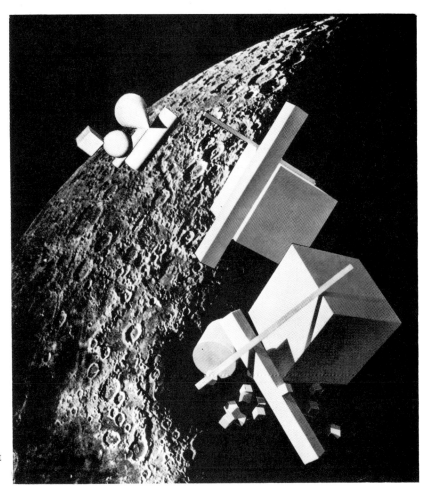

15-14 AL WUNDERLICH. *Light Flight Project.* Photo-collage simulation of sculptural forms in orbit in the presence of the moon. Concept: works of art put in orbit will be viewed from a space bus as commonly as one might fly to Europe today to see an exhibit. Space artists must be abreast of developing technology, and willing to work collaboratively. *Courtesy of the artist.*

Summary

Multimedia and intermedia visual statements including assemblage, happenings, conceptual art, environmental art, earth art, performance art, and collective art have no limit of possibility. These expressions developed as deliberate attempts to dissolve boundaries between art and nonart, between object and environment, between audience and creator. The legacy to us is the freedom to create visual statements with whatever we choose, and however we choose. Our visual literacy is challenged when either making multimedia creations or experiencing those made by others.

PART V SUMMARY

Media options, formats, tools, and techniques for drawing, the fine arts, crafts, design disciplines, mechnical and electronic media, and multimedia have been identified and defined as an introduction, and I hope as an enticement, for your engagement in visual statement making. It has, of necessity, been a very superficial overview, but one which should have given you a sense of the tremendous variety of visual expression available to us. Moreover, these disciplines offer viable opportunities for development and participation in rewarding professions and careers. Even the fine arts, the most notoriously difficult disciplines for making one's way financially, offer technical and educational options. Working in industry is one of the ways for a sculptor, printmaker, or craftsperson to gain technical skill and access to tools and equipment. Painters working as house painters may find clients for murals, woodcrafters make contacts through carpentry, and the list could go on.

Whether it is from inner necessity that you must make art and visual expression central to your life, or it is because you choose it as a path toward achieving balance with other parts of your life, to grapple with the process of expressing yourself visually, of verifying your visual literacy, is empowering and exciting.

213

VI Gregory Benson. *Visual Experience and Expression*. Photomontage. *Courtesy of the photographer*.

VI

YOU

AS VISUALLY LITERATE

Now that you have an overview of the forms of visual statements and of the media choices available for expressing yourself visually, where do *you* as maker, designer, artist fit in?

Self-knowledge is perhaps life's greatest and most compelling quest. Each of us has natural abilities, preferences, and predispositions that to a greater or lesser degree participate in determining who we are, what we think, do, feel, create. Knowing these qualities and abilities in their inherent uniqueness is vital to excellence in visual expression. There is a desire to uncover and develop perception and awareness of one's deeper feelings and inner resonance. These quests for inner truths enable us to transcend the physical properties and the subject matter of a visual statement and imbue it with character, substance, meaning, and a value of greater human, and perhaps universal, interest.

Much of visual expression is metaphorical in its transcendence of the literal and its search for the universal. Visual problem solving, by its nature, generates new ideas and insights. So what we are talking about is the development of *artistic consciousness*, that complex body of knowledge and abilities by which we experience and create art. The development of this level of consciousness takes place simultaneously with, and is dependent upon, our engagement with visual media and methods. We must *make, do, experience* in order to really know.

What are your own inclinations and characteristics with regard to visual expression?

Do you like working with concrete substances, or are you fascinated with illusion?

If you prefer the concrete, what materials, such as wood, fibers, clay, metals, plastics, do you feel an affinity for?

If you prefer illusion, do you want to create it manually through drawing/painting, or through the use of photomechanical or electronic devices?

Do you feel a passion to express your own visions and ideas, such as in sculpture, painting, art films?

Or do you prefer to solve visual problems presented by others, such as in graphic, industrial, or architectural design?

Self-awareness is essential in the effective making of visual statements on several levels of inquiry. When depicting objects in a drawing, your place in space relative to those objects is part of the drawing. The kind of marks you make convey your feelings, and the organization or composition of the drawing communicates your unique perceptions.

As beginning artists, we do what the teacher assigns us, having faith that the assignment is serving a purpose. At first that purpose seems to be technical proficiency. But gradually we awaken to the fact that it is *our own choices* that matter. In the process of coming

215

to know ourselves as visual statement makers, we trudge through uncertainties and insecurities until insights and confidences are reached. Each person's journey through this minimally charted land is unique. An important part of this journey is learning as well what we don't like.

Sometimes we try to measure ourselves by others who have gone before us, and wonder why we aren't getting the results that they got. Such comparisons can be both helpful and harmful. Self-awareness and acceptance of where you are in the ever-developing, never absolute process of becoming visually articulate is of enormous importance to both you and your audience. It is your personal engagement with your medium, the hidden agenda of your humanness and being, your accountability, achievement, and excellence that provide the only lasting reference and manifestation of your efforts.

Two of the chapters of part VI focus on you: your thinking processes when making visual statements, and your personal heritage and how that affects your visual perceptions and vocabulary.

VISUAL THINKING

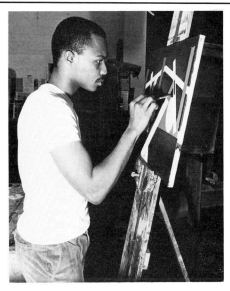

16-1 Student painting. *Courtesy of the School of the Art Institute of Chicago. Photo: Freedom Lialios.*

Few people, it seems, appreciate the powerful challenge and satisfaction of *visual thinking* when compared with, for example, literary or scientific thinking. Solving visual problems engages one's whole mind in such an inclusive and multilevel way that I have come to regard it (compared with my own study of philosophy and logic) as one of the most sophisticated and highest orders of cognitive thought.

Because of the relative non-verbal aspect of visual expressions, the intelligence of artists has often been misunderstood. To the uninitiated, solutions to visual problems can appear inchoate, incomprehensible, and/or enigmatic.

This chapter is offered as a door to understanding visual thinking, a path to increasing your intelligence relevant to spatial relations, pattern recognition, and visual literacy. The only way to fully understand visual thinking, however, is to *do* it, not just think about it. In the following pages visual thinking is defined and described, but unless you actively engage in making visual statements, and in so doing come to experience and understand your own visual thinking processes, visual thinking and problem solving will remain for you in the realm of speculation and uncertainty (as it has, alas, for many well-published estheticians and perception psychologists).

Visual thinking is the ability to receive, alter, and create visual statements through purely visual responses—that is, free from theory and preconceived ideas—to visual phenomena. While visual thinking may incorporate or be influenced by theory, any such theory will have already been learned and assimilated through experience. Thus visual thinking in its *purest* and ideal state is spontaneous and largely nonverbal. However, the ability to relate one's decision-making process after-the-fact is extremely helpful in completing and validating visual communication.

VISUAL THINKING AS VIEWER

Recall a time when you saw something that totally astonished you (**16-2**). It may have been light dancing among leaves of a tree, a building of intriguing design, or the refraction of light in a raindrop; or when you recognized a sibling as a separate entity from you, as a whole complete person, not just an indefinite extension of yourself. . . . These are times when you have perceived with *clarity*, when your perceptions have been unfettered by extraneous thoughts and concerns.

We first discover this kind of perception through happenstance—a sudden burst of awareness. But as we grow and choose to become conscious visual statement makers, we want to learn how to *intentionally*

16-2 SUSAN ROSENBERG. *Bottom of My Orange Juice Glass.* 1985. Photograph, $6\frac{1}{4} \times 9\frac{1}{2}''$. Magical visual experiences can be discovered in the most ordinary places. *Courtesy of the artist.*

create this kind of seeing, and also how to extend it over increasingly longer periods of time.

In this clarified visual perception, we are totally receptive—open to seeing without any editorial or censorial intervention or interference. Manfred Clynes, in *Sentics: The Touch of the Emotions*, gave this kind of perception a name: **apreene**. Clynes describes apreeneness as a

> total absence of fear and a willingness to accept whatever may come without fear of its implications. . . . Trust that whatever may come into [one's] awareness is worthy to be well received and even treasured. . .*

Being apreene is like becoming a window to let the light shine through, or a net waiting for fish to be caught. There is an element of passivity to it—creative passivity.

In being apreene, there are no extraneous thoughts. In fact, it can feel like you're not thinking at all, there is such a peaceful quiet in the mind. Nor are

there any preconceptions about what is being experienced. It is what it is. Only in this state of freedom from preconceived notions can true perception occur. Once we have a term for this unclouded perceptive state of being, it becomes easier for us to recreate that state at will.

As a concept, apreeneness can be useful. One can devise a scale from zero to ten, where ten represents total apreeneness and zero, no apreeneness whatsoever. **Zero apreeneness** is when you walk a mile and a half home without seeing a thing because you are preoccupied with some family issue or with how a class is going, or when you read eighteen pages and haven't the foggiest idea of what you read because your mind is elsewhere.

Ten apreeneness is when you experience something without a single extraneous thought, not even of your experiencing your apreeneness. Hopefully you have had this experience in a drawing or a design class where you have been so caught up with doing the assignment that you've lost awareness of time and your surroundings. Yet you have been keenly aware, nonverbally, of the different levels on which your project functions.

*Clynes, Manfred, *Sentics: The Touch of the Emotions* (Garden City, NY: Anchor/Doubleday, 1978), pp. 205–206.

When you go to a museum, watch a slide presentation, listen to music, work on a drawing, or study, you can assess your own level of apreeneness on this scale. By doing so, you become increasingly sensitized to the experience. With practice you become able to purify your apreeneness (raise it on the scale), and extend it over longer and longer periods of time. You can even bring it to interpersonal relations for better listening and interaction.

Apreeneness can include empathy, or identifying with whatever is being looked at. We can feel as if we are that object, take on its shape and form with our whole being. We can thus use all our senses, our *sensorium*, which is comprised of our total input from a subject, not only through vision, but through sound, smell, taste, touch, and somatic kinesthesia—total body awareness and identity. Incorporating all our senses into the process of perceiving enhances the quality of how we see, how we experience, and how we know.

In *Visual Thinking* Rudolf Arnheim discusses how our conceptual or thinking abilities are intricately interwoven with our perceptual or sensing abilities:

> . . . artistic activity is a form of reasoning, in which perceiving and thinking are indivisibly intertwined.*

Without **perception**, the receiving of impressions and experiences through our senses, we would have nothing to conceive or think about. And without thought, we would be unable to use our perceptions. **Conception** in visual statement making is the origin of ordering impressions, visions, and perceptions. Concepts embody intent, creative resourcefulness, and ideas.

VISUAL THINKING AS MAKER

The making of visual statements engages problem solving, and there are many ways to go about solving any given problem. One of the exciting aspects of visual expression is that there are no right or wrong answers. For any given problem, there are as many solutions as there are people who set out to solve the challenge. Some solutions may be more effective than others, but validity over a broad range is often discovered in classes having a number of students.

A common problem-solving process is that of **personal choice**. This may be a **subjective** process based solely upon personal preference and private symbolism, with no concern for how someone else

might respond to your choices. Or it may be more **objective**, an elusive concept that attempts to take into consideration what would be acceptable and/or pleasing to others (**16-3**).

Another familiar way of solving problems in the world of visual communication is that of **trial and error**, also known as empiricism. **Empirical thinking** is guided by experience. One makes educated guesses based upon prior experience and hopes for an appropriate outcome. If an effort does not work, one is challenged to learn why, to learn from one's errors. Perhaps several trials will be necessary before one achieves the desired result (**16-4**).

When making visual decisions empirically, it is necessary to be flexible and willing to acknowledge that inappropriate choices will sometimes be made. It is a challenge to art students to learn to accept that the explorations that appear to lead to failure, although time-consuming and discouraging, are really quite beneficial and increase the knowledge that will lead to more educated guesses in the future. It is helpful to develop a state of mind, based upon conscious decision, that is not too attached to an idea before seeing it realized. With continued detachment, one can then be more objective in assessing the effect of a visual endeavor.

In this way, visual creators change roles and become the audience of their own visual statements. In the receiver role, one looks at one's work as if through the eyes of a noninvolved viewer. This process is called **critical objectivity** and it is extremely important in becoming an effective visual statement maker. In art classes, critiques are given, both individually and in groups. **Critiques** enable us to look at our work more objectively, to see what is good about it, and what needs improvement. They enable us to expand our visual and verbal vocabularies through the exposure to the works and ideas of others, and through our own articulation of our perceptions and efforts (**16-5**).

Visual statements are rarely a simple cause-and-effect situation. More often there are many causes and many effects, and one must stand back and analyze just what works and why, and what doesn't and why. This analysis may engage any of several processes. From a number of trial-and-error attempts, we can establish a general situation from which we may **deduce** what will solve the problem adequately. The opposite of this **deductive process** is **inductive thinking**, where we have tested something on a small and limited scale, and decide it will work for a larger and more general situation.

Another thought process that visual creators use is the **dialectic method**. In this, one begins with a process that is anticipated, hypothesized, or conjectured to be appropriate. This is called the **thesis**. Then

*Arnheim, Rudolf, *Visual Thinking* (Berkeley, CA: University of California, 1969), p. v.

16-3 Selection is an ongoing process. Students weaving. *Courtesy of the School of the Art Institute of Chicago. Photo: Freedom Lialios.*

16-4 Striving for the best solution, the best print. Etching studio. *Courtesy of the School of the Art Institute of Chicago. Photo: Freedom Lialios.*

an opposite, or **antithesis**, is explored.* Through these investigations, the maker discovers a broad range of possibilities and may select from each aspect to combine into a synthesis. **Synthesis** means "bringing together"; it is the opposite of analysis—"taking apart" in order to better understand the constituent parts. To **syncretize** is to bring together in real form (same root as concrete, discrete).

These processes of hypothesizing or conjecturing, then testing or trying out, are known as the **scientific method**, and they are employed quite naturally and effectively by artists as well as by scientists. The main difference is that results are measured more qualitatively than quantitatively.

Whatever processes of problem solving are utilized, the generation of ideas is as natural to the human brain as coursing of blood is to the heart. But as the repository also for memory and emotions, our minds aren't always as free from extraneous information and feeling as the process of creative thinking ideally requires.

COMMON OBSTACLES TO VISUAL THINKING AND MAKING

One of the greatest impediments to effective visual thinking and creativity is when students try to do *only* what they think the teacher wants. In so doing, they deny their own involvement and opportunities for discovery.

A work must interest its creator first before it has any possibility of interesting someone else. But here is a difficult fact: that your solution to a visual problem interests you does not guarantee that it will be interesting to others. It only creates that *possibility*. On the other hand, a work that does not interest you, that is not imbued with caring and your most creative energy, has virtually no chance of affecting your audience positively. A clear, direct channel of personal involvement with the challenge at hand is imperative in becoming an effective visual statement maker.

Once willing to involve oneself, there are any number of obstacles one can encounter, all of which are fairly common. So you needn't feel alone when you get stuck. The following is a list of common blocks to creativity. It may help you in either avoiding them or identifying what you're dealing with. When solving a problem, the identity and clear statement of that problem is often 50 percent or more of the solution, the basis from which its completion falls into place (**16-6**).

*Note that an antithesis may be only one opposite. Visual concepts as well as words can have several possible opposites: Hard and loud for soft, for example.

Blocks to Creativity

Fear of failure: inability to take risks, settling for less.

Fear of criticism: thinking criticism means loss of acceptance and love, instead of what it is—an opportunity to help you see alternative solutions, to expand your awareness.

Fear of the unknown: insecurity—avoidance of unclear situations; the need to know the outcome, that something is worth your time and effort, before proceeding.

Fear of misunderstanding: thinking what will be received is not quite what you intended to communicate. (It probably won't be without verbal reinforcement.)

Fear of uniqueness: of being too much an individual—that it risks loss of acceptance, love, and results in aloneness.

Fear of frustration: avoidance of pain or discomfort that can accompany the novel; avoidance of being temporarily stymied; giving up in the face of obstacles.

Fear of being used: of being misused, of being associated with taboos, or of having your ideas used by someone else.

Reluctance to play: fear of experimenting; fear of being perceived as silly or foolish.

Reluctance to exert influence: fear of seeming pushy, aggressive; hesitant to stand up for your beliefs and perceptions.

Reluctance to let go: inability to let things incubate or happen naturally; lack of trust in others; trying to force situations and solutions.

Attachment to tradition: overconcern with balance, the tried and true, cliches and stereotypes; intolerance of uncertainty, ambiguity, complexity.

Attachment to habits: habitual reactions; unwillingness to question your assumptions; unwillingness to change.

Low self-esteem: lack of appreciation of your strengths and abilities.

Lack of acceptance: lack of appreciation of resources in your background, environment, family, friends, and possessions.

Lack of fantasy life: ignoring, mistrusting, or demeaning your visualizations and imaginings; overattachment to real-world objectivity; forgetting to ask, "What if?"

It is a daunting list of stumbling blocks. Most have to do with anxiety. And often, an overall anxiety that impedes effective creating is wondering whether one is *good* enough, has the talent to become a *great artist*. Finding solutions to visual problems always involves a high degree of uncertainty. One is constantly embarking upon uncharted paths into an unknown land. Very often we don't know what we're making until we've made it. With eyes and ears open,

16-5 When started early, critiquing visual statements can be a positive part of the learning process. Middle school students participating in a photo workshop conducted by Susan Rosenberg, H.B. duPont Middle School, Hockessin, DE. *Photo: Susan Rosenberg.*

16-6 Student and teacher at California Institute of the Arts, Valencia, CA.

16-7 *Courtesy of the School of the Art Institute of Chicago. Photo: Freedom Lialios.*

we have a good chance of making discoveries that will add to our body of knowledge. However, if we think that one is either born with or without talent, and for those who have it solutions come easily, naturally and automatically, then our awareness shuts off. The process of making visual statements engages deep personal dedication and involvement. It may come to feel natural, and it becomes easier with experience, but it is *never* automatic.

It may be sufficient to clear the blocks, but it can be further reinforcing to have qualities to reach for in nurturing our creativity.

PATHS TO CREATIVE ENDEAVOR

Curiosity, open-mindedness, interest in the unknown.

Flexibility, spontaneity, freedom to change, shift.

Delight, enthusiasm.

Serendipity, chance, accident: willingness to accept it, use it. If necessity is the mother of invention, accident is surely the father.

Experimentation.

Imagination, visualization, fantasy.

Dreams, accessibility to the unconscious, freedom from editing.

Appreciation of complexity and ambiguity.

Perspective: ability to see from differing points of view, keeping an eye to the long term, the broad context.

Persistence: willingness to work long, to believe in the process even when results have no guarantee.

Courage: to be yourself, to acknowledge the validity of what you do; to take chances.

Challenge: willingness to question, analyze, critique.

Holistic thinking: seeing the universe in a grain of sand; seeing how the grain of sand relates to the universe.

Combination, synthesis: integration of the unexpected.

Relatedness: willingness to relate responsively to a given situation (visual-spatial or otherwise); awareness that any format has its own existential reality with which one interacts, "receives from" as well as "gives to."

Recognition and acknowledgment of life-giving forces: (God, eros, creative generativity); willingness to integrate and nurture these energies both within oneself and into all creative acts.

Passion: acknowledgment and nurture of one's inner necessity to create; confidence that frustrations and sufferings encountered will lead to growth, strength, and significant breakthroughs.

16-8 *Courtesy of the School of the Art Institute of Chicago. Photo: Freedom Lialios.*

Celebration, taking time to savor accomplishments.

Using Both Sides of Your Brain

Since the 1960s, there has been a great deal of research on modes of thinking. It has even been discovered that the left and right hemispheres of the forebrain think differently from one another. Researchers have acknowledged that these two modes of thinking, while different in some ways, are also inextricably intertwined, and most effective when used simultaneously and interactively.*

For some years it was believed that the right hemisphere thought more spatially, holistically, globally, while the left hemisphere was more linear, pro-

gressing from point to point, and more adept at thinking analytically. Articles about the hemispheric split in thinking were published based upon data from patients whose brain hemispheres had been surgically separated. As a result, gross generalizations and false conclusions were popularized and never adequately redressed. It has subsequently been determined that the distinctions between the two modes of thinking are both less precise and more simple. The left hemisphere dominates in attending to issues of detail while the right hemisphere dominates in coping with larger, more general issues.* In essence, differences are between the general and specific, the forest-or-trees dichotomy known since ancient times. However, with today's awareness of the interactiveness of systems—synergy—we acknowledge these aspects of thinking to be complementary and inextricably interdependent. We are general *and* specific, we can see the forest *and* the trees.

As visual statement makers, we can be aware of these modes of thinking and use them as appropriate. In visual arts and visual communication there is both a great deal of detail *and* the more general issues of how

*Levy, Jerre, "Research Synthesis on Right and Left Hemispheres: We Think with Both Sides of the Brain," *Educational Leadership*, January 1983, pp. 66–72: reprinted from *NASSP Bulletin*.

16-9   Courtesy of the School of the Art Institute of Chicago. Photo: Freedom Lialios.

a work holds together as a whole. When one starts with the specific, it is easy to get stuck there and create a sequence of details that, when looked at from a distance, don't belong together. In drawing the human figure, for example, one might get so involved with drawing a foot that it has no relationship to the parts of the body that were drawn earlier. When learning to express oneself visually, therefore, work *from the general to the specific.* Plot out the overall organization and placement first, and then work out the details, referring frequently to the whole as you go along.

An architect doesn't start to design a 200,000 square foot building by designing the stairwells. Rather an architect begins with the overall building and its relationship to the site, roughing out the generalities before developing the specifics. A dialogue between the specifics and the whole begins to take over, and the final design reflects attention to both. Likewise, when designing a brochure, a graphic designer will gather all the information and lay it out generally before creating the final design of any one part.

When drawing a still-life, the same process is relevant. Plot out placement on the whole page first, and

then move into the detail. This is drawing with your *whole* brain. A visual statement worked out this way has a chance of unity and clout.

MAKING EFFECTIVE VISUAL STATEMENTS

What is it that a maker wants to accomplish with a visual statement? Certainly, there is a sense of satisfaction in the making, a love of process that is by itself quite meaningful to the creator. But that isn't the only reason the visual statement is made. As mentioned earlier, visual statements are primarily made to communicate, to share with others our visions and perceptions. To do so, we want to engage a viewer, seduce viewers as it were, and involve them in the process of experiencing and appreciating our work (**16-10**).

Technical mastery is one aspect of making good visual statements, but it is not the only one. In fact, a painting or photograph can be technically perfect and yet boring. Surprise, the unexpected, is a good way to

16-10 SUSAN ROSENBERG. Photo Show by Susan Rosenberg, Muse Gallery, Philadelphia, PA. 1979. Photograph $6\frac{1}{4}$ × $9\frac{1}{2}$". *Courtesy of the artist.*

capture attention. Leaving something out such as the edge of a form, to be completed mentally by the viewer, is a way to hold the viewer's attention for a longer time. When viewers have to employ a bit of their own creativity to fully appreciate a visual statement, they may feel gratified by the sense of exchange. They too have made an investment in the experience.

Beauty or esthetics, attractiveness of the visual statement, may also be an objective. **Esthetics** is a realm of philosophical inquiry that asks, "What is beautiful?" "What is art?" Because of its enormity, and the intrinsic complexity of these questions, esthetics cannot be explored in any depth here. But it is important to acknowledge that in the realm of visual statement making, how a thing looks and is experienced within some framework of esthetic merit is going to crop up.

Out of chaos, one creates order, and from order one can create form. Given form, one can create beauty, beauty can be destroyed, creating chaos, and the cycle repeats (**16-11**).

There is an idealism to the concept of beauty, and, too, a high degree of subjectivity, personal preference. Value judgments are inevitable in deciding upon

the esthetic merit of a visual statement. At a lecture at the Philadelphia Museum of Art, a highly regarded conceptual artist shocked the museum audience by saying, "99 percent of the art in this museum is not here because of esthetics, its visual attractiveness. It was selected because of historic significance." How true! Art is exhibited and chosen when it blazes new trails. In recent years there has been such an effort to surprise, to shock, and to redefine, that we've reached a time when anything goes and nothing startles. Almost daily art critics tout some new trend; but, like their predecessors, these trends soon fade and wait for the master judge of all, endurance and time. What strikes us as profound today may seem shallow tomorrow. And what seemed insignificant a few decades ago, now seems to have something special.

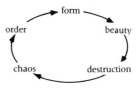

16-11 The ever moving cycle of chaos and beauty.

16-12 GREGORY BENSON. *Construction.* Photograph, $3\frac{1}{2}$ × $5\frac{1}{2}''$. *Courtesy of the photographer.*

Try as we might, neither philosophers nor art theorists have ever arrived at universal esthetic principles. Radically different esthetic values and systems exist throughout the world and from age to age, all of which have meaning and effectiveness for their place and time. In the absence of a persuasive, generally agreed upon esthetic, here is a list of issues to be absorbed and thought about when evaluating visual statements, both your own and those made by others:

Are the elements of a visual statement in some kind of meaningful dialogue with one another?

Does the overall composition or design have substance, purpose, splendidness, elegance, grace? Is it predicated upon harmonious dynamics?

Are the format and medium appropriate conveyors of the content?

Does the object serve its purpose well? Is it appropriate, related, vital?

Does its particular visual-spatial character inspire and/or enhance awareness, thought, feeling in the viewer?

Does it have *Gestalt*, that ineffable quality that provides unity, completeness, and transcends the commonplace?

SUMMARY

The making and experiencing of art engages the most complex and sophisticated thought processes known to humankind—thinking that engages the whole brain, including cognition, sensory perception, memory, emotions, and imagination. The visually literate have the potential and power to think clearly and to be intuitive; to think both analytically and holistically giving attention simultaneously to details and generalities. The interactive synergy of visual thinking is fundamental to making visual statements, to evaluating the visual expressions of others; and, this author posits, fundamental to being a fully educated person.

PERSONAL HERITAGE AND VISUAL AWARENESS

17

17-1 ARLENE and MICHAEL McGUIRE. Photomontage of Ethnic Celebrations. *Original photographs courtesy of the Balch Institute for Ethnic Studies, Philadelphia, PA; and Frances M. Cox.*

The extent to which our capacity for visual awareness, esthetic sensitivity, and artistic creativity has been nourished and nurtured greatly affects our facility in understanding visual statements and our ability to communicate visually. Such nurture might have come from our parents, who encouraged us to actively "look" at the visual phenomena around us. Our teachers may have encouraged us to express ourselves through making visual statements such as pictures or assembling environments with building blocks, furniture, and so forth. While these experiences are an important part of our personal heritage as it affects visual awareness, there are other factors that also affect what we see and what we choose to see.

These other factors include our gender, our religious and ethnic background, our level of education, our economic background, and the environment in which we were brought up or for which we have a preference (**17-1**). The effect of these factors upon our visual awareness will be variable in strength and may be positive or negative, but they are uniquely our own. Taking time to look at our heritage can restimulate our vast store of visual information and make it available to new visual experiences and expressions.

In this author's Visual Communication classes, students have been asked to form identity groups based upon the aspects of personal heritage just mentioned. These groups share their heritages and then report back to the class as a whole. From these reports

can be sketched out some generalizations that are offered here, not as facts or prescriptions, but as a means of stimulating you to think about your own experiences. Are yours similar or different?

FACTORS THAT AFFECT VISUAL AWARENESS

Gender

We are living at a time when societal attitudes about gender distinctions are undergoing rigorous challenge and change. Therefore, far fewer young people today are being subjected to the strict role expectations that once limited women to the home and men to the competitive workworld. With care to not perpetuate sexist restrictions, only these persistent distinctions of how your gender may have affected your visual awareness are offered. You may have experienced others.

Females tend to be brought up to be more conscious of colors, clothes, and the arrangement of the home. *Males,* who are encouraged to be active in sports, learn to perceive objects in motion with more acuity.

Do you have color preferences or prejudices that

228

you can attribute to your sex? Do you feel encouraged or discouraged to engage in certain visual creating that was instilled because of your sex?

Religion

Many persons have been awe-struck by the visual environment of places of worship. Candlelight, light colored and diffused by stained-glass, light glinting off gold and silver, faces of prophets, patterns of delicacy and intricacy, all have captured visual attention and provided visual learning.

The Roman Catholic Church through the Middle Ages was responsible for a remarkable tradition in the visual arts. The masses were illiterate, but Bible stories from both the Old and New Testaments were rendered over and over again in mosaics, frescoes, relief sculpture, and paintings so that people could learn the foundations of their religion. Thus a highly decorative and ornate tradition continues in most Roman Catholic churches—and in Eastern Orthodox and Anglican churches as well (**17-2**).

The Jewish faith rarely expresses itself through pictorial art, in keeping with the Old Testament admo-nition against making graven images or icons (**17-3**). But it does have a decorative tradition of embellishing the Torah spindles and cover, as well as the Star of David, and other traditional objects. For the most part, however, people reared in this faith tend to feel more nurtured by the rich storytelling heritage; listening to stories can engender visualization and imaging. The development of Jewish artists has been greatly stimulated by this rich verbally inspired imagery.

From its inception, Protestantism represented a simplification of the sometimes lavish visual tradition of Catholicism, and many Protestant churches and denominations reflect this. Some sects are especially simple, plain, and yet not lacking in a quiet beauty that their followers find peacegiving and inspiring (**17-4**). Others have a pictorial tradition expressed in stained-glass windows and decorative furnishings in the church.

Islam also prohibits pictorial images of any kind. Thus the embellishment of nonfigurative patterns—inspired by both mathematical and calligraphic forms—has evolved to a very high level (**17-5**).

In general, religions of the East have a rich visual iconography: Buddhism is replete with statues of Buddha and bodhisattvas (**17-6**). In Hinduism many mani-

17-2 San Lorenzo Roman Catholic Church, Florence, Italy. *Courtesy Alinari/Art Resource.*

17-3 FRANCES M. COX. *Studying the Torah.* 1982. Photograph, 6 × 8".
Courtesy of the artist.

17-4 Christ United Presbyterian Church, North Huntingdon, PA. *Courtesy of the Presbyterian Historical Society, Philadelphia, PA.*

230

17-5 A mosque antechamber, Istanbul, Turkey. *Photo: Eugene Gordon.*

17-6 A Chinatown, New York City, Buddhist Temple. *Courtesy of Laimute Druskis, New York.*

festations of Shiva are graphically and sculpturally depicted.

Ethnicity

One's ethnic heritage refers to the origin, classification, and characteristics of a cultural or national background. It can include religion, race, and language, as well as cultural characteristics. America is a great melting-pot of many cultures, and persons coming here from other countries are often eager to leave old ways behind and become Americanized quickly (**17-7**). Holidays are a time when ethnic traditions come to the fore, however, and some cultures value elaborate and highly visual displays of food, decorations around the home, and special attire for festivals, dances, and parades (**17-8**).

To think about your ethnic heritage and how it affected your visual awareness, remember the holiday celebrations, both religious and patriotic, in your family. Think too about family picnics, gatherings, and formal events such as weddings, funerals, or birthdays (**17-9**). All of these can be visually interesting and

inspiring experiences.

Some of these visual memories may be associated with cultures of other countries, but even if your family has been in the United States for many generations, the patriotic holidays such as Memorial Day and Independence Day, with their parades, decorations, and fireworks, offer a lot of visual stimulation.

Economic Background

Economic heritage is an area where generalizations are difficult. Persons from a background of economic deprivation have, in some cases, been too oppressed with hardship to be visually aware, whereas others, pressed by necessity into making their own furniture, clothing, and playthings, became visually stimulated in the process. If there was unemployment, the available time might have been spent in drawing pictures in the dirt of an empty lot, or making graffiti, both of which can awaken visual thinking and lead to better things (**17-10**).

Visual inventiveness seems to be the exception for children of working-class families. When there is a

17-7 BENEDICT TISA. *Feet on the Gangplank.* Photograph, 5 × 8". *Courtesy of the photographer.*

17-8 New Year's Celebration, Chinatown, New York City. *Courtesy of Laimute Druskis.*

17-9 Family Wedding. *Courtesy of the Balch Institute for Ethnic Studies, Philadelphia, PA, Yang Collection.*

17-10 Frances M. Cox. Philadelphia Neighborhood Mural Project. 1983. Photograph, 4 × 7¼″. *Courtesy of the artist.*

strong emphasis on working to survive, there is little time or energy to explore beyond daily needs. This is often reflected in the home and neighborhood. When time is available, television provides the passive viewer with rest and entertainment, and possibly learning and experience.

Upwardly mobile families tend to hold learning and the arts in high regard, so there is encouragement for offspring to visit museums and learn about art. There is often a concomitant discouragement of art as a profession, however, because of its erroneous associations with instability in earning a good living and getting ahead.

Many upper-middle-class and wealthy families provide opportunities for their children to learn about art and to make art, and it is often integrated into daily life without the sense that it is anything special. Curiously, this can result in a denegration of its value. Sometimes young people from a background of economic privilege reflect a lack of inventiveness and imagination; for others, the generous visual stimulation has provided a talent in making visual statements in a variety of media (**17-11**).

Education

There seems to be a direct correlation between the level of education in a family and its visual awareness and regard for art. However, this doesn't mean

that one must have formal training to become sensitized. People who have never thought about art beyond its factual information, when encouraged and challenged, can often respond with sensitivity to, say, the formal and metaphorical relationships of a painting.

In looking at one's educational heritage, the goals met by our parents, and the goals set by them for us, are relevant. Add together the visual arts opportunities we had in the home, neighborhood, community, and school, and one can explore the effect these educational experiences had upon one's visual awareness.

What kind of art classes did you have in school? For how many years? How did you feel about the classes? About the work you did? Were visual experiences shared and valued by teachers, peers, and/or family? Was your visual education integrated into your education as a whole, or was it separate (**17-12**)?

Environment

In this mobile age, few of us have an upbringing comprised of one type of environment: rural, suburban, or urban. In exploring the effects of your environment upon visual awareness, it is helpful to identify preferences—where you would ideally like to live, as well as where you were actually brought up (**17-13**).

A person living in or preferring the mountains, will be more adept at making distinctions in rocks and

17-11 Art/Music graduate student at California Institute of the Arts, Valencia, CA. *Photo: Debra Richardson.*

17-12 FRANCES M. COX. *Child Painting.* 1984 Photograph, $6\frac{1}{2} \times 9\frac{1}{2}''$. *Courtesy of the artist.*

17-13 SUSAN ROSENBERG. *Mother and Son Walking.* 1980. Photograph, $6\frac{1}{4} \times 9\frac{1}{2}''$. *Courtesy of the artist.*

17-14 SUSAN ROSENBERG. *Cows.* 1980. Photograph, $6\frac{1}{4}$ × $9\frac{1}{2}''$. *Courtesy of the artist.*

17-15 SUSAN ROSENBERG. *Skyline, Hawaii.* 1982. Photograph, $6\frac{1}{4}$ × $9\frac{1}{2}''$. *Courtesy of the artist.*

17-16 Ron Williams. *Hershey.* 1983. Photograph, $6\frac{1}{4} \times 9\frac{1}{2}''$. *Courtesy of Flash a.k.a. Susan Rosenberg.*

trees than an urbanite (**17-14**). The urban dweller, however, is more sensitive to architectural styles. Such experiences and preferences affect how one sees (**17-15**).

But remember, the descriptions above are only examples of possible discoveries a person might make in studying his or her visual heritage. Each person has a unique history. When we get in touch with our own heritage, accept and validate it, and shake loose some visual memories, we discover a treasure trove that can enrich our visual vocabulary in countless ways.

VISUAL PREFERENCE AND BIAS

While exploring your heritage you probably uncovered some early *preferences* toward certain kinds of visual phenomena. For example, dressing up for Halloween might have triggered a lifelong fascination with costuming and creative apparel (**17-16**); or light filtering through stained glass may have given you an interest in color and luminosity. You also may have discovered some things for which you developed a dislike. For example, graphic renditions of the passion of Christ that you saw as a child may have been so frightening and abhorrent that you have never liked explicit realism since.

These are clues to our visual *biases*, which we all have. Each of us has such a complex array of preferences and dislikes that it is no wonder that we interpret visual statements differently. Graphic design, the integration and mutual reinforcement of word and image, attempts to thwart any ambiguity or confusion. Yet try showing an advertisement to your classmates and have them write their interpretations: You may be surprised by the range of their responses.

While precision will never be the purpose of visual expression, there are so many qualities of feeling, intuition, excitement; of enduring interest or unabashed sensory delight that owe their existence to this shortcoming of personal preference and bias, that this complexity is cause for celebration.

SUMMARY

Each of us has a heritage that has affected the way we respond to visual phenomena. By taking the time to bring that heritage into conscious awareness, we find a store of visual experience that can expand and enrich our vocabularies for expressing ourselves with visual means. Moreover, we gain a clearer understanding of our biases and how they affect our responses and abilities in receiving and making visual statements.

VISUAL LITERACY FOR ALL

18-1 FRANCES M. COX. *Untitled.* 1984. Photograph, $9\frac{1}{4} \times 6\frac{1}{4}$". *Courtesy of the artist.*

Visual awareness offers a wealth of discovery and entertainment. As a student of this author once exclaimed: "I'll never be bored again! I found myself sitting on my bed wondering what to do, when I looked at the edge of my crumpled blanket against the dark woodwork beyond, and I saw this amazing dance of colors along the fuzzy edge. I mean I got high, man, just looking!"

With visual literacy—the ability to both understand and make visual statements—we become sensitized to the world around us, the relationships and systems of which we are a part. Visual literacy integrates personal experience, knowledge, and imagination with social experience, technology, and esthetics. Accessible to us is the world of art, that direction of power and excellence toward things and experiences that are transcendent and wonderful, a realm which is both at our spiritual center and exemplifies the highest achievements of human endeavor (18-1). Through the experience of understanding and making art we develop a creative vision that is comprised of judgments, feelings, and intuitions. This vision and creative ability can only be developed through active inquiry and participation in viewing and making visual statements of the highest merit our abilities will allow.

There is no formula for achieving excellence in the arts. However, we do know some basic ingredients of that formula. They include motivation, inner necessity, passion for one's medium, and intense desire for

exploration and creative activity (18-2). In making art in any discipline—music, dance, poetry, as well as the visual arts—one encounters opportunities to discover, create new possibilities, unify opposites, transform chaos into order, and transport ourselves into as yet unknown realms of accomplishment and experience.

Part of this creative activity can be inspired by the visual expression that has preceded us. It is necessary to know about art history to appreciate its accomplish-

18-2 An artist working. *Courtesy of the art department, East Tennessee State University. Photo: James W. Sledge.*

ments and avoid its failures. Yet we must not enslave ourselves to that past. There simply isn't time for us to master all that has gone before us prior to permitting ourselves to express our own vision. So we use today to simultaneously build upon the past and look to the future.

In recent times there has been a questioning and refutation of the processes and institutions involved in the teaching, making, exhibiting, and selling of art. Much art since 1960 has rejected and refuted Modernism and the concept of the exquisite art object. It is not clear where we are going. Modernism itself grew out of a rejection of the Academic esthetic tradition, and a time of great artistic upheaval and wildness, from 1850 to 1920, before it was finally codified by the Bauhaus. Some new esthetic probably will evolve out of our own wild and exciting time, too.

Semiotics—the science and art of interpreting a culture by its expressions, behavior, and artifacts—is providing us with a tool with which to analyze and understand. My projection is that a combination of systems technology, information theory, and semiotics will strongly influence the underlying structure of visual statements of the future. Meanwhile today's artists are already mounting attacks on the organizational principles of art outlined in chapter 5.

As visual statement makers, we can celebrate this time today when no restrictions of any type or consequence are authoritatively imposed upon our artistic activities. We are as free as we allow ourselves to be to choose any idea, theme, emotion, or subject, and to express it with any materials, formats, or techniques within our reach (**18-3**). Such freedom, in order to be meaningfully experienced, entails a responsibility to both our own and to our collective cultural standards of quality; and to the avoidance of creating waste or pollution.

In addition to thoughtful visual statement making, we can support visual literacy as an integral part of human education and experience. The evidence of history is that when the masses became verbally literate, there was a desensitization to visual stimuli. Today among educators there is a concern that the passivity of TV viewing and the addictiveness of computer and video games (which are highly visual-spatial) have reduced verbal literacy. Need this verbal-visual conflict continue? I think not. Visual literacy, as presented herein, is a *synthesis* of verbal and visual experience and expression. With our knowledge of the different modes of thinking we have the power to educate ourselves more fully.*

*See Gardner, Howard, *Frames of Mind: The Theory of Multiple Intelligences* (New York: Basic Books, 1983).

18-3 Lenna Haug. *Untitled.* Low-fire ceramic with acrylic overglaze, 36 × 15 × 21″. *Courtesy of the artist.*

As we have observed before, approximately 90 percent of vision is mental and, indeed, 60 percent of thinking is tied in with seeing. It becomes evident that facilitating visual literacy would contribute significantly to human intelligence. Instruction for visual literacy should not be left only to art classes or professional postsecondary education. It should be an integral part of our training and experience in life from birth onwards (**18-4**).

One of the ways we can express our visual literacy on a daily basis is to respond to the visual world by sharing these experiences with others. And with a little more effort, we can discover the significant visual statements that artists of today are making. If we don't "read" these statements and respond to them, we relegate them to a closed self-referential system with communicative power limited to initiates (**18-5**). By

18-4 Student and teacher. *Courtesy of the art department, Beaver College, Glenside, PA.*

18-5 Students reviewing 24 × 20″ polaroid photographs. *Courtesy of the California Institute of the Arts, Valencia, CA. Photo: Dennis Gilbert.*

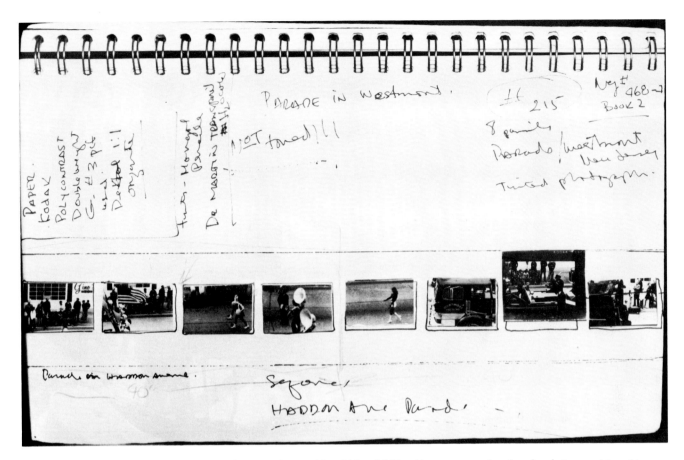

18-6 BENEDICT TISA. *Parade in Westmont.* Page from visual journal in which exhibition ideas are notated and explored. *Courtesy of the artist.*

experiencing visual statements in a variety of media we make a bridge—a connection between these statements as isolated abstractions and the "real world" of alive, thinking, social human beings. Artists, designers, the print media, galleries and museums (many of which you can visit free of charge)—and to a lesser extent, television—are making these works available to us. They are ours, an entry into another world, just by looking and being there with them.

As visual literates, we have the ability and confidence to appreciate and evaluate the relationships of shapes, forms, colors, and values. We are able to visualize and organize many components into a coherent whole. We can both make and interpret the marks of drawing. We know how to see freshly and objectively as a means to break free of old habits and patterns of seeing.

The visual arts, a manifestation of a continual attempt to make sense of life and beingness, present endless evidence of our creative spirit; and make joyous our common humanity. Visual literacy therefore, is a basic component of this humanity (**18-6**).

Let us work for the day when fluent visual *and* verbal literacy will have equal importance for every human being. For it would mean a consciousness of our whole environment, a treasuring of its assets, the shared enjoyment and enrichment of the whole planet, not just for a few privileged people, but for all.

18-7 Vito Acconci. *People's Wall.* 1985. Painted wood, quilted fabric, rubber flooring, mirrored plexiglass, 8′ × 16′ × 27″. *Courtesy of the artist and Carpenter + Hochman Gallery, New York.*

EXERCISES FOR BECOMING VISUALLY LITERATE

In the process of encouraging students toward visual literacy, a variety of exercises have been developed by this author, many of which are presented below according to chapter. These exercises follow a progression from a focus on oneself as a visual statement receiver to an emphasis on becoming visually expressive and articulate. Most should be accessible to the independent reader.

In many cases the exercises call for an analysis of visual statements. Accessible visual statements that can be passed around, and written and drawn upon, are pictures from magazines. The pictures may be representational or abstract, black-and-white or color, photographs, graphic design and illustration, or reproductions of works of art. . . . There need be no prior judgment on their merit—that will evolve with the exercises themselves.

Some exercises call for a good deal of writing. It should be simple and direct. Flowery phrases and big words are of no use. Writing down one's perceptions and discoveries provides for the assimilation of concepts and also for integrating our visual and verbal modes of thinking and expression.

CHAPTER 1

1. Write an evaluation of your own visual awareness. How aware are you of the visual world around you? How important is visual experience to you? Do you go out of your way to experience nature? To experience art?
2. Select three to five pictures cut from magazines and describe (a) who you think made the visual statement, (b) why he or she made it and for what purpose, and (c) the audience to which you think the visual statement is directed.
3. Select several pictures and describe the *content* as you understand it.
4. Using the same pictures as in exercise 3, (a) conjecture about what the visual statement maker intended to communicate, and (b) conjecture how the picture might be interpreted differently by other people (real or imagined).
5. Select several visual statements in your immediate environment. They may be any objects such as a chair, bowl, TV (or TV picture), a painting, a piece of jewelry, etc. To the best of your knowledge (different now from what it will be when you've read and understood all of this book), identify and describe the *format*, the *medium/materials* and the *techniques/tools* you think have been used to create each.

CHAPTER 2

See the exercises contained in text of chapter. Do them daily for three weeks and then weekly for optimal seeing strength.

CHAPTER 3

1. Select three to five magazine pictures and analyze each for its use of the *point* (*dot*). Indicate graphically on the

picture where dots have been used. Write a paragraph that describes the use of dots in each; use as much of the verbal vocabulary you have read as is appropriate.

2. Select another group of pictures and similarly analyze graphically for the use of *line*. Describe the kinds of lines and their uses.
3. With another group of pictures analyze and describe the use of *shape*.
4. Do the same for 3-D *form/volume/mass*.
5. Do the same for *texture*.
6. And do the same for the *illusion of space/depth*.
7. Analyze several pictures for their use of *perspective*. Draw lines of *convergence* on the picture; indicate uses of *diminution* and *foreshortening*. Write a description of the kinds and methods of perspective that have been used in each.
8. Find several visual statements that depict the illusion of *time* and *movement*. Write a description of how this is done in each.
9. Select one or more visual statements you have created yourself. Apply the above analyses (1-8) to it.
10. Create visual statements such as drawings, collages, or photographs for each dimension element, in which that element is explored, exploited, and celebrated.

CHAPTER 4

Select pictures from magazines, mostly in color.

1. Analyze several for their use of *color*, identifying the *hues* used, their *saturation*, and *value*. Describe.
2. Analyze several of the pictures for their use of *color mixture*, identifying the *primary*, *secondary*, and *tertiary* colors; *analogous* and *complementary* colors; and *co-mixes*. Describe the relationships.
3. Analyze several black-and-white pictures for their use of *value*. How many degrees of gray do you see, and where are they? Identify the kinds of *shadow*.
4. Analyze *value* in the color pictures. What are the relationships of colored shadows to the objects that are casting them?
5. Describe the *color schemes* of several visual statements.
6. Find pictures that have *simultaneous contrast, color vibration, color harmony,* and *color dissonance*. Identify and describe.
7. Analyze and describe the *temperature* of the colors used in several visual statements.
8. Induce an *after-image* in your own visual experience. Write a detailed description of it.
9. Analyze a number of your own pictures for their use of *color*, as in the above exercises.
10. Using marking pens, paints, or colored papers, create visual statements that demonstrate each and all of the above color phenomena.

CHAPTER 5

Evaluation is a three-step process:

1. What is good about something?
2. What is not good?
3. Suggestions for improvement.

Cut-out pictures from magazines are also employed for these exercises. Use several examples for each of the following.

1. Identify and describe the use of *orientation*. Superimpose *vertical* and *horizontal* lines that clearly indicate the orientation (or disorientation) of the statement as a whole. Do the same for components within the whole (such as figures or buildings).
2. Indicate and describe the use of *scale*.
3. Evaluate several pictures for *balance*. Draw a central vertical line through each composition and describe whether it is balanced and why. Be specific: What balances with what?
4. Evaluate *proportion*. What do you identify as providing the significant proportional relationships in the composition?
5. Identify and describe *dominance* and *subordination*, and *positive* and *negative*.
6. Circle the *primary focal point* (with a large or dark circle) and the *secondary focal points* (with small or light circles). Evaluate their relationship to one another and to the format in terms of balance and connectedness.
7. Highlight examples of *repetition, pattern,* and *rhythm*.
8. Find examples of high *contrast, variety,* and *energy*. Evaluate what these qualities do for the composition as a whole.
9. Evaluate pictures for their *unity* or disunity. What elements or compositional principles provide the primary unifying force?

CHAPTER 6

1. Do *diagrammatic tracings*, as outlined in chapter 6, on a number of magazine pictures.
2. Apply these analyses to some of your own visual works.
3. Evaluate some of your own visual statements for all of the compositional principles (those in chapter 5). Include with each an evaluation of overall *unity*.
4. Making deliberately "bad" visual statements can be extremely edifying. Create visual statements—with whatever materials you wish—that are boringly unified. Do others that contain horrendous conflicts. Likewise create, side-by-side, examples that demonstrate excellent and awful uses of: orientation, scale, proportion, balance (especially radical balance); placement of focal points, rhythm, and arrhythm.
5. Create a visual statement that is disorganized compositionally but that you unify through the use of one of the elements (chapters 3 and 4).

CHAPTER 7

1. While making a visual statement in the medium of your choice, keep a log of *every* decision you make. Make note of whether the decision was a spontaneous act (recognized only after the fact) or involved prior thought, such as weighing of options. Note: Neither spontaneous or planned acts are better, both are employed extensively in visual statement making.

CHAPTER 8

1. Using visual statements from magazines, analyze them for *representation, abstraction,* and *nonrepresentation.*
2. Analyze some examples of your own work for their degree of *realism* and *abstraction.*
3. Create examples of *objective* and *non-objective* abstraction.

CHAPTER 9

1. With several visual statements, select the terms of this chapter that you think apply to each and state why. Note: If you use the suffix *-ist,* such as Fauvist, that places the work specifically in that historical time and context, such as France 1905-1908. But when you use the suffix *-istic* (Fauvistic) it could be a work created anywhere at any time that is in the spirit of that movement (Fau*vism*).
2. Choose a *style* that interests you especially and create a work in that style. (You'll need to see and read more about your chosen style than is discussed in the chapter.)
3. Do the same with a style that you find repellent.

CHAPTER 10

1. Do at least one drawing every day of things you are looking at. Represent them as accurately as you can.
2. Go to a museum and copy a master drawing stroke-by-stroke. If possible, use the same medium as the artist used.
3. Make a spontaneous mark on a page of drawing paper. From it, develop an abstract drawing that creates the illusion of volume and/or depth.
4. Do quick sketches of people in groups as they eat, study, walk, play sports, and so forth.

CHAPTER 11

1. Visit a museum or gallery and select a work of art to analyze thoroughly.
   a. State title of work, visual statement maker, date created.
   b. What is the *format?* Give dimensions: height, width, depth, and time as relevant.
   c. What is the work's *medium?* The *methods, tools,* and *processes* utilized in its making?
   d. What is the *content*—its subject and meaning—to you?
   e. Analyze for the use of *elements.* Which are used? Where and how? Draw sketches to illustrate.
   f. Analyze the *composition,* again using diagrammatic sketches to demonstrate the use of the compositional principles. Evaluate the composition's uses and effectiveness.
   g. Describe the *stylistic* aspects and qualities.
   h. Evaluate the work as a whole—its *Gestalt.*
2. Make paintings, prints, and/or sculpture in the media available to you.

CHAPTER 12

1. Visit a craft gallery or museum and do an analysis of an original craftwork, following the exercises outlined under chapter 11.
2. Make craft works in the media to which you are attracted.

CHAPTER 13

1. Analyze your own *home—exterior* and one or more of its *interior* spaces—using the analysis outline under the exercises for chapter 11.
2. Do the same for a public *building,* your workplace, a public space or park. How do they relate to human needs and scale?
3. Use this analysis procedure with a *designed object* from your home environment, one from your work environment, and one from the public environment (such as a bus, park bench, lighting fixtures, etc.).
4. Analyze the *clothes* you are wearing right now. How did you choose them? What do they communicate? How visually literate are you, at this moment, as a visual statement?
5. Do analyses/evaluations of several *graphic designs, illustrations, advertisements.* How objectively are you analyzing *form* in the face of strong, intentional, emotional, and persuasive communication?

CHAPTER 14

1. Limit yourself to one roll of film, a small geographical area (one city block or less), and a one-hour shooting time. Take up to thirty-six carefully composed *photos*— scan the entire scope of the viewfinder and assess balance and composition *before* shooting. Process and develop pictures. (Commercial processing is all right, but ask that the full negative be printed.)
2. Analyze and evaluate each of the above photos.
3. Reshoot same photos to improve upon composition and to correct any mistakes, oversights, etc.
4. Plan, shoot, edit, and present a super-8 *film* or a six-minute *video* tape (borrow or rent equipment if necessary).
5. Create a visually arresting *computer graphics* program. Evaluate it rigorously on its esthetic merits.
6. Make a portfolio of six visually literate *electrographic* images.

CHAPTER 15

1. Using found materials, make a visually interesting *collage.*
2. Similarly, make a visually literate *assemblage.*
3. Describe in detail a visual statement you would like to make, that would cost a million dollars or more.
4. Create a five-minute *happening* or *performance piece* in which visual expression is central.

CHAPTER 16

1. Write a profile of yourself as a visual statement maker that addresses your preference for:
   a. the concrete or the illusionary;
   b. working with 2-D, 3-D, or 4-D formats;
   c. what materials you have an interest in and affinity for; and
   d. what kind of tools and implements you like to use or want to explore.
2. Go to a museum or gallery with the intention of seeing *apreenely* (see chapter 16 for definition of term). Free yourself from obligations to see specific things or to respond in a certain way. Wander slowly around until a particular work ''calls'' to you to spend more time. Allow yourself to enter into the work. Allow it to communicate with you whatever it has to express and you have to experience. After you leave the museum or gallery, evaluate your apreeneness on a scale from zero to ten. When were you least apreene? When most? How can you extend your apreeneness?
3. After you have made a visual statement, review your process. To what extent were your decisions conscious and preconceived, and to what extent were they unconscious and evolving out of the process? To what extent were your decisions based upon personal choice, and to what extent were they based upon what you thought your teacher or your intended audience would like? How many trials and errors did you make on your path to completing the work? How many times did you stand back and view your visual statement objectively, as a viewer rather than as a maker?
4. Make a list of the *blocks to creativity* that you have felt, both while making visual statements and while engaging in any creative activity.
5. Make a list of the *paths to creative endeavor* that you possess (curiosity, flexibility, etc.). List those you feel weak in. Explore how you can use your strengths to shore up and eliminate your weaknesses.
6. Do a drawing of any subject in which you plot out the whole space lightly before going into any detail. Finish the drawing to your satisfaction, remembering that what you leave out is as important as what you include.
7. Choose an original work of art that you especially like. Do a thorough analysis of it:
   a. Identify the *format, dimensions, media,* and *techniques.*
   b. Write your interpretation of the *content.*
   c. Plot and identify the use and relationships of the *elements.*
   d. Plot and identify the *compositional principles* that have been used and how.
   e. *Evaluate* the composition.
   f. Describe the *style*(s).
   g. Write an overall *evaluation:* what you think is good about it, what is not good about it, what you suggest to improve it.
8. Using the same outline as in exercise 7, do a thorough analysis of one or more of your own visual statements.

CHAPTER 17

1. Close your eyes and visualize yourself growing up. Think of at least five experiences that address each of the following questions or directions:
   a. What are some of the *images* that come to your mind that pertain to your being a girl or a boy?
   b. What *scenarios* do you get about religion, yours or others?
   c. Remember your family at holidays; what were some especially *visually* memorable occasions that relate to your ethnic and racial heritage?
   d. Identify your economic class and recall some *visual* experiences you have had that you associate with your economic status.
   e. Recall the art classes you had before college. How did you feel about them?
   f. Visualize the environment(s) in which you have lived.
   g. Visualize the one of your dreams.
2. Write a description of the most vivid visual memory for each category: gender, religion, ethnicity, economic background, education, and environment. For each memory, describe how it affected your visual awareness, your preferences for and biases against particular kinds of visual experience.
3. From memory, make informal drawings or sketches, using color, that illustrate your keenest visual memories.
4. You have just tapped an enormous store of visual information—your *own* memory and imagination. Use it to make a visual statement in the medium of your choice.

CHAPTER 18

1. Write an evaluation of your visual literacy: (a) your ability to receive and understand visual messages in any medium; (b) your ability to create visual messages in at least one visual medium; (c) where there is room for improvement—be specific; and (d) what you plan to do about it.
2. Write a description of what your life would be like if you were living in a visually literate world. Start with your own immediate environment (bedroom, etc.), progress to your building/home, to your neighborhood, to your town or city, to your state, country, continent, planet, solar system, universe . . .
3. What are you doing to contribute to a visually literate world?
4. Celebrate your creativity!

BIBLIOGRAPHY

GENERAL

ARNHEIM, RUDOLF. *Art and Visual Perception.* Berkeley, CA: University of California, 1974.

CURTISS, DEBORAH. *Contemporary Research in Brain Hemispheric Specialization for Artists and Art Educators: An Annotated Bibliography,* master's thesis, Philadelphia College of Art, 1982.

DONDIS, DONIS A. *A Primer of Visual Literacy.* Cambridge, MA: M.I.T., 1973.

Encyclopedia of World Art, 16 vols. New York: McGraw-Hill, 1959–1968.

FELDMAN, EDMUND B. *Varieties of Visual Experience.* New York/Englewood Cliffs, NJ: Prentice-Hall/Abrams, 1971.

GOODMAN, NELSON. *Languages of Art,* 2nd ed.. Indianapolis, IN: Hackett, 1976.

KEPES, GYORGY, ed. *Vision + Value Series: Education of Vision.* New York: Braziller, 1965.

LANGER, SUSANNE K. *Problems of Art.* New York: Scribner's, 1957.

MURRAY, PETER and LINDA. *A Dictionary of Art and Artists.* New York: Penguin, 1976.

OSBORNE, H., ed. *Oxford Companion to Art.* Oxford, England: Oxford University, 1970.

WALKER, J.A. *Glossary of Art, Architecture, and Design Since 1945.* London: Clive Bingley, 1977.

CHAPTER 1, Visual Literacy

SHAHN, BEN. *The Shape of Content.* Cambridge, MA: Harvard University, 1957.

CHAPTER 2, Seeing Awareness

FRANCK, FREDERICK. *The Awakened Eye.* New York: Vintage/Knopf, 1979.

_____ . *The Zen of Seeing.* New York: Vintage/Knopf, 1973.

GREGORY, RICHARD L.. *Eye and Brain.* New York: McGraw-Hill, 1973.

_____ . *The Intelligent Eye.* New York: McGraw-Hill, 1970.

CHAPTER 3, Dimension Elements

CLARK, KENNETH. *The Nude: A Study in Ideal Form.* New York: Pantheon, 1956.

D'AMELIO, JOSEPH. *Perspective Drawing Handbook.* New York: Van Nostrand-Reinhold, 1984.

KANDINSKY, WASSILY. *Point and Line to Plane.* New York: Dover, 1979.

CHAPTER 4, Color and Value

ALBERS, JOSEF. *Interaction of Color.* New Haven, CT: Yale, 1975, 1960.

BIRREN, FABER. *Color, Form, and Space.* New York: Reinhold, 1961.

GERRITSEN, F. *Theory and Practice of Color.* New York: Van Nostrand-Reinhold, 1975.

ITTEN, JOHANNES. *The Elements of Color.* New York: Van Nostrand-Reinhold, 1970.

OSTWALD, W. *The Color Primer.* New York: Van Nostrand-Reinhold, 1969.

SIDELINGER, S. *Color Manual.* Englewood Cliffs, NJ: Prentice-Hall, 1985.

VERITY, ENID. *Color Observed.* New York: Van Nostrand-Reinhold, 1982.

CHAPTERS 5, 6, and 7, Composition and Design

BEHRENS, ROY R.. *Design in the Visual Arts.* Englewood Cliffs, NJ: Prentice-Hall, 1984.

BEVLIN, MARJORIE E.. *Design Through Discovery.* New York: Holt, Rinehart & Winston, 1977.
CHEATHAM, FRANK, JANE CHEATHAM, and SHERYL HALER. *Design Concepts and Applications.* Englewood Cliffs, NJ: Prentice-Hall, 1983.
LAUER, DAVID A.. *Design Basics,* 2nd ed. New York: Holt, Rinehart & Winston, 1985.

CHAPTERS 8 and 9, Style

HONOUR, H., and J. FLEMING. *The Visual Arts: A History.* Englewood Cliffs, NJ: Prentice-Hall, 1982.
POTHORN, H.. *Architectural Styles: An Historical Guide to World Design.* New York: Facts on File, 1979.

PART V: Media Options

CAPLIN, LEE EVANS. *The Business of Art.* Englewood Cliffs, NJ: Prentice-Hall, 1982.
Careers in the Arts: A Resource Guide. Center for Arts Information. 625 Broadway, New York, NY.
HOLDEN, DONALD. *Art Career Guide.* 4th ed. New York: Watson-Guptill, 1984. Choosing an art career, planning art education, and finding a job in all visual art and design fields.
KATCHEN, CAROLE. *Promoting and Selling Your Art.* New York: Watson-Guptill, 1978.
MAYER, RALPH. *A Dictionary of Art Terms and Techniques.* New York: Crowell, 1975.
MCCANN, MICHAEL. *Health Hazards Manual for Artists,* 3rd ed. New York: Watson-Guptill, 1985.
MICHELS, CAROLL. *How to Survive and Prosper as an Artist.* New York: Holt, Rinehart & Winston, 1983.

CHAPTER 10, Drawing

COLLIER, GRAHAM. *Form, Space, and Vision: Understanding Art—A Discourse on Drawing,* 3rd ed. Englewood Cliffs, NJ: Prentice-Hall, 1972.
EDWARDS, BETTY. *Drawing on the Right Side of the Brain.* Los Angeles: J. P. Tarcher, 1979.
GOLDSTEIN, NATHAN. *The Art of Responsive Drawing.* Englewood Cliffs, NJ: Prentice-Hall, 1984.
HALE, R. B. *Drawing Lessons from the Great Masters.* New York: Watson-Guptill, 1964.
LAMBERT, SUSAN. *Reading Drawings: An Introduction to Looking at Drawings.* New York: Pantheon, 1984.
NICOLAIDES, KIMON. *The Natural Way to Draw.* Boston: Houghton Mifflin, 1960, 1941. A classic.
O'CONNOR, C. *Perspective Drawing and Applications.* Englewood Cliffs, NJ: Prentice-Hall, 1985.
RAWSON, PHILIP. *The Art of Drawing.* Englewood Cliffs, NJ: 1984.
SIMMONS III, S., and M.S.A. WINER. *Drawing—The Creative Process.* Englewood Cliffs, NJ: Prentice-Hall, 1977. An excellent perceptual approach.

CHAPTER 11, Fine Arts

Fine Arts Periodicals

Art Forum, P.O. Box 980, Farmingdale, NY, 11737.
Art in America, 850 Third Avenue, New York, NY, 10022.
Artnews, P.O. Box 969, Farmingdale, NY, 11737.
Arts Magazine, 23 East 26th Street, New York, NY, 10010. These lavishly illustrated magazines follow current developments in the fine arts. More practically oriented toward materials, techniques and tools is:
American Artist, 1515 Broadway, New York, NY, 10036.
New Art Examiner, 300 W. Grand Street, Suite 620, Chicago, IL, 60610. Exhibit opportunities and other than mainstream art. Also, subscribe to local art newsletters.

Painting

GOLDSTEIN, NATHAN. *Painting: Visual and Technical Fundamentals.* Englewood Cliffs, NJ: Prentice-Hall, 1979.
KAY, REED. *The Painter's Guide to Studio Methods and Materials.* Englewood Cliffs, NJ: Prentice-Hall, 1983.
LECLAIR, CHARLES. *The Art of Watercolor.* Englewood Cliffs, NJ: Prentice-Hall, 1985.
MAYER, RALPH. *The Artist's Handbook of Materials and Techniques.* New York: Viking, 1970.

Printmaking

ANTREASIAN, GARO Z.. *The Tamarind Book of Lithography: Art & Techniques.* Los Angeles: Tamarind Lithography Workshop, 1971.
AUVIL, K. *Serigraphy: Silk Screen Techniques for the Artist.* Englewood Cliffs, NJ: Prentice-Hall, 1965.
BRUNNER, FELIX. *Handbook of Graphic Reproduction Processes: Technical Guide for Art Collectors, Artists, and Printmakers.* New York: Hastings, 1984.
HELLER, JULES. *Paper Making.* New York: Watson-Guptill, 1978.
————. *Printmaking Today.* New York: Holt, Rinehart & Winston, 1972.
PETERDI, GABOR. *Printing Methods Old and New.* New York: Macmillan, 1961.
SENEFELDER, ALOIS. *A Complete Course of Lithography.* New York: DaCapo, 1968.
WENNINGER, M. *Lithography: A Complete Guide.* Englewood Cliffs, NJ: Prentice-Hall, 1983.

Sculpture

ANDERSON, WAYNE V. *American Sculpture in Process.* New York: Graphic Society, 1975.
HOFFMAN, MALVINA. *Sculpture Inside and Out.* New York: Norton, 1939.
HOLLANDER, HARRY B. *Plastics for Artists and Craftsmen.* New York: Watson-Guptill, 1972.
KELLY, JAMES J. *The Sculptural Idea.* 3rd ed. Minneapolis, MN: Burgess, 1981.
NEWMAN, THELMA R. *Plastics as Sculpture.* Philadelphia, PA: Chilton, 1974.
VERHELST, WILBERT. *Sculpture: Tools, Materials, and Techniques.* Englewood Cliffs, NJ: Prentice-Hall, 1973.

CHAPTER 12, Crafts

Craft Periodicals

American Crafts, The American Crafts Council, 401 Park Avenue South, New York, NY, 10016.
Ceramics Monthly, Box 12448, Columbus, OH, 43212.
Crafts, Crafts Council, 8 Waterloo Place, London SW1Y 4AT, England.
Fiber Arts, Lark Communications, 50 College Street, Asheville, NC, 28801.
Fine Woodworking, The Taunton Press, 52 Church Hill Road, Newtown, CT, 06470.
Glass Magazine, P.O. Box 23383, Portland, OR, 97223.
Metalsmith, Society of North American Goldsmiths, 6707 North Santa Marta Blvd., Milwaukee, WI, 53217.
Shuttle, Spindle and Dyepot, Handweavers Guild of America, P.O. Box 7-374, West Hartford, CT, 06107.

Ceramics

BERENSOHN, PAULUS. *Finding One's Way with Clay.* New York: Simon & Schuster, 1972.

CLARK, GARTH. *A Century of Ceramics in the United States, 1878–1978.* New York: Dutton, 1979.

NELSON, GLENN. *Ceramics: A Potter's Handbook,* 5th ed. New York: Holt, Rinehart & Winston, 1984.

RAWSON, PHILIP. *Ceramics.* Philadelphia: University of Pennsylvania, 1984.

RICHARDS, M. C. *Centering.* Middletown, CT: Wesleyan, 1964.

RIEGGER, HAL. *Raku: Art & Technique.* New York: Van Nostrand-Reinhold, 1970.

ROSSI, FERNANDO. *Mosaics: Painting in Stone: History and Techniques.* New York: Praeger, 1970.

WECSHLER, SUSAN. *Lowfire Ceramics.* New York: Watson-Guptill, 1981.

Glass

LABINO, DOMENICK. *Visual Art in Glass.* Dubuque, IA: Wm. C. Brown, 1968.

LITTLETON, HARVEY K. *Glassblowing: A Search for Form.* New York: Van Nostrand-Reinhold, 1971.

O'BRIEN, VINCENT. *Techniques of Stained Glass.* New York: Van Nostrand-Reinhold, 1977.

SCHULER, FREDERIC. *Glassforming: Glassmaking for the Craftsman.* New York: Chilton, 1968.

Fibers

ALBERS, ANNI. *On Weaving.* Middletown, CT: Wesleyan, 1965.

CONSTANTINE, M., and J. L. LARSEN. *The Art Fabric: Mainstream.* New York: Van Nostrand-Reinhold, 1981.

_____. *Beyond Craft: The Art Fabric.* New York: Van Nostrand-Reinhold, 1972.

HELD, SHIRLEY E. *Weaving: A Handbook for Fiber Craftsmen.* New York: Holt, Rinehart & Winston, 1972.

HELLER, JULES. *Paper Making.* New York: Watson-Guptill, 1978.

ROSSBACH, ED. *The Art of Paisley.* New York: Van Nostrand-Reinhold, 1980.

_____. *The New Basketry.* New York: Van Nostrand-Reinhold, 1980.

WALLER, IRENE. *Textile Sculptures.* New York: Taplinger, 1977.

Metalcraft and Jewelry

MORTON, PHILIP. *Contemporary Jewelry.* New York: Holt, Rinehart & Winston, 1976.

UNTRACHT, OPPI. *Jewelry Concepts and Technology.* New York: Doubleday, 1982.

Woodcraft

CASTLE, WENDELL, and DAVID EDMAN. *The Wendell Castle Book of Wood Lamination.* New York: Van Nostrand-Reinhold, 1980.

Fine Woodworking Techniques. Newtown, CT: Taunton, 1981. Selected articles from the magazine present methods of various woodworkers.

FRID, TAGE, *Tage Frid Teaches Woodworking: 1—Joinery Tools and Techniques.* Newtown, CT: Taunton, 1979; *2—Bending, Shaping, Veneering, Finishing.* New York: Van Nostrand-Reinhold, 1981.

CHAPTER 13, Design

Periodicals

American Illustration 1982/83, New York: American Illustration Inc., 1983. An annual publication.

American Institute of Graphic Artists, *Graphic Design USA 1, 2, 3, 4, . . . ,* New York: Watson-Guptill, annual from 1980.

Architect's Handbook of Professional Practice, The American Institute of Architects, 1735 New York Avenue, Washington, DC, 20006.

Architectural Record, 1221 Avenue of the Americas, New York, NY, 10020.

Design Perspectives, Industrial Designers Society of America, 6802 Poplar Place, Suite 303, McLean, VA, 22101.

Fine Print, P.O. Box 7741, San Francisco, CA, 94120.

Graphic Arts Monthly and the Printing Industry, Technical Publishing Corp., 666 Fifth Avenue, New York, NY, 10013.

Graphis, Graphis Press, Dufourstrasse 107, Zurich, Switzerland.

ID, Industrial Design, 330 West 42nd Street, New York, NY, 10036.

Illustrators 1–25 . . . , New York: Madison Square, annual from 1960.

Interior Design, 150 East 58th Street, New York, NY, 10022.

Italix, Haywood House, P.O. Box 279, Fairlawn, NJ, 07410.

Landscape Architecture, 1190 East Broadway, Louisville, KY, 40204.

Planning, American Planning Association, 113 East 60th Street, Chicago, IL, 60637.

Print, R. C. Publications Inc., 355 Lexington Avenue, New York, NY, 10017.

Progressive Architecture, 600 Summer Street, Stamford, CT, 06904.

Theatre Design and Technology, 1501 Broadway, New York, NY, 10036.

Environmental Design

ARNHEIM, RUDOLF. *Dynamics of Architectural Form.* Berkeley, CA: University of California, 1977.

BACON, EDMUND N. *Design of Cities.* New York: Penguin, 1974.

BALL, VICTORIA K. *Opportunities in Interior Design.* Lincolnwood, IL: National Textbook, 1977.

BLAKE, PETER. *Form Follows Fiasco.* Boston: Little Brown, 1977.

BLOOMER, KENT C., and CHARLES W. MOORE. *Body, Memory, and Architecture.* New Haven, CT: Yale, 1977.

FRIEDMAN, A., J. F. PILE, and F. WILSON. *Interior Design,* 2nd ed. New York: Elsevier, 1976.

GREENBIE, BARRIE. *Spaces, Dimensions of the Human Landscape.* New Haven, CT: Yale, 1981.

GRISWOLD, RALPH E. *Opportunities in Landscape Architecture.* Lincolnwood, IL: National Textbook, 1978.

HALPRIN, LAURENCE. *The R.S.V.P. Cycles.* New York: Braziller, 1970. The interrelationship of people and designed spaces.

_____. *Cities.* Cambridge, MA: M.I.T., 1973.

JERRIS, SIMON. *Dictionary of Design and Designers.* New York: Penguin, 1984.

McHARG, IAN L. *Design with Nature.* Garden City, NY: Doubleday, 1971.

MOORE, CHARLES, and GERALD ALLEN. *Dimensions: Space, Scale and Shape in Architecture.* New York: McGraw-Hill, 1976.

PIPER, ROBERT J. *Opportunities in Architecture Today.* Lincolnwood, IL: National Textbook, 1975.

ROSSBACH, SARAH. *Feng Shui: The Art of Chinese Placement.* New York: Dutton, 1983.

SIMONDS, JOHN O. *Landscape Architecture.* New York: McGraw-Hill, 1961.

TRACHTENBERG, M., and I. HYMAN. *Architecture: From Prehistory to Post Modernism.* Englewood Cliffs, NJ: Prentice-Hall, 1986.

VENTURI, ROBERT. *Complexity and Contradiction in Architecture.* 2nd ed. New York: Museum of Modern Art, 1977.

Graphic Design

BEHRENS, ROY. *Illustration as an Art.* Englewood Cliffs, NJ: Prentice-Hall, 1986.

BLANCHARD, RUSSELL W. *Graphic Design.* Englewood Cliffs, NJ: Prentice-Hall, 1984.

CRAIG, JAMES. *Graphic Design Career Guide.* New York: Watson-Guptill, 1983.

CROY, PETER. *Graphic Design and Reproduction Techniques.* New York: Hastings, 1968.

DALLEY, TERENCE, ed. *The Complete Guide to Illustration and Design: Techniques and Materials.* Oxford, England: Phaidon, 1980.

HART, HAROLD, comp. *The Illustrator's Handbook.* San Rafael, CA: Artists & Writers, 1981.

REINFELD, GEORGE. *Opportunities in Graphic Communications.* Lincolnwood, IL: National Textbook, 1983.

SMITH, R. *Basic Graphic Design.* Englewood Cliffs, NJ: Prentice-Hall, 1986.

SWANN, CAL. *Techniques of Typography.* New York: Watson-Guptill, 1969.

THOMA, MARTA. *Graphic Illustration.* Englewood-Cliffs, NJ: Prentice-Hall, 1982.

Industrial Design

CAPLAN, RALPH. *By Design.* New York: St. Martin's, 1982.

LOEWY, RAYMOND. *Industrial Design.* Woodstock, NY: Overlook, 1979.

PAPANEK, VICTOR. *Design for Human Scale.* New York: Van Nostrand-Reinhold, 1983.

———. *Design for the Real World.* New York: Van Nostrand-Reinhold, 1984.

PULOS, ARTHUR J. *American Design Ethic: A History of Industrial Design.* Cambridge, MA: M.I.T., 1983.

———. *Opportunities in Industrial Design.* Lincolnwood, IL: National Textbook, 1983.

Clothing Design

DAVIS, MARIAN L. *Visual Design in Dress.* Englewood Cliffs, NJ: Prentice-Hall, 1980.

DOBLER, ROSLYN. *Opportunities in Fashion.* Lincolnwood, IL: National Textbook, 1983.

McDERMOTT, I. E., and J. L. NORRIS. *Opportunities in Clothing.* New York: Bennett, 1972.

CHAPTER 14, Electronic Media

Periodicals

Afterimage, 31 Prince Street, Rochester, NY, 14607.
Amazing Cinema, 12 Moray Court, Baltimore, MD, 21236.
American Cinematographer, 1782 North Orange Drive, Los Angeles, CA, 90028.
American Photographer, 1515 Broadway, New York, NY, 10036.
Art Com: Contemporary Art Communications, Box 3123, San Francisco, CA, 94119.
Byte, P.O. Box 590, Martinsville, NJ, 08836.
Computers and Graphics, Maxwell House, Fairview Parks, Elmsford, NY, 10523.
Creative Computing, P.O. Box 789-M, Morristown, NJ, 07412.
Filmakers' Film and Video Monthly, P.O. Box 115, Ward Hill, MA, 01830.
Holosphere, Museum of Holography, 11 Mercer Street, New York, NY, 10013.
Home Video, 475 Park Avenue South, New York, NY, 10016.

The Independent Film and Video Monthly, 625 Broadway, New York, NY, 10012.
Modern Photography, 825 Seventh Avenue, New York, NY, 10019.
Popular Photography, P.O. Box 2775, Boulder, CO, 80302.
Video, 235 Park Avenue South, New York, NY, 10003.

Photography

CRAVEN, GEORGE M. *How Photography Works.* Englewood Cliffs, NJ: Prentice-Hall, 1986.

———. *Object and Image,* 2nd ed. Englewood Cliffs, NJ: Prentice-Hall, 1982.

CRAWFORD, WILLIAM. *The Keepers of Light.* Dobbs Ferry, NY: Morgan & Morgan, 1979.

DuBOIS, WILLIAM W., and BARBARA HODIK. *A Guide to Photographic Design.* Englewood Cliffs, NJ: Prentice-Hall, 1983.

GREEN, JONATHAN. *American Photography.* New York: Abrams, 1984.

JOHNSON, B. A., and FREDERICK SCHMIDT. *Opportunities in Photographic Careers.* Lincolnwood, IL: National Textbook, 1978.

Filmmaking

BONE, JAN. *Opportunities in Film.* Lincolnwood, IL: National Textbook, 1983.

Factfile: Careers in Film and Television. American Film Institute, John F. Kennedy Center for the Performing Arts, Washington, DC, 20566.

LAYBOURNE, KIT. *The Animation Book.* New York: Crown, 1979.

LIPTON, LEONARD. *Independent Filmmaking.* San Francisco: Straight Arrow, 1972.

MALKIEWICZ, J. KRIS, and ROBERT E. ROGERS. *Cinematography: A Guide for Filmmakers and Film Teachers.* New York: Van Nostrand-Reinhold, 1973.

PINCUS, EDWARD, and STEPHEN ASHER. *The Filmmaker's Handbook.* New York: New American Library, 1984.

RUBIN, S. *Animation: The Art and the Industry.* Englewood Cliffs, NJ: Prentice-Hall, 1984.

SHARFF, STEFAN. *The Elements of Cinema.* New York: Columbia University, 1982.

Video and Television

BARNOUW, E. *Tube of Plenty: The Evolution of American Television.* London: Oxford University, 1977.

BATTCOCK, GREGORY, ed. *New Artists Video.* New York: Dutton, 1978.

DAVIS, DOUGLAS. *Video.* Berlin: Neuer Berlinner Kunstverein, 1978.

SELLERS, L. L., and others. *Mass Media Issues.* Englewood Cliffs, NJ: Prentice-Hall, 1977.

SKORNIA, H. J. *Television and Society.* New York: McGraw-Hill, 1965.

Computer Graphics

KATZEN, HARRY. *Microcomputer Graphics and Programming Techniques.* New York: Van Nostrand-Reinhold, 1982.

LEAVITT, ed. *Artist and Computer.* New York: Harmony, 1976.

PETERSON, DALE. *Big Things from Little Computers: A Layperson's Guide to Personal Computing.* Englewood Cliffs, NJ: Prentice-Hall, 1982.

———. *Genesis II: Creation and Recreation with Computers.* Reston, VA: Reston, 1983.

WILSON, S. *Using Computers to Create Art.* Englewood Cliffs, NJ: Prentice-Hall, 1986.

Electrographic Art

FIRPO, PATRICK, and others. *Copy Art.* New York: Marek, 1978.

Holography

DOWBENKO. *Homegrown Holography.* Garden City, NY: Amphoto, 1978.

HOLOCO. *Light 2 Fantastic.* London: Bergstrom & Boyle, 1978.

JEONG, T. H. *A Study Guide on Holography.* Washington, DC: American Association for the Advancement of Science, 1975.

CHAPTER 15, Multimedia

BATTCOCK, GREGORY, ed. *Idea Art.* New York: Dutton, 1973.

————, and ROBERT NICKAS, eds. *The Art of Performance.* New York: Dutton, 1984.

KAPROW, ALLAN. *Assemblage, Environments, and Happenings.* New York: Abrams, 1965.

McCABE, CYNTHIA JAFFEE. *Artistic Collaboration in the Twentieth Century.* Washington, D.C.: Smithsonian Institute, 1984.

MEILACH, DONA Z. *Collage and Assemblage.* New York: Crown, 1973.

MEYER, URSULA. *Conceptual Art.* New York: Dutton, 1972.

SEITZ, WILLIAM C. *The Art of Assemblage.* New York: Doubleday, 1961.

SMAGULA, HOWARD. *Currents—Contemporary Directions in the Visual Arts.* Englewood-Cliffs, NJ: Prentice-Hall, 1983.

CHAPTERS 16, 17, and 18, Visual Thinking and Creating

ADAMS, JAMES J. *Conceptual Blockbusting.* New York: W. W. Norton, 1976.

ARGUELLES, JOSÉ A. *The Transformative Vision: Reflections on the Nature and History of Human Expression.* Berkeley, CA: Shambala, 1975.

ARNHEIM, RUDOLF. *Visual Thinking.* Berkeley, CA: University of California, 1971.

CLYNES, MANFRED. *Sentics: The Touch of the Emotions.* New York: Anchor, 1978.

EDWARDS, BETTY. *Drawing on the Artist Within.* New York: Simon & Schuster, 1986.

HANKS, KURT, and others. *Design Yourself.* Los Altos, CA: William Kaufmann, 1978.

JOHNSON, MARY FRISBEE. *Visual Workouts.* Englewood Cliffs, NJ: Prentice-Hall, 1983.

KOBERG, DON, and JIM BAGNALL. *The Universal Traveler.* Los Altos, CA: William Kaufmann, 1976.

MAY, ROLLO. *The Courage to Create.* New York: Bantam, 1976.

McKIM, ROBERT H. *Experiences in Visual Thinking.* Belmont, CA: Wadsworth/Brooks-Cole, 1980.

————. *Thinking Visually: A Strategy Manual for Problem-Solving.* rev. ed. Belmont, CA: Wadsworth/Lifetime Learn, 1980.

SAMUELS, MIKE and NANCY. *Seeing with the Mind's Eye.* New York: Random House, 1975.

STORR, ANTHONY. *The Dynamics of Creation.* New York: Atheneum, 1972.

ARTISTS REPRESENTED

INDEX OF TERMS AND CONCEPTS

*Important terms are indicated by **bold-face** type.

This book was set in Meridien,
a face designed by Adrian Frutiger in 1957,
and first cast by Deberny and Peignot.
The display type was set in Eurostyle with Meridien initial caps.

Designed by Lisa A. Domínguez
Cover underpainting by Deborah Curtiss
Manufacturing buyer: Ray Keating